DRAMA

WITHDRAWN

Translation and Adaptation in Theatre and Film

This book provides a pioneering and provocative exploration of the rich synergies between Adaptation Studies and Translation Studies and is the first genuine attempt to discuss the rather loose usage of the concepts of translation and adaptation in terms of theatre and film. At the heart of this collection is the proposition that Translation Studies and Adaptation Studies have much to offer each other in practical and theoretical terms and can no longer exist independently from one another. As a result, it generates productive ideas within the contact zone between these two fields of study, both through new theoretical paradigms and detailed case studies. Such closely intertwined areas as translation and adaptation need to encounter each other's methodologies and perspectives in order to develop ever more rigorous approaches to the study of adaptation and translation phenomena, challenging current assumptions and prejudices in terms of both. The book includes contributions as diverse yet interrelated as Bakhtin's notion of translation and adaptation, Bollywood adaptations of Shakespeare's *Othello*, and an analysis of performance practice, itself arguably an adaptive practice, which uses a variety of languages from English and Greek to British and International Sign-Language. As translation and adaptation practices are an integral part of global cultural and political activities and agendas, it is ever more important to study such occurrences of rewriting and reshaping. By exploring and investigating interdisciplinary and cross-cultural perspectives and approaches, this volume investigates the impact such occurrences of rewriting have on the constructions and experiences of cultures while at the same time developing a rigorous methodological framework which will form the basis of future scholarship on performance and film, translation and adaptation.

Katja Krebs is Senior Lecturer in Theatre and Performance Studies at the University of Bristol, UK.

Routledge Advances in Theatre and Performance Studies

Translation and Adaptation in Theatre and Film

Edited by Katja Krebs

Routledge
Taylor & Francis Group

NEW YORK   LONDON

First published 2014
by Routledge
711 Third Avenue, New York, NY 10017

Simultaneously published in the UK
by Routledge
2 Park Square, Milton Park, Abingdon, Oxon OX14 4RN

*Routledge is an imprint of the Taylor & Francis Group,
an informa business*

Library of Congress Cataloging-in-Publication Data
    Translation and adaptation in theatre and film / edited by Katja Krebs.
        pages cm. — (Routledge advances in theatre and performance
studies ; 30)
    Includes bibliographical references and index.
    1. Literature—Translations—History and criticism. 2. Film
adaptations—History and criticism.   I. Krebs, Katja, editor of
compilation.
    PN241.T83 2013
    418'.02—dc23
    2013003420

ISBN: 978-0-415-82968-7 (hbk)
ISBN: 978-0-203-40554-3 (ebk)

Typeset in Sabon
by IBT Global.

Für Millie

Contents

Figures

1 Introduction
Collisions, Diversions and Meeting Points

Katja Krebs

"Cast as an act of love, and as an act of disruption, translation becomes a means of repositioning the subject in the world and in history" (Emily Apter 2006: 6)

"For better or worse, every adaptation is an expression of love, however selfish or perverted that love may seem." (Thomas Leitch 2011: 10)

Translation and adaptation—as both practices and products—are an integral and intrinsic part of our global and local political and cultural experiences, activities and agendas. Translation is pivotal to our understanding of ideologies, politics as well as cultures, as it simultaneously constructs and reflects positions taken. Similarly, adaptation offers insights into, as well as helps to establish, cultural and political hegemonies. Within Translation Studies, the relationship between translation and political agendas has been, and continues to be, discussed in detail—most recently by scholars such as Mona Baker and Emily Apter, for example, who argue convincingly that "translation is central to the ability of all parties [in our conflict-ridden and globalized world] to legitimize their events" (Baker 2006: 1) and "a concrete particular of the art of war, crucial to strategy and tactics, part and parcel of the way in which images of bodies are read" (Apter 2006: 15). Both studies are based upon the analysis of a large corpus of material which consists of news items, statements by governments, literatures and so on relating to historic as well as contemporaneous conflicts. And both include examples of translation, which in another context may be regarded as adaptation: the rewriting of texts.

COLLISIONS

It is ever-more important to study such rewritings in order to understand more fully the impact such occurrences of translation and adaptation have on the construction and the experience of culture as well as politics. Popular culture, for example, has seen an exponential proliferation of adaptation and translation (see Hand and Krebs 2007): Stieg Larsson's *Millennium Trilogy* (2008–2010)[1] has been a translation and adaptation phenomena *par excellence* with translations of both the novels and the film adaptations permeating global popular culture in less than five years; J. K. Rowling's *Harry Potter* series, in its various media permutations, including film, stage, cartoon, games and so on, has been translated into more than 60 languages; and Steven Spielberg's and Peter Jackson's *The Adventures of Tintin* (2011) celebrates Hergè's *Les Aventures de Tintin*, which have appeared on screen, stage and page in over 50 languages for at least 70 years. One of the latest examples, at the time of writing, is located on the small screen: an analysis of Anglo-American television's embrace of, and possibly obsession with, contemporary Scandinavian crime drama, such as the Danish series *The Killing*, both in subtitled form (BBC4) as well as rewritten form (Fox Television), can only be understood in terms of both translation and adaptation. Somewhat randomly chosen from a plethora of available examples, these instances are all truly global translation *and* adaptation phenomena which have contributed significantly to the shape of a popular cinematic landscape; all involve a rewriting and reshaping with regards their form, that is cartoon to stage, novel to film, and with regard their language, that is from Swedish, English and French into a number of other languages. The theatre has also seen a resurgence of work based on translations and adaptations: popular films are being turned into stage musicals on a regular basis (see, e.g., Krebs 2011; Symons 2008), and respected theatre companies, such as Kneehigh in the UK, have an entire repertoire consisting of translations and adaptations from a number of different media and genres, including opera, fairytale and film (see Radosavljević 2010). In the 2010–2011 season at the National Theatre, an adaptation of Mary Shelly's *Frankenstein* caused international interest: Directed by Danny Boyle, who is primarily known for feature films such as *Trainspotting* (itself an adaptation from Irvine Welsh's novel of the same title) and *Slumdog Millionaire*, it was shown in cinemas in parts of Europe, the United States, Canada, South Africa, New Zealand and Australia. Interestingly, the actors Benedict Cumberbatch and Johnny Lee Miller alternated the roles of the creature and Victor Frankenstein, thus further blurring the boundaries between source and adaptation. The list of countries which offered screenings of the stage production is noteworthy: Southern European countries such as Spain, France and Italy were notable by their absence, while screenings were clustered in Northern and Eastern Europe: Romania, Poland, Estonia, Finland, Sweden, and Germany all participated in this experiment where screen and stage converge. What this means with regard the hegemony of the English language, cultural expectations of stage and screen, and European cultural relations—North/East versus South/West, new members versus old members—remains to be seen and needs to be examined in more detail. What is already becoming clear, however, is that both adaptation and translation are not merely innocent bystanders in cultural relations.

So far, studies of such hybrid texts as mentioned above have discussed them exclusively in terms of adaptation *or* translation. Yet all these examples make it impossible to hold on to what seems a somewhat arbitrary distinction between the act of adaptation and the act of translation. Both translation and adaptation—as (creative) process, as product or artefact, and as academic discipline—are interdisciplinary by their very nature; both discuss phenomena of constructing cultures through acts of rewriting, and both are concerned with the collaborative nature of such acts and the subsequent critique of notions of authorship. Whether translation and adaptation are twins or indeed first cousins, however, is not the main concern of this book. Rather than necessarily argue that adaptation and translation are quintessentially the same, what this collection of essays aims to do is enrich our critical vocabularies and approaches by opening up a dialogue between these two fields of enquiry.

DIVERSIONS

It seems a curious state of affairs that two distinct academic fields and discourses have developed which investigate such closely related acts of rewriting as adaptation and translation, without engaging with each other's critical perspectives and methodologies. Such emphasis on division and lines of separation is not exclusive to the academy. Popular, and some academic, western discourse tends to view adaptation as a creative version of, rewriting of or commentary on a source text, as opposed to translation which, it is assumed, offers sameness and strives for equivalence. Thus, a binary is constructed around these two acts of rewriting: creative freedom versus linguistic confinement, or piracy versus trustworthiness and faithfulness, depending on which side of the fence you sit on. Of course, this view "betrays an ignorance of developments in Translation Studies over the past three decades" (Venuti 2007: 9) as well as Adaptation Studies, both of which have gone beyond discussions of equivalence, faithfulness and fidelity (see, e.g., Hermans 2007; Hutcheon 2006; Oittinen 2000; and Sanders 2006).

In her influential work *Adaptation and Appropriation* (2006), Julie Sanders proposes that adaptations are "reinterpretations of established texts in new generic contexts or . . . with relocations of . . . a source text's cultural and/or temporal setting, which may or may not involve a generic shift" (19). However useful Sanders' emphasis on relocation and reinterpretation may be, to what extent this specific definition allows for a clear distinction between adaptation and translation is questionable. Depending on the generic contexts and forms, reinterpretation and relocation are also commonplace in translation practices. Translation history is witness to a plethora of examples which comply with Sanders' definition of adaptation (see, e.g., Hale 1999; Krebs 2007; Milton 2009; Tymoczko 1999), and contemporaneous examples can be found in large numbers particularly in translation practices for the screen and stage.

MEETING POINTS

Screen and stage offer an abundance of case studies that blur the boundaries between adaptation and translation. The dramaturgical processes necessary, the practices employed by directors, writers, actors, and so on, and the nature of film and theatre that destabilises notions of single authorship (see Lehmann 2006) and 'original' in the first place, disallows a distinction between adaptation and translation more decisively than other forms and genres. According to Sirkku Aaltonen, "translation for the stage probably employs adaptation more frequently than does printed literature" (2000: 75) not only because of artistic decisions and subsequent claims of ownership made by director, performer, and/or dramaturg but also because theatrical systems themselves are "living organisms coexisting in a symbiotic relationship with other cultural and social systems . . . and part of a complex network of subsystems, mainstream and fringe theatres as well as various consumer and producer organisations" (5) and so on. In addition to theatre's complexities as a creative practice and as a site of performance, Gunilla Andermann observes, when discussing the difference between a reader and a spectator, that "members of the audience are left to fend for themselves when, during the course of a performance, they are confronted with unfamiliar and often bewildering information" (2005: 7). Footnotes or explanatory introductions which are sometimes made use of in published translations are not available to the audience of a live performance or indeed a film.

Let us turn our attention for a moment to a pertinent theatre example which makes a clear distinction between translation and adaptation impossible: Mike Pearson's production of Aeschylus' *The Persians* formed part of the National Theatre of Wales' 2010 season. It used a so-called 'version' by Kaite O'Reilly for its performance on a military site in the Brecon Beacons, Wales. Not normally accessible to the public, the site includes a mock (west) German village, constructed at the height of the Cold War, which is still used as a place for testing battlefield scenarios. At no point, either on posters, in the programme or any other written material relating to the performance, is *The Persians* labelled an adaptation. Kaite O'Reilly is no stranger to adaptation, however: for example, 2002 saw the premiere of *peeling*, her adaptation of *Trojan Women*, noteworthy for its multilingual text which includes British Sign Language alongside spoken English. Yet, she insists that *The Persians* is not to be viewed as an adaptation by describing her writing process in the programme accompanying the performance: "Although I'm not a linguist and therefore unable to read the text in Ancient Greek, through my close reading of 23 translations, made across three centuries, I like to think I caught a sense of the bass line" (O'Reilly 2010: n. pg.).

Emphasising the importance of the socio-political contexts of those 23 translations, she describes the process of writing as one akin to translation in all but linguistic competence:

I chose not to reinvent. I chose to be as faithful as far as I could perceive it, to that 'initial' voice and to trust that extraordinary location in
which the performance takes place would create a context with more
resonance than anything I could ever fabricate. (O'Reilly 2010: n. pg.)

By employing terminology such as 'reinvention' as a negative and 'faithfulness' as a positive description of the translation process, O'Reilly operates
within popular western discourse of translation. Despite her attempts to
distance her work from notions of adaptation and instead align it with
ideals of translation, both her process of rewriting and the performance
comply with Sanders' definition of adaptation: the production of *The Persians*, including O'Reilly's text, is a "reinterpretation of [an] established
text . . . with relocations of the source text's cultural and/or temporal setting" (2006: 19). Thus, O'Reilly's and Pearson's production of *The Persians* raises a number of intriguing questions. Is this a performance of a
'translation' so long as the audience does not read O'Reilly's programme
notes? Or is it an 'adaptation' even though it labels itself a 'version'? How
can distinctions be drawn and what would their consequences be, both
for watching and for performing? Does the experience of the performance
change according to the nomenclature used for the rewriting? Or has *The
Persians*, belonging to the canon of classic western drama, surpassed such
labelling? Has the text and the production been authenticated by the title
alone? It is such questions that the essays in this collection investigate.

Examples which complicate the relationship between adaptation and
translation can be found in abundance not only in the theatre but also on
the screen, if only because the two regularly translate and adapt each other.
Film adaptation as an academic discipline has quite recently established
itself as an area of scholarship in its own right, independent from comparative literature and English departments. However, the ever-growing
body of work investigating adaptation on screen tends to ignore translation
issues and Translation Studies. This may partly reflect the monolingualism typical of Film Studies in its Anglo-American context as well as the
dominant position North America holds with regards accepted film practice. Either way, matters of translation tend to become the butt of the joke
as in Sofia Coppola's *Lost in Translation* (2003) or regular column fillers
whereby titles are translated back so to speak from the target language to
the source language:

Eternal Sunshine of the Spotless Mind: If You Leave Me, You're Erased
    Not as poetic as the original title but the Italian audiences were left
in no doubt about what Jim Carry wanted to tell Kate Winslet.
    . . .
Basic Instincts: Ice Smile
    An ice pick was the weapon of choice for Sharon Stone in Basic
Instinct. But that only partly explains the Japanese title, especially

since the original title was the best thing about the film. (*Observer* 3 February 2008)

Of course, the majority of examples such as these only serve to emphasise English language hegemony. What is important, however, is that Translation Studies and Adaptation Studies have much to offer each other in practical and theoretical terms and should not exist independently from one another. Such closely intertwined areas need to encounter each other's methodologies and perspectives if only to develop ever more rigorous approaches to the study of translation and adaptation phenomena. Once it has become clear that we are dealing with converging agendas—a tendency towards common conclusions and findings rather than disparate discourses—the merging of ideas and the emergence of creative practices will challenge current assumptions and prejudices in terms of both adaptation and translation. And thus the structure of this collection reflects three stages of such encounters. The essays that follow fall into (and sometimes necessarily go beyond) the following categories: converging agendas, merging ideas and emerging practices.

CONVERGING AGENDAS

The first section, 'Converging Agendas', consists of three chapters, all of which identify areas of convergence from varying perspectives. Márta Minier's 'Definitions, Dyads, Triads and Other Points of Connection in Translation and Adaptation Discourse' offers a historical account of various points at which critical concerns of Adaptation Studies and Translation Studies overlap. Minier argues that both academic disciplines share a great deal in terms of methodologies, terminologies and objects of critical investigation, yet do not communicate extensively with one another, and more often than not fail to recognise what links them together. Minier's chapter surveys overlapping conceptual and methodological areas, typologies and definitions in particular, from seminal moments in the histories of both disciplines. This is done with the explicit aim of bringing the disciplines in question closer, while maintaining an awareness of the medium-specific aspects of research ongoing in these fields that may justify the current division between these interdisciplinary areas.

While Minier starts from the premise of Translation Studies, Dennis Cutchins's foregrounds his work in Adaptation Studies' historical expectation that film adaptations 'translated' or even 'transposed' literary content. Using Bakhtin's seminal work on language and culture, 'Bakhtin, Translation and Adaptation' challenges such assumptions. Cutchins's demonstrates the profound effects Bakhtin's notions about the gap between language and expressive material had on early adaptation theorists. He also shows, however, that these theorists failed to grasp the rest of Bakhtin's logic: that as materials are divorced from language by translation, they are simultaneously wedded to a particular style.

Moving on from the more traditional forms of translation and adaptation, that is film adaptation and stage translation, Eckart Voigts-Virtchow's 'Anti-Essentialist Versions of Aggregate Alice: A Grin Without a Cat' takes the discussion into the realm of intertextuality and intermediality. While acknowledging the close relationship between translation and adaptation, this chapter's analysis of the rewriting and rebranding of popular texts such as *Alice in Wonderland* necessitates a rigorous and critical engagement with terminologies used within Adaptation Studies. It argues that by observing adaptational change and intertextual proliferation, Adaptation Studies renders notions of essence in cultural production untenable, investigating instead the play of 'brands' and the citability and iterability of cultural texts and processes.

MERGING IDEAS

The second section of this collection, 'Merging Ideas', offers in-depth analyses of case studies which rely on a merging of translation and adaptation practices and theories. All three chapters examine canonical texts and authors, whether in relation to classics or indeed popular culture, and all three chapters demonstrate clearly the importance of merging translation and adaptation perspectives. John Milton's 'Theorising *Omkara*' investigates a Bollywood adaptation of Shakespeare's *Othello* in order to further develop Lawrence Venuti's theories of formal and thematic interpretants in adaptation and translation. Jessica Wiest's '*The Thief of Baghdad*: Foreigneising Adaptations' appropriates Venuti's notion of foreignisation in her reading of film adaptations of *The Thief of Baghdad*. Leaving behind performance practice and film adaptation, Adrienne Mason adds an important perspective when she offers an insightful account of the relationship between the iconic Penguin Classic series and translation of French theatre into English in the chapter 'Molière Among the Penguins: John Wood's Translations for the Early Penguin Classics'. Focusing on the general editor of the series, E. V. Rieu's relationship with the translators and his emphasis on readability and enjoyment above scholarship, this chapter explores the translation and reception of the early choices of plays for translation. Material in the Penguin Archive, housed in the University of Bristol, allows a rare glimpse of the complex relationship between translator and publisher and Mason concludes that it is such a network of relations which underpin the choice of texts for translation and the way in which they are rewritten.

EMERGING PRACTICES

It is with the rewriting of French classic theatre that the third section, 'Emerging Practices', starts. Richard Hand's 'Half-Masks and Stage Blood: Translating, Adapting and Performing French Historical Theatre Forms' emphasizes the specificities of theatrical practices and the role such systems play in translation and adaptation for performance. Drawing on his own experience of translating, adapting and, crucially, staging of historical theatre for a 21st-century Anglophone performer and audience, Hand considers issues of genre and modification in translation and adaptation on page and stage. In particular, Hand emphasizes a three-level symbiotic journey of translating plays: from source into target language, followed by the development through adaptation of a performance script, and eventual stage production.

In 'Bridging the Translation/Adaptation Divide: A Pedagogical View', Laurence Raw and Tony Gurr turn to the use of translation and adaptation in the context of teaching English language and culture in Turkish higher education institutions. While translation is primarily if not exclusively used as a tool for language teaching as well as a means of assessment of language proficiency, instances of adaptation do not necessarily play a role in a 'lecture-driven university environment'. Raw and Gurr argue translation and adaptation are fundamental to the process of constructing knowledge for learners and educators alike.

While Hand and Raw and Gurr offer an analysis of their own creative and pedagogic practices as translators and adaptors, Ildikó Ungvári Zrínyi, in 'Scenic Narration: Between Film and Theatre', turns her attention to the work of Andrei Şerban, whose stage adaptation of Ingrid Bergman's feature film *Cries and Whispers* won three awards given by the Union of Theatre People of Romania. Her contribution offers a detailed analysis of the adaptation and translation processes in Serban's theatrical practice and what these practices may mean for our understanding of pastiche, translation and adaptation on stage.

Last but not least, 'Emerging Practices' concludes with Pedro de Senna's 'When Creation, Translation and Adaptation Meet: SignDance Collective's *New Gold*'. SignDance Collective is an international ensemble working at the crossroads between dance, theatre and Sign Language. In the company's challenging aesthetic, these systems of signification collapse into a hybrid form, where English (and sometimes Spanish) is translated into British and International Sign Language, which are then adapted into choreography. In their devising processes, this continuum is at times reversed or disrupted, and the creative act originates in a choreographic idea, which may then be put into words, in an intersemiotic dialogue which is constantly translating and adapting, under what H-Dirksen L. Bauman termed a 'Poetics of Vision, Space and the Body'. De Senna participated in *New Gold* as performer and dramaturg, translator and adaptor, and it is this dual function which allowed him to negotiate his way between Graham Ley's notion of theatre as 'Discursive Embodiment' and Tim Etchells's 'Performance Writing'. Within this context, the perceived dichotomy between Ley's logocentrism and Etchell's performative approach is resolved through a new way of conceiving and perceiving, one which Kanta Kochhar-Lindgren calls the

'Third Ear'. *New Gold* is of particular note in that it contains moments in four different spoken languages as well as British and International Sign Languages. This aspect of SignDance's work makes for an interesting case study in the possibilities of translation and adaptation taking place within a performance, as well as during its inception. During their residency in Greece (Spring and Summer 2011), these processes are further complicated by the requirement that the (English) spoken text is translated into Greek—while the Sign Language is only partly altered—highlighting some of the issues that arise in the translation of multilingual texts. While embracing the converging of ideas, merging of agendas and exploring emerging practices of translation and adaptation practices and theories, this chapter also points the way towards future perspectives: it argues that through their habitual dealing with alteration, Deaf and Disability Studies have a significant contribution to make towards the debates around the phenomenology of performance, translation and adaptation.

As diverse as the list of contributors to *Encounters* may be, ranging from such apparently colliding cultural backgrounds as Brazil and Romania, Turkey and the US, Germany and the UK, where all chapters within this book meet is the tenet of the opening quotes: both adaptation and translation are acts of love—a form of love that may show itself to be disruptive, selfish, and perverse yet is central to the (re)writing, (re)construction and reception of cultural positions and ideologies. If anything this collection of essays hopes to achieve, it is to disrupt and rethink some of the entrenched positions our analysis of these acts of love find themselves in.

NOTES

1. The dates refer to the publication of the English translations in paperback. The Swedish novels were published between 2005 and 2006; they appeared in French between 2006 and 2008 and in German between 2007 and 2009, to give just a couple of examples of differing translation journeys and speeds.

WORKS CITED

Aaltonen, Sirkku. 2000. *Time-Sharing on Stage: Drama Translation in Theatre and Society*. Clevedon, England: Multilingual Matters.
Andermann, Gunilla. 2006. *Europe on Stage: Translation and Theatre*. London: Oberon Books.
Apter, Emily. 2006. *The Translation Zone: A New Comparative Literature*. Princeton, NJ: Princeton University Press.
Baker, Mona. 2006. *Translation and Conflict: A Narrative Account*. London: Routledge.
Hale, Terry. 1999. 'The Imaginary Quay From Waterloo Bridge to London Bridge: Translation, Adaptation and Genre'. In: Myriam Salama-Carr (ed.), *On Translating French Literature and Film II*. Amsterdam: Rodopi, pp. 219–238.
Hand, Richard and Katja Krebs. 2007. 'Editorial'. *Journal of Adaptation in Film and Performance*, 1:1, pp. 3–4.

Hermans, Theo. 2007. *Conference of the Tongues*. Manchester, England: St. Jerome.

Hutcheon, Linda. 2006. *A Theory of Adaptation*. London: Routledge.

Krebs, Katja. 2007. *Cultural Dissemination and Translational Communities: German Drama in English Translation, 1900–1914*. Manchester, England: St. Jerome.

Krebs, Katja. 2011. 'Megamusicals, Memory and Haunted Audiences: *The Producers* in Berlin's Admiralspalast'. *Quaderns de Filologia Estudis Literaris*, 15, pp. 41–54.

Lehmann, Hans-Thies. 2006. *Postdramatic Theatre*. Translated by Karen Jürs-Munby. London: Routledge.

Leitch, Thomas. 2011. 'Vampire Adaptation'. *Journal of Adaptation in Film and Performance*, 4:1, pp. 5–16.

Milton, John. 2009. 'Between the Cat and the Devil: Adaptation Studies and Translation Studies'. *Journal of Adaptation in Film and Performance*, 2:1, pp. 47–64.

Oittinen, Ritta. 2000. *Translating for Children*. London: Routledge.

O'Reilly, Kaite. 2010. *Programme Notes: The Persians*. National Theatre of Wales.

Radosavljević, Duška. 2010. 'Emma Rice in Interview With Duška Radosavljević'. *Journal of Adaptation in Film and Performance*, 3:1, pp. 89–98.

Sanders, Julie. 2006. *Adaptation and Appropriation*. London: Routledge.

Symons, Alex. 2008. 'Mass-Market Comdey: How Mel Brooks Adapted *The Producers* for Broadway and Made a Billion Dollars 2001–2007'. *Journal of Adaptation in Film and Performance*, 1:2, pp. 133–145.

Tymoczko, Maria. 1999. *Translation in a Postcolonial Context*. Manchester, England: St. Jerome.

Part I
Converging Agendas

2 Definitions, Dyads, Triads and Other Points of Connection in Translation and Adaptation Discourse

Márta Minier

Various theories of translation date back to the beginning of western civilisation (among others to Horace, Cicero, St Jerome or St Augustine), yet Translation Studies as a relatively coherent discipline established itself in the latter part of the past century. On careful scrutiny, it appears that much of early translation theory—for instance, the 17th-century John Dryden's famous tripartite typology (*metaphrasis*, *paraphrasis* and *imitatio*), and even the Prague linguist Roman Jakobson's three-fold notion of translation (interlingual, intralingual and intersemiotic) from 1959—point towards several conjectures that have been theorised more recently within the younger yet sinewy body of work termed Adaptation Studies (e.g., Wagner 1975; Andrew 1984; Desmond and Hawkes 2005; Cahir 2006). This is understandable as adaptation—be it in a theatre, small screen, big-screen or computer-screen context—has become more prevalent from the 20th century onwards, since the emergence of the moving image. This contribution will draw attention to various overlapping critical concerns between two closely related fields of research—Adaptation Studies[1] and Translation Studies—which have a lot in common in terms of methodologies, terminologies (including dyads and triads) and objects of critical investigation, yet do not communicate extensively with one another, and more often than not fail to recognise what links them together. In the spirit of interdisciplinarity and interdiscursivity, this article takes a kaleidoscopic format rather than a very linear one as it aims to paint a composite, multichrome picture of the translation/adaptation spectrum. It will look at clusters of issues, look for convergences and divergences, and highlight the rapid changeability of the picture (without hoping to keep up the pace).

In an article that aims to infuse Film Adaptation Studies with theoretical models and configurations well matured by Translation Studies, Lawrence

Venuti admits, "Today, to be sure, translation and adaptation are carefully distinguished by publishers and translators, filmmakers and screenwriters, even if copyright law classifies both cultural practices as 'derivative works'" (2007: 29). However, speaking from as diverse disciplinary backgrounds as children's literature in/as translation and adaptation and the contemporary reception of ancient classics, respectively, both Riitta Oittinen and Joanne Paul envisage some commonality between translation and adaptation. As the eminent Finnish translation scholar Riitta Oittinen puts it, "[T]he main difference between translation and adaptation lies in our attitudes and points of view, not in any concrete difference between the two" (2000: 80). Joanne Paul also asserts in her conclusion to her exploration of the film adaptation *Le Mépris* as a translation:

> My initial suspicion . . . that it is dishonest and oversimplifying to use translation and adaptation somewhat interchangeably proves to be overcautious. Though not synonymous, the two terms do form a critically productive partnership. There is, in fact, much to be gained from considering the two in tandem, so long as we recognize that framing adaptation as translation (and vice versa) should be used to illuminate the complexities of each, rather than elide them. (2008: 163)

In his essay 'Theatre Pragmatics', the drama translator and academic David Johnston perceives translation and adaptation as two stages of the same transformative process. The punning title of the collection where his essay was published—*Stages of Translation*—suggests the same:

> [I]n the final analysis, every act of translation for the stage is an act of transformation. The distinction between translation and adaptation is one which is difficult to understand fully, unless it is to refer to translation as the first stage of linguistic and broadly literary interrogation of the source text, and adaptation as the process of dramaturgical analysis, the preparation for re-enactment. (1996: 66)

Indeed, it is practically impossible to decide (even with a purely descriptive purpose) how much and what kind of freedom a rewriter/reimaginer is allowed to exercise in order for the artefact to be called a translation rather than an adaptation, a version and so on. Although taxonomies are numerous, there are no objective criteria for the separation of these notions. A great deal depends on what a certain receiving community regards as one or the other at a given historical time. For example, Ferenc Kazinczy's 1790 less-than-tragic prose Hungarian *Hamlet*—based on Friedrich Ludwig Schröder's rather free-handed and highly politicised rewrite (see, e.g., Kiséry 1996)—was viewed as a translation at the time; public opinion today would tend to consider such a work an adaptation, due to the radical alterations in terms of plot and character (including the excision of some characters and the introduction of a felicitous ending). A systematic, international, comparative/parallel and—emphatically—historical study of the two concepts is long overdue, but existing sporadic accounts promise a much more intertwined kinship than some contemporary scholars would surmise. For example, Corinne Lhermitte's (2004) insightful overview of the French discourse on translation in relation to film adaptation underlines that from medieval times onwards, there has been a strong tradition in French culture that has respected the act of translation as a creative and genuinely intellectual (rather than mechanical) activity. The famous-infamous *Les belles infidèles* school itself testifies to the role and prestige of adaptive translation in the literary (and cultural) polysystem, if we may borrow this rather useful term from Even-Zohar (1978) and his collaborators.[2]

This chapter will survey overlapping conceptual and methodological areas—typologies and definitions in particular, from historical landmarks of theorising both concepts, extending the scope of enquiry to tendencies in conceptualising in the even younger disciplinary area of remediation. This will be done with the explicit aim of bringing the disciplines in question closer, while remaining aware of the great degree of medium-specificity in the research ongoing in these fields that may justify the current division between these interdisciplinary areas. The vantage point from which the article is written is marked by recent contributions to Adaptation Studies through the reading of which returning to a cornucopia of translation theories seems appropriate and potentially mutually enriching for the two fields.

In spite of ample shared ground—which this brief study aims only to begin charting with somewhat big brushstrokes—the two concepts are rarely mentioned alongside one another in the same academic study or practitioner's account today. An exception is, for instance, Phyllis Zatlin's 2005 work *Theatrical Translation and Film Adaptation: A Practitioner's View*, which discusses the two practices within the same book, while broadly maintaining their separation. The essay collection *Genre Matters* (2006) also dedicates a joint section (albeit completely separate articles) to the two concepts.

If one may consider questions for a broad and systematic research project, first and foremost one should ask the question, what is adaptation? What is the scope of the term in its various definitions? In what context or contexts is it used and defined? If it is defined against another concept, what is that? Translation? Appropriation? Version? Transposition? Transformation? Supplement? Paraphrase? Parody? Allusion? Intertextuality? Is the term source or target oriented primarily in terms of text as well as context (although these polar opposites are odious)? Is it in service of a communication model, a hermeneutic model—I am using shortcuts adopted from Venuti (2007)[3] here—or some other critical apparatus? And conversely, does adaptation also appear as a term in translation discourse? In what contexts? Alongside what notions? While the scope and applicability of all these concepts is time and space specific, it also appears that they frequently appear synonymously and critics often feel the need to explain their usage. Mary H. Snyder, a creative writer and scholar, for example, is not in favour of the term 'version'—for her this phrase carries a belittling connotation which "isn't fair on the literary work, and it isn't fair to the film" (2011: 149). André Lefevere's anthology of translation criticism *Translation/History/Culture* (1992) lists 'versions' and 'adaptations' in its index, with one reference for each. This underlines the recourse to these concepts at various points during the history of translation criticism. Chantal Zabus prepares a rich list of creative transformations without explaining them in detail, in order to offer the umbrella term 'rewriting' for them (which she defines with the aid of another critical term, 'appropriation'). The absence of translation from the nomenclature is telling:

> As a genuine category of *textual transformation* that is different from but that possesses the ability to encompass sources, *imitation*, *parody*, *pastiche*, *satire*, *duplication*, *repetition* (both as debasement and challenging recurrence), *allusion*, *revision*, and *inversion*, "*rewriting*" is the *appropriation* of a text that it simultaneously authorizes and critiques for its own ideological uses. (2002: 3, my emphases)

There are numerous further terms for modes of cultural re-creation (Fischlin and Fortier 2000: 2), such as *alteration* (18th century), *imitation* (18th century), *spinoff* (contemporary), *tradaptation* (Garneau). Ruby Cohn (1976) opts for the term *offshoot*, with subcategories such as *reduction/emendation*, *adaptation* and *transformation*. Other, often title-giving, terms in use are *repositioning* (Cartelli 1999), *reinventing* (Taylor 1990), *reimagining* (Marsden 1995;[4] Miller 2003), *making fit* (Clark, in Fischlin and Fortier 2000: 1).[5] To add a few more related terms from Mary Orr's three-page-long inventory in *Intertextuality: Debates and Contexts*: *permutation*, *reappraisal*, *rejuvenation*, *reverberation*, *transfiguration*, *transplantation* (2003, 'Directory of Alternative Terms'). Fischlin and Fortier dismiss the term *appropriation* (used extensively for example in Marsden 1991; Vickers 1993; Desmet and Sawyer 1999; Sanders 2006) for connoting "a hostile takeover" (2000: 3). Adapting something implies adjusting it, making it suitable for a certain receiving community, even if that involves the possibility of changes that break away from the 'source text', while still fulfilling a duty of care towards it, communicating it to an audience in a more palatable or topical way (than the 'source' itself may come across). Fischlin and Fortier choose adaptation as a "working label", because this is the term they believe to be in most common use, and it also emphasises the process involved (2000: 3): the practice of adjusting, making something fit or suitable for a different context and audience/readership. (Interlingual translation, however, is not included in their definition.) In an attempt to distinguish adaptation from appropriation, they point out that the latter can materialise without the actual alteration of a text—for instance, quoting a Shakespearean sonnet on a Valentine's card, or quoting a sentence from Shakespeare in a collection of aphorisms—while the cases of adaptation they examine include textual modifications rather than 'mere' recontextualisation. It is noteworthy, however, that David Lane in the chapter he dedicates to adaptation in *Contemporary British Drama* (2010) also places emphasis on the element of recontextualisation when defining and categorising adaptations for the purposes of his overview:

> Adaptation is best understood . . . as the act of taking an existing book, play text or screenplay and transposing it to another context. It is useful to consider context here in three different ways. First, the context of the medium: a book might be transposed to the stage. . . . Second, one can consider the context of the story within the original source text: the world in which the characters of the drama are placed. . . . Third, one needs to consider context as a factor that lies outside either the source text's story or its medium, looking instead at the time and place in which it was originally encountered by an audience. (157–159)

It is to be regretted that the academic disciplines examining texts of a 'translational' modality are so compartmentalised, and thus, their critical attention so divided. Fischlin and Fortier are among the noticeably few critics working on adaptation who very briefly draw a parallel between Adaptation Studies and translation theory: "Adaptation, like translation and parody, is part of a generalized cultural activity that posits reworking in new contexts as more characteristic of cultural development than are originality in creation and fidelity in interpretation" (2000: 5).

As we have seen, adaptation—just as translation—is far from being an unproblematic concept to define whether the focus is on practice or product, on strategy or context. In the prolific field of Adaptation Studies, there seems to have developed an understanding—not shared by any means by all practitioners of this field of criticism—that the term 'adaptation' refers to filmic reimaginings of literature, mainly novels but also other fiction (short stories or epics) with drama included as a potential source rather marginally in adaptation-focused discourse—for instance, by Roger Manvell (1979), Peter Reynolds (1993) or Linda Costanzo Cahir (2006).[6]

To illustrate this phenomenon, let me cite a recent 'reel Shakespeare' book (which I consider generally excellent and only use it as an example of a discursive gesture here), Carolyn Jess-Cooke's *Shakespeare on Film: Such Things as Dreams Are Made Of*: "Adaptation is a blanket term for the process by which a text is visualised on screen" (2007: 34). This is by far not the only example of the slightly exclusive usage of this term in recent criticism, and this provocative discursive praxis calls for some altercation.

A tendency is thus in formulation to use Adaptation Studies to refer to the study of films—rather than works from any medium—based on literature—rather than texts in any medium and genre, such as plays, novels, musicals, operas, dance pieces, cartoons, comic books, paintings or any other textual phenomena in the broad sense of the term. Speaking from within Film Adaptation Studies, James Naremore highlights a considerable imbalance in his very own field of research:

> [W]e immediately think of the film *Mrs Dalloway* (1998) or even of the more freely derivative *Orlando* (1993) as adaptations, but not of *The Set Up* (1949, based on a narrative poem), *Batman* (1989, based on a comic book), *His Girl Friday* (1940, based on a play), *Mission Impossible* (1996, based on a television series), or *Twelve Monkeys* (1995, based on an art film). (2000: 1)

The practice thus criticised is not based on a consensus by any means in contemporary scholarship: Daniel Fischlin and Mark Fortier, in their highly influential anthology titled *Adaptations of Shakespeare*, collect a number of plays that are reworkings of Shakespearean drama, for instance Federico García Lorca's slightly lesser-known *El público* (1930) as a metadramatic rewriting of *Romeo and Juliet* (see Fischlin and Fortier 2000: 103–105). Manuela Perteghella's 2008 article 'Adaptation: "Bastard Child" or Critique: Putting Terminology Centre Stage' also engages with the concept of adaptation in relation to the realm of the theatre only. Accomplished children's author, director and actor David Wood finds it entirely appropriate to use the term 'adaptation' in his *Theatre for Children: Guide to Writing, Adapting, Directing and Acting* (1997) written with Janet Grant, where a separate chapter is dedicated to his adaptation methods and advice. Other applications of the concept in drama include work by Philip Cox—*Reading Adaptations: Novels and Verse Narratives on the Stage, 1790–1840* (2000)—and various contributions to the *Journal of Adaptation in Film and Performance*, for instance by Michael Fry (2008) and Graham Ley (2009). *Novel Images: Literature in Performance* (1993), edited by Peter Reynolds, divides its attention between big-screen, small-screen and theatrical reimaginings of primarily classic novels ranging from *Wuthering Heights* and *Little Dorrit* to *The Color Purple* and *Nice Work*.

What is intriguing is not necessarily whether the term 'adaptation' is applied to drama, film, literature or something else but whether a certain definition implies intersemiotic transfer or not. For the majority of film adaptation scholars, the concept does involve a transfer across different artistic media, while for a few others, it may also be a case of interlingual or intralingual/intrasemiotic transfer (see, e.g., Lhermitte 2005) or even a combination of interlingual and intrasemiotic transposition.

Bringing a plethora of uses and contexts together, Linda Hutcheon's much-cited 2006 study, *A Theory of Adaptation*, opens up the concept of adaptation so that it encompasses potentially any medium both as an adapted and as an adaptive text. Examining transfers across what she labels as the telling, showing and interactive modes of expression, Hutcheon's recent publication, perhaps unwittingly, reappropriates the term 'adaptation', and 'Adaptation Studies', taking it from film adaptation discourse and placing it in the no man's land of textual transformations of varied sorts. While Hutcheon's perspective liberally allows for the embracement of theatrical reworking as well as adaptations in and from various other media, her study makes relatively little reference to translation (and that is mainly through Benjamin, Bassnett and Lefevere).

DYADS IN TRANSLATION AND ADAPTATION DISCOURSE

From a more ontological point of view, it is illuminating that both translation theory and adaptation theory—if we treat them as self-contained areas—use the other concept as a trope when elaborating on the nature of transformative practices of the kind.[7] This is recognised by Hutcheon: "As openly acknowledged and extended reworkings of particular other texts, adaptations are often compared to translations" (2006: 16). To bring a much earlier example, André Bazin also uses the metaphor of translation when elaborating on a film's relationship with its adapted material (see Nánay 2000: 35).

Putting metaphorical usage to one side, some translation scholars—acting mainly in the interest of clarity—insist on the use of 'translation' even when a considerable degree of reshaping is visible in what is broadly labelled as the 'target text' in Translation Studies. Susan Bassnett (2002), for instance, defends Wyatt's and Surrey's respective works as translations (against the designation 'adaptation' used by some critics to reflect on the remarkable degree of poetic license applied). Bassnett is adamant that "such a distinction [adaptation] is misleading [whereby] [a]n investigation of Wyatt's translations of Petrarch, for example, shows a faithfulness not to individual words or sentence structures but to a notion of the meaning of the poem in its relationship to its readers" (60–62).

The concepts of translation and adaptation have both been recruited to help define the other, and they are both utilised as an analogy in illustrating intrinsic features of the other: "Just as there is no such thing as a literal translation, there can be no literal adaptation" (Hutcheon 2006: 16). They both appear in various classifications of the other one as subcategories. Georges L. Bastin sees adaptation as a translation method and contrasts it with "forms of conventional translation" (1998: 8). Drawing on Malmkjaer, Newmark, and Vinay and Darbelnet, among others, Manuela Perteghella's aforementioned article, too, presents the practice as a subcategory of translation: "The use of the term 'adaptation' has become so widespread and denotes such diverse aspects and practices of translation in the theatre that this has grown to be problematic for any study in the field of theatre translation" (2008: 51). Patrick Cattrysse's influential 1992 article also encourages a broader, Jakobsonean scope to the term translation so that it embraces film adaptations. As we know, the noted Slavicist and general linguist Jakobson introduced the terms *intralingual translation* for rewording, *interlingual translation* for translation proper, and *intersemiotic translation* for the transmission of verbal signs into a nonverbal system (1992: 145). The latter includes translation between media, for example, "from verbal art into music, dance, cinema, or painting" (1992, p. 151). Intralingual translation and intersemiotic translation seem to correspond to what we may term as adaptation today in everyday discourse.

Cattrysse's proposal for a translational film adaptation model has influenced the work of Corinne Lhermitte, Vincenza Minutella and others.[8] Lhermitte, for instance, emphasises the importance of "lay[ing] the foundations of an aesthetics of adaptation derived from the theory of translation" (2005: 98). As she asserts, "[W]e can assume that the long tradition of Translation Studies, spanning from Plato to Derrida, provides a helpful background for the building of a film adaptation theory" (99). Translation is also evoked in Robert Stam's overview of adaptation theory as a metaphor that may appear in adaptation discourse (2000: 62).

James Naremore, too, reflects on translation as a metaphor for adaptation, and discerns it as one of two dominant critical approaches to adaptation—the other being the auterist approach—both steeped in fidelity-orientated discourse in his reading and therefore rather limited (2000: especially 7–9). Yet such a view betrays a conceptualising of translation that does not engage with up-to-date translation theories which, in turn, rescue the notion from the restrictive straitjacket of faithfulness or equivalence.

R. Barton Palmer, yet another expert on film adaptations, also turns to the metaphor of translation but finds its applicability limited and "distorting" as it "makes it difficult to theorize any adaptation as a separate entity" (2008: 29). Palmer—among some other film adaptation scholars—in spite of paying some lip service to translation as a metaphor, turns out to be dismissing translation as a more or less straightforward and merely interlingual process yielding an unproblematic product that, in Palmer's view, is far too attached to its source, whereas, in Cahir's opinion, it is comfortably independent of it.

In *Filmmaking by the Book: Italian Cinema and Literary Adaptation* (1993), the film scholar Millicent Marcus refers to translation theory, more specifically André Lefevere's concept of refraction (first introduced in 1982) when questioning the validity of fidelity criticism. In an interdisciplinary and interdiscursive gesture Marcus borrows insights from the sister discipline of Translation Studies (rather than merely using translation in an analogous way) to highlight how a shared critical crux may be resolved:

> André Lefevre's [sic] essay on translated literature offers perhaps the best rebuttal to attacks on film adaptations as "unoriginal." Lefevre coins the term refraction to talk about the way a text is reworked to suit the needs of a particular public. Refractions can thus include Biblical stories retold for an audience of children, Classic Comics, *Reader's*

Digest condensations, anthologized masterworks, Monarch notes and study guides, opera libretti as well as foreign language translations. Lefevre argues against the absolutist thinking that posits a textual source a supreme authority to be strictly followed in any translation process and suggests instead that all texts are refractions–that the poetics of a literature is its central refracted text. . . . Lefevre's comments serve to relativize the argument about translation and, by extension, about adaptation, justifying the kinds of accommodations that refractors must make to the evolving ideological and aesthetic demands of the publics whom they address. (1993: 21–22)

Linda Costanzo Cahir aims to identify a common ground upon which source and adaptation can be compared: "The first step in exploring the merits of literature-based films is to see them as *translations* of the source material and to understand the difference between 'adaptation' and 'translation'" (2006: 14). This is then how she defines adaptation and subsequently translation:

While literature-based films are often, customarily and understandably, referred to as adaptations, the term 'to adapt' means to alter the structure or function of an entity so that it is better fitted to survive and to multiply in its new environment. To adapt is to move *that same entity* into a new environment. In the process of adaptation, the same substantive entity which entered the process exits, even as it undergoes modification—sometimes radical mutation—in its efforts to *accommodate* itself to its new environment. (14)

'To translate,' in contrast to 'to adapt,' is to move a text from one language to another. It is a *process of language*, not a process of survival and generation. Through the process of translation a fully new text— *a materially different entity*—is made, one that simultaneously has a strong relationship with its original source, yet is fully independent from it. Simply put: we are able to appreciate the translation without reading the original source. If we think of a literature-based film as a translation we will come to see that the filmmakers are moving the language of literature—made up of words—into the language of film . . . In doing so, they make choices from within film's syntax and vocabulary. (14)

It is important to recognise that Cahir here describes intersemiotic translation. While I fully agree with Cahir's emphasis that translation is "a fully new work" rather than "a mutation of the original matter" (2006: 14), from the perspective of translation theory, one may still challenge Cahir's definition of translation and the contrast she sets up between adaptation and translation. Translation can certainly be seen as a process of text generation that has a pivotal role in the afterlife and overall reception of a particular source text—we only need to remind ourselves of the connection Walter Benjamin envisages between translation and a work's afterlife. Such a function is also attributed to adaptation in various contexts, deservedly.[9] Even though it is important to stress that adaptation involves placing a work in "a new environment", the new cultural and linguistic context in which an interlingual translation is embedded is likewise a key factor when we analyse translations—so this does not necessarily work as a distinguishing feature between translation and adaptation.

An obvious shared tendency within critical thinking on translation and that on adaptation is a preoccupation with what adaptation and intermediality scholar Kara McKechnie (2009) calls the F-word of Adaptation Studies, namely the rather fuzzy concept of fidelity.[10] Even though Desmond and Hawkes associate this fidelity-orientated discourse primarily with newspaper and magazine reviews (2005: 44), one must note how much they also permeate academic writings on the subject. Linda Cahir's recent monograph *Literature Into Film: Theory and Practical Approaches*, despite discouraging the reader from scolding adaptations for not living up to their originals, features sentences such as, "Sometimes the film is the flawed translation of the literature" (2006: 13). Cahir also insists, "In translating a literary text into another language, faithfulness of translation is generally the overall goal". She does, however, acknowledge that "the matter of 'faithfulness' is a complex one, as there are multiple features of the parent text which a translator needs to consider" (15). Writing on adapting for stage performance, Govan, Nicholson and Normington also opine,

> [H]ow can devised performance possibly adapt fiction to create an authentic replica? Or indeed should it? The format of the original, as a piece of narrative, and the copy, as a dramatic form, dictates that there will be a number of differences. The characteristics of these two modes meant that it is impossible for a stage version of a piece of fiction to be faithful, or authentic. (94)

As scholars of film adaptation, taking inspiration from structuralism, poststructuralism, Cultural Studies and other critical theories, approaches and systems of thought, wrestle with the near-omnipresence of fidelity discourse one cannot help recalling Translation Studies' combating the concept of equivalence by way of criticising, contextualising, qualifying, further typifying it—suffice it to refer to dynamic/functional and formal equivalence as conceptualised by Bible translator and translation theorist Eugene Nida (see, e.g., Nida 2000: especially 134–140).

Desmond and Hawkes emphasise that pursuing fidelity in a concerted effort of comparing source and adaptation is like comparing apples with oranges: they will never be identical or even systematically, structurally alike (2005: 34). They call film adaptation "the case of apples and oranges" (34), suggesting that there is no shared, universally agreed method for a systematic, objective comparison of adaptation and source. This ties in with Linda Hutcheon's urge from 2006, which calls for foregrounding the contextual elements of the adaptive progress: the why, how, when and so on of the process of adaptation as opposed to a futile obsession with fidelity. In relation to translation, too, Minier (2005) proposes the consideration of the *when, what, who* and *how* of the reworking process (63).

Apart from the contextual aspect, the intertextual also brings the two practices closer to each other. This may be an area where translation criticism could perhaps take some inspiration from adaptation discourse. In (film) Adaptation Studies, the theories of intertextuality have been broadly applied by leading scholars of the field (especially—and increasingly—over the past two decades). As R. Barton Palmer elucidates, "As an archly postmodernist critical protocol, intertextuality provides an ideal theoretical basis from which can proceed an account of the shared identity of the literary source and its cinematic reflex" (2008: 258). In translation theory, too, the concept of intertextuality has been applied in several publications (Józan 1997; Szegedy-Maszák 1998; Minier 2005; Federici 2007), yet the incorporation of translational activities (alongside 'adaptive' ones) under the broader framework of intertextuality may not appeal to all translation scholars.

A serious consideration of intertextuality with regard to translation radically alters the way we view the ontology of a translated text/a text in transit. It is bound to undermine the age-old dichotomy of 'original'/'source' and 'translation', or—as Translation Studies scholars tend to put it—*source text* and *target text*. These traditional terms may well be used in inverted commas, partly for mere reasons of philology (it is not always evident what source was used by a translator in cases of interlingual translation), and partly in keeping with an intertextual notion of translation. The widely used traditional terms 'target language', 'target culture' and 'target text' are problematic, since they imply that the process of textual production ends with the appearance of a translation, while it is evident that the translation will have its own afterlife. This chapter intends to work on the deconstruction of such terms and supports the use of the term 'receiving culture' (adopted in accordance with hermeneutics and reception aesthetics), which indicates more aptly that the translation is received by a different community to that which received the 'source text', and it will obviously be subject to very different readings to those of the respective foreign-language 'source'.

The intertextual approach to translation encourages the receiver to question the dichotomy of 'translation' and 'original'. It is not only the so-called 'original' that is rewritten, but other texts and artefacts may be woven into the so-called 'translation'. These influences can come from the 'source', the receiving, or even totally extraneous cultures. Here is an illuminating example from the Hungarian translation history of *A Midsummer Night's Dream*. The expression in question is "my life for yours" (III/1, 40–41), which is spoken by one of the tradesmen, Bottom, instructing Quince at a rehearsal. In a contemporary Hungarian translation of the play this is mediated as "életemet és véremet ajánlom" [I offer my life and blood] (Shakespeare 1995: 76–77). The translator's choice is playfully intertextual, since it recalls a famous anecdote from the history of Hungary under Austrian domination. When, before the Silesian war of 1756–1763, the Empress Maria Theresa asked the Hungarian nobility for an army, they offered their lives and blood ("Vitam et sanguinem!"), provided that they received exemption from taxation for their lands. When retranslating the comedy, Ádám Nádasdy makes use of the analogous situation in a daring, tongue-in-cheek way: both the tradesmen and the noblemen want to receive something in return. This event takes place well after Shakespeare's time, and it clearly belongs to the receiving culture. This very apparent rewriting gesture—in which cultural allusion is made to a much later event—does not allow the receiver to identify the translation with the original, and it highlights the creative aspect of translation.

Two more binary sets—one from the study of interlingual (and, at the same time, intralingual) translation, and one from the realm of media—that may be seen as expressions of kindred thinking on creative refashioning. Lawrence Venuti (2007, 2008), revitalising Schleiermacher's related concepts (namely taking the writer to the reader and taking the reader to the writer), puts forward the much contested but, I feel, still immensely helpful, notions of foreignisation and domestication (the latter strategy may be perceived as of a more adaptive nature, if not a synonym for 'adaptation' as rewording, rearticulation). Modes and degrees of retaining/re-introducing foreignness and infusing a text with features recognisable as the receiver's own are valid fields of research—and strategies of practice—especially if one considers these attitudes, as Venuti himself later emphatically clarifies, as two ends of a broad spectrum. The fact itself that a translation is written in a language different from that of its (main but not necessarily only) 'source' is a gesture of domestication in itself, even if the text otherwise abounds with signs of otherness. Schleiermacher and Venuti, understandably, conceptualise in terms of language and literature. Jay David Bolter and Richard Grusin (2000), however, think, admittedly, along the lines of visual technologies primarily when they launch a likewise binary system: immediacy and hypermediacy as two sides of the process of remediation. As foreignisation in interlingual processes, hypermediacy makes the borrowing from other media explicit, purposefully visible. As domestication, immediacy also wishes to delete the traces of the main source of borrowing and aims to provide (the impression of) a seamless, unmediated or little mediated experience to the receiver. While without doubt it is the foreignising and hypermediatic decisions that are overtly metatextual, for a retranslator (who reads existing translations alongside 'originals') the domesticating and immediatic choices may also come across as self-referential, since they also comment on the translation/repurposing process, or more precisely, the attempt of camouflaging the practice of translation (by way of making the texture of a text smooth and quasi-familiar) reveals itself as a significantly intrusive process when caught red-handed. The metaphoric phrase 'intrusive' (which is often used when criticising translations) is, of course, in a sense faulty. A translation rewrites its (main) source; it is a new text written in a different language rather than the 'original' with changes. A translation's identity, however, is determined to a considerable extent by the 'original' so much so that many of the receivers would identify it with that. Talking of interlingual translation, in these cases the perception of translation as rewriting (with an emphasis on translation itself being writing, a form of creative writing) is, in such a context, inevitable.

TRIADS IN TRANSLATION AND ADAPTATION DISCOURSE

Having highlighted some analogous dyads in translation and adaptation discourse, let me highlight a few three-fold taxonomies that tend to appear in typologies of both translation and adaptation. The primary perspective once again is that of Adaptation Studies, into which I will graft translation criticism. Part Three of Geoffrey Wagner's *The Novel and the Cinema* (1975), titled 'Methods', explores three modes of adaptation, taking inspiration from Béla Balázs's film theory: *transposition* (exemplified by the 1939 *Wuthering Heights* and the 1944 *Jane Eyre* among others), *commentary* (with examples such as the 1970 *Catch-22* and the 1972 *A Clockwork Orange*) and *analogy* (illustrated for instance by the 1960 *Candide* and the 1971 *Death in Venice*). Wagner—a novelist (and a bilingual one at that), translator, literary critic and cultural commentator—defines *transposition* as the novel "directly given on the screen, with the minimum of apparent interference" (1975: 222–223). Wagner, who himself admits that some of the examples reduce their sources to some bare components, considerably undermines his definition by giving examples that noticeably truncate and alter their source text, for instance the 1939 *Wuthering Heights* and the 1944 *Jane Eyre*. For Wagner, *commentary* is "where an original is taken and either purposely or inadvertently altered in some respect. It could also be called a re-emphasis or re-structure" (223). And he adds, "Sometimes a change in character or scene may actually fortify the values of its original on the printed page. . . . It is when there has been a different intention on the part of the film-maker, rather than an infidelity or outright violation, that I would class the result as a commentary" (224). The most liberal of the three, *analogy*, involves "a fairly considerable departure" (227). It may be a "violation" (227) or it may "take but the merest hints from their sources" (230). Even though Wagner does not offer a concise definition of this type, it appears that examples of analogy may range from a very loose connection—a mere inspiration—to a more systematic template in a domesticating or transculturation approach.

Dudley Andrew's famous trichotomy—*borrowing, intersection* and *fidelity of transformation*—laid out in his seminal study *Concepts in Film*

Theory (1984) is, importantly, set up for "those cases where the adaptation process is foregrounded, that is, where the original is held up as a worthy source or goal" (98).[11] In *intersecting* "the uniqueness of the original text is preserved to such an extent that it is intentionally left unassimilated in adaptation" (99). When describing this mode, Andrew turns to Bazin, who claimed that this type of adaptation gives us the novel itself as seen by cinema. Bazin uses the conceptual metaphor of refraction to illustrate this type, and he also turns to the metaphors of the crystal chandelier as opposed to a flashlight when examining the relationship between novel and such a filmic take on it.[12] Such works, Andrew claims, "fear or refuse to adapt" (100). An illuminating overlapping area with translation theory emerges from Andrew's discussion of *fidelity of transformation*—a discussion that uncannily echoes the classical 'word for word' and 'sense for sense' distinction from centuries of translation theory:

> Fidelity of adaptation is conventionally treated in relation to the 'letter' and to the 'spirit' of the text, as though adaptation were the rendering of an interpretation of a legal precedent. The letter would appear to be within the reach of cinema for it can be emulated in mechanical fashion. It includes aspects of fiction generally elaborated in any film script: the characters and their inter-relation, the geographical, sociological, and cultural information providing the fiction's context, and the basic narrational aspects that determine the point of view of the narrator (tense, degree of participation and knowledge of the storyteller, and so on). . . . The skeleton of the original can, more or less thoroughly, become the skeleton of a film. (100)

He goes on to argue,

> More difficult is fidelity to the spirit, to the original's tone, values, imagery, and rhythm, since finding stylistic equivalents in film for these intangible aspects is the opposite of a mechanical process. The cineaste presumably must intuit and reproduce the feeling of the original. It has been argued variously that this is frankly impossible, or that it involves the systematic replacement of verbal signifiers by cinematic signifiers, or that it is the product of artistic intuition. (100–101)

Andrew suggests that *borrowing* is a frequently used mode over the course of art history as it implies building on the iconic, sacred or respectable status and force of the respective original, be it the Bible, Shakespeare or *Don Quixote*. In such adaptations "the audience is expected to enjoy basking in a certain pre-established presence and to call up new or especially powerful aspects of a cherished work" (98). The adaptation benefits from the "generality" and "wide and varied appeal" of the source. Andrew goes so far as to make a connection with archetypes and myths in this regard (and this is not far from the perspective taken in Julie Sanders' recent work in the field), not only by suggesting that such originals have obtained mythic status—a status as "a continuing form or archetype in culture" (98) but also allowing for the centrality of "the great fructifying symbols and mythic patterns of civilization" (99) as discussed by Jung or Fry to cycles of adaptations, which considerably broadens the concept of adaptation.

John M. Desmond and Peter Hawkes in *Adaptation: Studying Film and Literature* (2005) divide adaptations into *close*, *loose* and *intermediate* ones.[13] As they claim, "A film is a close adaptation when most of the narrative elements in the literary text are kept in the film, few elements are dropped, and not many elements are added". They exemplify this type with *Harry Potter and the Philosopher's Stone* (or, to be more precise, its American version: *Harry Potter and the Sorcerer's Stone*). According to their taxonomy "a film is a loose adaptation when most of the story elements in the literary text are dropped from the film and most elements in the film are substituted or added. A loose adaptation uses the literary text as a point of departure" (2005: 44). Their examples are *To Have and Have Not*, directed by Howard Hawks and inspired by Hemingway's novel, and *Memento*, directed by Christopher Nolan, borrowing the "basic premise" of his brother Jonathan's short story.

They then conveniently place intermediate adaptation "in the fluid middle of the sliding scale between close and loose. In this type, some elements of the story are kept in the film, other elements are dropped, and still more elements are added. An intermediate adaptation neither conforms exactly not departs entirely" (Desmond and Hawkes 2005: 44). The authors illustrate this with *What's Eating Gilbert Grape*, Lasse Hallström's adaptation of Peter Hedges's novel, which, as they observe, omits some lesser characters and plotlines (44). As the authors themselves admit, "Like the language of fidelity, these words carry their own implications". They associate 'close' adaptation with rather positive and 'loose' with more negative connotations.

Linda Cahir defines *literal* translation as "reproduc[ing] the plot and all its attending details as closely as possible to the letter of the book" (2006: 16). She brings the 1956 *Moby Dick* as an example of this. In her view, *traditional* translation "maintains the overall traits of the book (its plot, settings, and stylistic conventions) but revamps particular details in those particular ways that the filmmakers see as necessary and fitting" (16–17). The 1998 *Moby Dick* is seen as an example of this. She asserts that *radical* translation "reshapes the book in extreme and revolutionary ways both as a means of interpreting the literature and of making the film a more fully independent work" (17). Her two examples from the filmic adaptations of *Moby Dick* are the 1926 silent film *The Sea Beast* and its 1930 readaptation.[14]

When teaching translation and adaptation as creative-interpretive processes I tend to 'smuggle in' John Dryden's tripartite taxonomy of translation from his 1680 preface to *Ovid's Epistles* in the middle of the table that I have compiled of the abovementioned adaptation scholars' classifications (see Table 2.1). It is revealing to see the connection between the semi-contemporary taxonomies (which also display commonalities in between them)

Table 2.1   Translation and Adaptation Classifications

Wagner (1975)	Andrew (1984)	Dryden (1680)	Desmond and Hawkes (2005)	Cahir (2006)
transposition	intersecting	metaphrasis	close	literal
commentary	fidelity of transformation	paraphrasis	intermediate	traditional
analogy	borrowing	imitatio	loose	radical

and the one from the late 17th century. The three different approaches to translation (as the rewriting of a text) appear to have influenced the way we think about 'translation' (as Jakobson does in his own three-fold definition of the concept) as well as 'adaptation': the mode of rearticulation as well as the distance taken from the source (which an intertextual perspective on the process may re-label as the 'main/most overt' source of intertextual connection) are both pivotal to defining the kind of creative and critical work that constitutes the new text.

Linda Cahir herself points out the connection with John Dryden's work:

> The antecedents of such attempts are in literary theory, the most pronounced of which is John Dryden's categorizing translations into three types: line-by-line, paraphrasing, and imitation. . . . Similarly to Dryden's categories, this text asserts that film fundamentally translates literature in three distinctive ways. Each of these three different methods bears distinct translation values, aims, and ambitions, and each regards different features of the source text as most vital to preserve when translating the literature into film. (16)

Dryden's ideas, of course, constitute not only literary theory but translation theory too, and the critical heritage defined by translation theory and revisited up to our day is easy to note.

ADAPTATION, TRANSLATION AND THE ONTOLOGY OF THE TEXT

It is noteworthy that both translation and adaptation have appeared recently in discussions of genre. It is broadly acknowledged that genre in a more traditional sense of the term has moved considerably from the realm of literature towards film, television and other newer media since the beginning of the 20th century (see Dowd 2006, among many others), although it still has considerable use in marketing books (see Bassnett 2002: 94; Frow 2006: 128). Genre appears more relevant when categorising contemporary popular film than in relation to a great deal of contemporary literature (except for instance 'genre books' on the more popular end of the market), where longstanding generic categories do not often apply any more. The subtitle of the academic journal *Genre* (established in 1968, revamped in 1992)—*Forms of Discourse and Culture*—itself reveals that the scope of the concept has broadened considerably under the aegis of the postmodern. That said, I still find it a little misleading when adaptation is presented as a genre in some contemporary criticism. In a recent BFI genre reader, *They Went Thataway* (a collection of edited trade journalism on the most common contemporary film genres), the editor Richard T. Jameson distinguishes between two kinds of adaptation: literary adaptations and movie adaptations (in the latter category he assembles articles on remakes and sequels). This is how he approaches adaptation as a genre:

> The 'genre' of Literary Adaptations is as miscellaneous as the variety of works adapted to the screen. We include it here to stimulate reflection on the subtle art of translating literature to film, but also to propose that Literary Adaptations do have something in common—a quality of *expectation* ("Are they going to ruin my favourite novel or make me love it all the more?") that can be more powerful than any generic presuppositions we bring to a new Western, horror film, or film noir. Indeed, it often transpires that, when one has read the book on which a film is based, one ought to see the film at least twice: the first time, to get one's curiosity about the adaptation out of the way; the second time, to see the movie in its own right. (Jameson 1994: 308)

Let me also cite a couple of academic and, at the same time, considerably more specific recourses to the idea of the adaptation genre. In a 2008 article published in *Adaptation*, Thomas Leitch argues very persuasively that adaptation is a genre. As one is expected when introducing concepts (or new usage for a concept), he throws light on what he perceives as "markers" of the genre which is adaptation, and provides ample exemplary material (mainly of female-orientated romances and male-orientated adventure films). These markers or conventions are period setting, period music, a preoccupation with "authors, books, and words" (2008: 112) and distinctive intertitles. Deborah Cartmell proposes to take Leitch's work one step further, adding some more criteria to Leitch's system in her analysis of screen adaptations of *Pride and Prejudice*, which novel and its screen afterlife Cartmell considers "a template for such a genre" (2011: 227, abstract). Building on Leitch as well as Geraghty, who adds the foregrounding of media to the conventions identified by Leitch (see Cartmell 2011: 229), Cartmell introduces the use of pictures and other art forms, "the makeover of the author to screen" and the appeal to female audiences (229–230). Corinne Lhermitte (2005) also suggests that film adaptation be viewed as a genre, yet she does not set this genre against other filmic genres recognized by academy and the industry.

While the use of the term 'genre' in this "regime of reading" (Frow 2005: 139) is carefully considered and systematically presented, one may also observe that it only applies to a small fraction of what we refer to as adaptations either in everyday or scholarly discourse. It excludes all sorts of adaptations or reworkings that are not in the filmic (or televisual) medium; it may even exclude filmic adaptations that are not particularly popular or middlebrow but on the arthouse, auterist end of the spectrum. The "evolving definition of an adaptation genre" (Cartmell 2011: 227, abstract), despite being a clever and enticing critical construct, is altogether confusing. Adaptation can hardly be considered a genre in the way, say, horrors, thrillers, romantic comedies or biopics can be.[15] A film adaptation—the way I would perceive it—may belong to one of many genres: it may be a romantic comedy or a biographical film (adapted from a source or—as it is more likely to be the case—reworking or evoking a broad range of material). It may, of course, be a generic hybrid, for instance both a teenpic and a comedy (*Ten Things I Hate About You*).[16] What makes such a film an adaptation is the intertextual relationship with pre-existing or rather co-existing texts, yet those texts and the adaptations themselves may belong to various genres. Still, the process of adaptation is something that leaves marks on the 'text' (the text we 'freeze' for our scrutiny in its intertextual flow for our purposes so as to call it adaptation). These marks are to do with the ontology of the mid-flow scrutinized text and can indeed be very similar in nature to the markers identified by Leitch and subsequently Cartmell but they are not necessarily reflective of individual genres as text types. Yes, a certain type of period music or period typeface in the intertitles may be markers of adaptation—not of adaptation as a genre (alongside the sci-fi or the woman's film for instance) but adaptation as a way of being of a travelling text. As discussed before with regard to translation and intertextuality, translations indeed bear marks of their status as translations (some perhaps more so than others). They unavoidably have self-referential traits, for instance a poem may be translated in a verse that is indigenous to the receiving language and cannot demonstrate an aspect of the 'original', therefore emphatically displays itself as a translation. An utterly alien verse form may have a similar effect, so both domesticating and foreignising strategies may act as self-referential markers. These metatextual markers contribute to the discussion of the ontology of such texts—their being as translations—but in a similar vein, they would not make translation as such a genre. Translations (that is, textual translations), just as adaptations, can be examples of numerous genres: a translation may be a memoir, an elegy, an ode, a Künstlerroman or a campus novel, but translation is not their genre, unless we replace (but why would we?) the working definition of genre as 'text type' with genre as 'way-of-being/ontology' of a product of creativity.

In his landmark Adaptation Studies collection of essays, *Film Adaptation*, the editor James Naremore recognises,

The study of adaptation needs to be joined with the study of recycling, remaking, and every other form of retelling in the age of mechanical reproduction and electronic communication. By this means, adaptation will become part of a general theory of repetition, and adaptation study will move from the margins to the centre of contemporary media studies. (2000: 15)

Whilst fidelity- and equivalence-centred approaches persist and make valuable contributions especially to case-study based research enterprises, those regimes of reading that focus on inter- or transtextuality and inter- or transmediality enrich the contemporary way of thinking both of translation and adaptation. Such approaches problematise the kindred features of the two modes of creative and critical rearticulation of texts—modes that do not necessarily entail distinctly separate processes.

NOTES

1. The term 'Adaptation Studies' appears in literary criticism proper as well; it is used for instance by John Joughin (2003: 145) in a collection entitled *The New Aestheticism*.
2. Itamar Even-Zohar, a representative voice of the Israeli school of Translation Studies, is credited, alongside his colleagues, with the establishment of polysystem studies. This approach entails analysing a culture's literary outputs as part of a complex, multi-branching polysystem with translation playing a significant role in three particular stages of any polysystem's history: in the phase of establishment, times of weakness or moments of crisis/at turning points (Even-Zohar 1978). Recently Even-Zohar has been investigating culture as a polysystem more holistically rather than literature only, and he has been specifically interested in exploring minority cultures.
3. Venuti (2007: 25–28) is critical of what he terms the 'communicative' model in Film Adaptation Studies (apparent, for instance, in McFarlane 1996) where the adaptation is seen a complex transfer of narrative and enunciation. He perceives the 'hermeneutic' model (exemplified by Stam 2005, among others) focusing on intertextuality and a plethora of operations more inclusive, but still somewhat limited. In Venuti's reading, the communicative model tends to maintain the primacy of the text, while the hermeneutic model seems merely to reverse the hierarchy. It may not be an exaggeration to suggest that the theories of translation can also be broadly divided into these two approaches: the more semiotically oriented, equivalence-focused communicative approaches and those that interpret translations as texts in their own right and also examine them as readings of prior/co-existent texts.
4. The word is spelt as *re-imagining* in Marsden's study.
5. Many of these examples are from Shakespeare Reception Studies; a study of the afterlife of further (especially canonical) *oeuvres*, such as Austen and the Brontë sisters, will reveal more attempts at naming modes of reworking.
6. Thomas Leitch (2008) sheds light on the fact that Hollywood cinema first used stage plays for source materials before turning to the novel as a predominant inspirational form. Stage plays, being conceived in/for the performative mode, were almost ready-made materials for the cinema industry

before it took up the challenge offered by the novel and other primarily narrative forms.

7. On metaphors in translation discourse see Chamberlain (1992) for an excellent account. Naremore's observation echoes Chamberlain's findings: ". . . most writing on adaptation as translation, even when it assumes a tone of quasi-scientific objectivity, betrays certain unexamined ideological concerns because it deals of necessity with sexually charged materials and cannot avoid a gendered language associated with the notion of 'fidelity'" (Naremore 2000: 8). Shelley Cobbs's recent article "Adaptation, Fidelity, and Gendered Discourses" (2011) explores this phenomenon in contemporary criticism.

8. Joanne Paul (2008) also acknowledges the work of Cattrysse in the area.

9. John Joughin's 2003 article on adaptation and *Hamlet* is a case in point.

10. McKechnie refers to "the flawed taxonomies of 'faithfulness' (sometimes flippantly termed 'the F-word by frustrated scholars')" (2009: 193).

11. Andrew's *Concepts in Film Theory* (1984) devotes an entire chapter to adaptation, which is divided into sections entitled "The Sources of Films", "Borrowing, Intersecting and Transforming Sources" and "The Sociology and Aesthetics of Adaptation".

12. Among other examples, Andrew uses one that Bazin himself elaborated on: Robert Bresson's filmic reworking of Bernanos's novel.

13. As the authors themselves admit, "Like the language of fidelity, these words carry their own implications." They associate 'close' with rather positive and 'loose' with more negative connotations.

14. These all happen to be threefold conceptualisations yet it is important to note that for instance Kamilla Elliott's six item categorisation in her *Rethinking the Novel/Film Debate* (2003) and Thomas Leitch's (2009) extensive ten-strong inventory—explored in his chapter "From Adaptation to Allusion"—are also very helpful and theoretically grounded models.

15. Interestingly, Leitch considers what he terms the adaptation genre in the vicinity of (but not fully overlapping) the genres of heritage film and costume drama (both particularly contentious categories).

16. It is revealing to note that on the one hand, there is a contemporary tendency to use genre in a very broad sense, even to encompass types of shops as "genres of shop" (see Frow 2005: 126–128, particularly 127), on the other hand, other usages intend to restrict the term to a very specific frame of use.

WORKS CITED

Andrew, Dudley. 1984. *Concepts in Film Theory*. New York: Oxford University Press.

Bassnett, Susan. 2002. *Translation Studies*. 3rd ed., New York and London: Routledge.

Bastin, Georges L. 1998. 'Adaptation'. In: Mona Baker (ed.), *Routledge Encyclopedia of Translation Studies*. London: Routledge, pp. 5–8.

Bolter, Jay David and Richard Grusin. 2000. *Remediation: Understanding New Media*. 2nd ed. Cambridge, Massachusetts: MIT Press.

Cahir, Linda Costanzo. 2006. *Literature Into Film: Theory and Practical Approaches*. Jefferson, NC: McFarland.

Cartelli, Thomas. 1999. *Repositioning Shakespeare: National Formations, Postcolonial Appropriations*. London: Routledge.

Cartmell, Deborah. 2011. '*Pride and Prejudice* and the Adaptation Genre'. *Journal of Adaptation in Film and Performance*, 3:3, pp. 227–243.

Cattrysse, Patrick. 1992. 'Film (Adaptation) as Translation: Some Methodological Proposals'. *Target*, 4:1, pp. 53–70.

Chamberlain, Lori. 1992. 'Gender and the Metaphorics of Translation'. In: Lawrence Venuti (ed.), *Rethinking Translation: Discourse, Subjectivity, Ideology*. London: Routledge, pp. 57–74.

Cobbs, Shelley. 2011. 'Adaptation, Fidelity, and Gendered Discourses'. *Adaptation*, 4:1, pp. 28–37.

Cohn, Ruby. 1976. *Modern Shakespeare Offshoots*. Princeton, NJ: Princeton University Press.

Cox, Philip. 2000. *Reading Adaptations: Novels and Verse Narratives on the Stage, 1790–1840*. Manchester: Manchester University Press.

Desmet, Christie and Sawyer, Robert (eds.). 1999. *Shakespeare and Appropriation*. London: Routledge.

Desmond, John M. and Peter Hawkes. 2005. *Adaptation: Studying Film and Literature*. New York: McGraw-Hill Higher Education.

Dowd, Garin. 2006. 'Introduction: Genre Matters in Theory and Criticism'. In: Garin Dowd, Lesley Stephenson and Jeremy Strong (eds.), *Genre Matters: Essays in Theory and Criticism*. Bristol: Intellect, pp. 11–27.

Dryden, John. 1992 [1680]. 'Extracts From the Preface to His Translation of *Ovid's Epistles* Published in 1680'. In: André Lefevere (ed.), *Translation/History/Culture: A Sourcebook*. London: Routledge, pp. 102–105.

Elliott, Kamilla. 2003. *Rethinking the Novel/Film Debate*. Cambridge: Cambridge University Press.

Even-Zohar, Itamar. 1978. *Papers in Historical Poetics*. Tel Aviv: Tel Aviv University.

Federici, Eleonora. 2007. 'The Translator's Intertextual Baggage'. *Forum for Modern Language Studies*, 43:2, pp. 147–160.

Fischlin, Daniel and Mark Fortier (eds.). 2000. *Adaptations of Shakespeare: A Critical Anthology of Plays from the Seventeenth Century to the Present*. London: Routledge.

Frow, John. 2006. *Genre*. London: Routledge.

Fry, Michael. 2008. 'Researching the Method: Some Personal Strategies'. *Journal of Adaptation in Film and Performance*, 1:2, pp. 147–159.

Hutcheon, Linda. 2006. *A Theory of Adaptation*. New York: Routledge.

Jakobson, Roman. [1959] 1992. 'On Linguistic Aspects of Translation'. In: Rainer Schulte and John Biguenet (eds.), *Theories of Translation*. Chicago: University of Chicago Press, pp. 144–151.

Jameson, Richard T. 1994. 'Literary Adaptations'. In: Richard T. Jameson (ed.), *They Went Thataway: Redefining Film Genres: A National Society of Film Critics Video Guide*. San Francisco: Mercury House, pp. 307–308.

Jess-Cooke, Carolyn. 2007. *Shakespeare on Film: Such Things as Dreams Are Made Of*. London: Wallflower.

Johnston, David. 1996. 'Theatre Pragmatics'. In: *Stages of Translation: Translators on Translating for the Stage*. Bath, England: Absolute Classics, pp. 57–66.

Joughin, John. 2003. 'Shakespeare's Genius: *Hamlet*, Adaptation and the Work of Following'. In: John J. Joughin and Simon Malpas (eds.), *The New Aestheticism*. Manchester: Manchester University Press, pp. 131–150.

Józan, Ildikó. 1997. 'Műfordítás és intertextualitás'. *Alföld* (November), pp. 45–53.

Kiséry, András. 1996. 'Hamletizing the Spirit of the Nation: Political Uses of Kazinczy's 1790 Translation'. In: Holgar Klein and Péter Dávidházi (eds.), *Shakespeare and Hungary* (*Shakespeare Yearbook*, Vol. 7). Lewiston, NY: Edwin Mellen, pp. 11–35.

Lane, David. 2010. *Contemporary British Drama*. Edinburgh: Edinburgh University Press.

Lefevere, André (ed.). 1992. *Translation/History/Culture: A Sourcebook*. London: Routledge.

Leitch, Thomas. 2008. 'Adaptation, the Genre'. *Adaptation*, 1:2, pp. 106–120.

Leitch, Thomas. 2009. 'Between Adaptation and Allusion'. In: *Film Adaptation and Its Discontents: From Gone With the Wind to The Passion of Christ*. Baltimore: Johns Hopkins University Press, pp. 93–126.

Ley, Graham. 2009. '"Discursive Embodiment": The Theatre as Adaptation'. *Journal of Adaptation in Film and Performance*, 2:3, pp. 201–209.

Lhermitte, Corinne. 2004. 'Adaptation as Rewriting: Evolution of a Concept'. *Revue LISA/LISA e-journal*, 2:5. http://lisa.revues.org/2897 (accessed on 4 December 2011).

Lhermitte, Corinne. 2005. 'A Jakobsonian Approach to Film Adaptations of Hugo's *Les Misérables*'. *Nebula*, 2:1, pp. 97–107.

Littau, Karin. 2011. 'First Steps Towards a Media History of Translation'. *Translation Studies*, 4:3, pp. 261–281.

MacCabe, Colin, Katherine Murray and Rick Warner (eds.). 2011. *True to the Spirit: Film Adaptation and the Question of Fidelity*. Oxford: Oxford University Press.

Manvell, Roger. 1979. *Theater and Film: A Comparative Study of the Two Forms of Dramatic Art, and of the Problems of Adaptation of Stage Plays Into Films*. Rutherford, NJ: Farleigh Dickinson University Press.

Marcus, Millicent. 1993. *Filmmaking by the Book: Italian Cinema and Literary Adaptation*. Baltimore: Johns Hopkins University Press.

Marsden, Jean I. 1991. *The Appropriation of Shakespeare: Post-Renaissance Reconstructions of the Works and the Myth*. New York: Harvester Wheatsheaf.

McKechnie, Kara. 2009. '*Gloriana*—the Queen's Two Selves: Agency, Context and Adaptation Studies'. In: Monika Pietrzak-Franger and Eckart Voigts-Virchow (eds.), *Adaptations: Performing Across Media and Genres*. Trier: Wissenschaftlicher Verlag Trier, pp. 193–209.

Miller, Naomi J. (ed.). 2003. *Reimagining Shakespeare for Children and Young Adults*. London: Routledge.

Minier, Márta. 2005. 'Reconsidering Translation From the Vantage Point of Gender Studies'. In: Patsy Stoneman and Ana María Sánchez-Arce (with Angela Leighton) (eds.), *European Intertexts: Women's Writing in English in a European Context*. Bern: Peter Lang, pp. 59–83.

Minutella, Vincenza. 2012. '*Romeo and Juliet* From Page to Screen: A Multilateral Model for the Analysis of Three Italian Films'. *Journal of Adaptation in Film and Performance*, 5:1, pp. 25–40.

Nánay, Bence. 2000. 'Túl az adaptáción' [Beyond Adaptation]. In: Anna Gács and Gábor Gelencsér (eds.), *Adoptációk: Film és irodalom egymásra hatása* [Adoptions: How Film and Literature Influence Each Other]. Budapest: József Attila Kör, Kijárat, pp. 21–45.

Naremore, James. 2000. 'Introduction: Film and the Reign of Adaptation'. In: James Naremore (ed.), *Film Adaptation*. London: Athlone Press, pp. 1–16.

Nida, Eugene. 2000 [1964]. 'Principles of Correspondence'. In: Lawrence Venuti (ed.), *The Translation Studies Reader*. London: Routledge, pp. 126–140.

Oittinen, Riitta. 2000. *Translating for Children*. New York: Garland Publishing.

Orr, Mary. 2003. *Intertextuality: Debates and Contexts*. Cambridge: Polity.

Palmer, R. Barton. 2008 [2004]. 'The Sociological Turn in Adaptation Studies: The Example of Film Noir'. In: Robert Stam and Alexandra Raengo (eds.), *A Companion to Literature and Film*.

Malden, MA: Blackwell, pp. 258–277.

Paul, Joanna. 2008. 'Homer and Cinema: Translation and Adaptation in *Le Mépris*'. In: Alexandra Lianeri and Vanda Zajko (eds.), *Translation and the*

Classic: Identity As Change in the History of Culture. Oxford: Oxford University Press. pp. 148165.

Perteghella, Manuela. 2008. 'Adaptation: "Bastard Child" or Critique? Putting Terminology Centre Stage'. *Journal of Romance Studies*, 8:3, pp. 51–65.

Reader, Keith A. 'Literature/Cinema/Television: Intertextuality in Jean Renoir's *Le Testament du docteur Cordelier*'. In: Judith Still and Michael Worton (eds.), *Intertextuality: Theories and Practice*. Manchester: Manchester University Press, pp. 176–189.

Reynolds, Peter (ed.). 1993. *Novel Images: Literature in Performance*. London: Routledge.

Sanders, Julie. 2006. *Adaptation and Appropriation*. London: Routledge.

Sarris, Andrew. 1994. 'Orlando'. In: Richard T. Jameson (ed.), *They Went That-away: Redefining Film Genres: A National Society of Film Critics Video Guide*. San Francisco: Mercury House, pp. 325–326.

Shakespeare, William. 1995. *Szentivánéji álom* [A Midsummer Night's Dream]. Trans. Ádám Nádasdy. Budapest: Ikon.

Snyder, Mary H. 2011. *Analyzing Literature-to-Film Adaptations: A Novelist's Exploration and Guide*. New York: Continuum.

Stam, Robert. 2000. 'Beyond Fidelity: the Dialogics of Adaptation'. In: James Naremore (ed.), *Film Adaptation*. London: Athlone, pp. 54–76.

Szegedy-Maszák, Mihály. 1998. 'Fordítás és kánon'. In: *Irodalmi kánonok*. Debrecen, Hungary: Csokonai Kiadó, pp. 47–71.

Taylor, Gary. 1989. *Reinventing Shakespeare: A Cultural History from the Restoration to the Present*. London: The Hogarth Press.

Venuti, Lawrence. 2007. 'Adaptation, Translation, Critique'. *Journal of Visual Culture*, 6:1, pp. 25–43.

Venuti, Lawrence. 2008. *The Translator's Invisibility: A History of Translation*. 2nd ed. London: Routledge.

Vickers, Brian. 1993. *Appropriating Shakespeare: Contemporary Critical Quarrels*. New Haven, CT: Yale University Press.

Wagner, Geoffrey. 1975. *The Novel and the Cinema*. Rutherford, NJ: Fairleigh Dickinson University Press.

Wood, David (with Janet Grant). 1997. *Theatre for Children: Guide to Writing, Adapting, Directing and Acting*. London: Faber and Faber.

Zatlin, Phyllis. 2005. *Theatrical Translation and Film Adaptation: A Practitioner's View*. Clevedon, England: Multilingual Matters.

3   Bakhtin, Translation and Adaptation

Dennis Cutchins

TRANSLATION AND ADAPTATION

I must begin this chapter with a confession. Although I am writing about Bakhtinian theory, adaptation and translation, I have very little practical knowledge about the last item on that list. In addition to my native English, I speak a little bit of Italian and a little bit of Spanish. I took classes in Japanese and French in college, but I have forgotten most of the former, and I believe I am still under an injunction, delivered by my French teacher one afternoon in 1994, never to speak French again in public. Thus I approach translation, at least in terms of national languages, as a theoretical prospect, rather than a practical exercise. Despite my ignorance, Bakhtin might argue that I am an experienced translator nonetheless. This is true, in part, because he conceives of languages more broadly than most, and he argues that within a given national language, there might be different 'languages' spoken according to region, occupation, age, and other factors. He writes,

> At any given moment in its evolution, language[1] is stratified not only into linguistic dialects in the strict sense of the word (according to formal linguistic markers, especially phonetic), but also—and for us this is the essential point—into languages that are socio-ideological: languages of social groups, 'professional' and 'generic' languages, languages of generations and so forth. (Bakhtin 1981: 271–272)

This broader definition of language suggests that we are all, every day, engaged in more or less constant acts of translation. The languages my children experience at school, family languages and professional languages all must be translated before they can be understood by those who are not a part of the group that uses them. I will discuss translation in terms of national languages in this chapter, but 'translation' is used primarily in this sub-linguistic, Bakhtinian sense.[2] Ultimately, I'd like to understand translation as an analog of adaptation, and Bakhtin's broader understanding of language and translation suggests that this may be appropriate.

Although he did not seem concerned with adaptation proper, Bakhtin's notions about the gap between language and expressive material, what we might call a gap between language and content, was taken up eagerly by early adaptation theorists. Adaptations, particularly film adaptations, were seen by some theorists as 'translations' or even 'transpositions' of literary content to the screen. It was as if the language of a novel or other text was simply a container that carried a particular material that might just as easily be converted (translated) into a play, a film or an opera. These theorists failed to grasp the rest of Bakhtin's logic: translation is not simply the changing of the container; it literally creates the content. Katerina Clark and Michael Holquist have argued that the common understanding of 'translation', the notion that the 'same idea' might be expressed in different languages, was one of the central questions in all of Bakhtin's thought. But he did not assume the 'sameness' of translated texts,[3] and he was fascinated with the notion of difference within similarity, or similarity within difference. "A question that fuels Bakhtin's whole enterprise, then, is, What makes differences different?" (Clark and Holquist 1984: 9). These differences seemed to generate meaning, and that intrigued Bakhtin. He worked throughout his career to understand how something could be the same and different simultaneously, and this dynamic became a central feature of his notion of 'dialogue'. "Ultimately", Clark and Holquist argue, "dialogue means communication between simultaneous differences" (1984: 9). It is, perhaps, here, at this basic level of thought, that the relationship between Bakhtin's ideas about dialogue and translation and the more recent study of adaptation become clear. Bakhtin wanted to understand how something like a film could be utterly and completely different from something like a novel, and yet be perceived by an audience or readers as somehow the same. Understanding relationships like that, of course, is the central goal of Adaptation Studies.

THE IMPORTANCE OF TRANSLATION

The word I have often heard used to describe Bakhtin's writings is 'uneven', and that word is fitting. As a reader, I find myself easily mired in Bakhtin's details and in his esoteric examples. Nevertheless, amid the sometimes confusing and often dry passages are plenty of absolute gems, and those moments are worth the effort. I read Bakhtin because he inspires me and his work regularly changes my perspective on the way humans make meaning in language and art. That was the case a few years ago when I stumbled on a passage he had written about the translation of chivalric romances from one national language to another. Bakhtin argued that the act of translation forced the translators of these texts to recognise the relational, rather than absolute, status of one language to another. Subject matter, or "material and language were not given as a seamless whole (as they were for the creators of the epic), but were rather fragmented, separated from each other, had to seek each other out" (1990: 377). This gap between the material and the language helped to engender the very idea of literature, what he calls "literary consciousness", at least in terms of these romances. "Translation, reworking, re-conceptualizing, re-accenting—manifold degrees of mutual inter-orientation with alien discourse, alien intentions—these were the activities shaping the literary consciousness that created the chivalric romance" (1981: 377). Later he expands this line of thought to suggest that "the first prose novels were in an analogous situation with regard to language". He concludes, "It could even be said that European novel prose is born and shaped in the process of a free (that is reformulating) translation of others' works" (377–378).

Since tales or stories already existed in this history Bakhtin describes, it's not immediately clear what Bakhtin meant when he said that the idea of literature or "literary consciousness" as well as "novel prose" were invented in an act of translation. The answer lies in Bakhtin's understanding of 'literature'. One might tell a story in a culture that did not recognise other languages, but the story would not be *literature*, at least as far as Bakhtin is concerned. It would, instead, tend to be scriptural (a story drawn from sacred texts), prosaic (something that had happened to the teller) or mythic (a story representing a deeply seated belief). Bakhtin argues that for monoglot or single-language cultures unfamiliar with the concept of translation, literature, as we know it, cannot exist (1981: 370).[4] Monoglot cultures might have myths, scriptures or even epics, but not novels, not literature. This is because both the teller and the listener in these situations conceive of the tale both as utterly and completely true and as closed to interpretation. In other words, monoglot texts are unable to generate 'readings'. Language in these situations is understood as having what must be considered a magical quality that connects it more or less directly to that which it represents. The assumed magical power of knowing someone's true name, common in many cultures, is a reflection of this view of language.

Literary language, on the other hand, is quite different from the language of personal experience, scripture, myth or epic. For Bakhtin literary language requires "a complete rupture between language and its material" (1981: 378). Words, in literary language, are no longer magically connected to the things they represent. This rupture creates literature by allowing a story to exist not as an absolute truth, but "as a rejoinder in a given dialogue, whose style is determined by its interrelationships with other rejoinders in the same dialogue" (274). Literature, in short, always understands itself as relative, rather than absolute, and thus always generates multiple readings. In this way Bakhtin's very definition of literature required interrelationships with other languages. Keep in mind, however, that Bakhtin did not limit his idea of language to national language. We are all engaged in translation acts as we move between the various languages we speak.

This awareness seems potentially productive and empowering for adaptation theory since adaptations are, in effect, free translations or reworkings of existent texts into new 'languages'. More to the point, this notion places adaptation not at the edges of the study of literature, but at its centre, since the very idea of literature is a result of translation. At the end of *The Dialogic Imagination* Bakhtin suggests that "great novelistic images continue to grow and develop even after the moment of their creation; they are capable of being creatively transformed in different eras, far distant from the day and hour of their original birth" (1981: 422). It's possible that some of the concepts defined by Bakhtin as he explored literature and translation will provide at least a partial foundation for a theory of adaptation. Like his notion of novelistic images, his own ideas may prove capable of being creatively transformed to work in ways that are "far distant from the day and hour of their original birth". Perhaps more to the point, Bakhtin's broader understanding of 'translation', as well as the potential ramifications of this understanding, fit in well with the way the term has been used by at least some contemporary scholars. Wai Chee Dimock claimed in 2006, for instance, that when he wrote *Walden* and 'Civil Disobedience', Henry David Thoreau was actually 'translating' the *Bhagavad Gita*. "Translated in just this way, its volatile truth betraying its literal monument, the *Bhagavad Gita* is threaded into an American context unthinkable at its moment of genesis" (in Gentzler 2008: 39).

Although Bakhtin's assertions about the genesis of literature are, insofar as I am concerned, unprovable,[5] they do make sense. I am intrigued by the basic idea that literary consciousness was born in moments of translating alien discourse, and the implications of the passage cited above are both complex and stunning. Bakhtin's often revolutionary notions about language, meaning, dialogism and literature are implicit in this statement. This simple declaration of the central role translation plays in literature is the logical result of several of Bakhtin's most repeated themes. In other words, although I can't verify the historical truth of what he is suggesting, I can see the clear and relatively simple logic that leads him to this conclusion. I'd like to spend most of the rest of this essay unpacking the logic that led Bakhtin to this conclusion, and exploring the implications of what he is suggesting in terms of adaptation. I'll note first, however, that Bakhtin's stress on the importance of translation helps to unlock the chains that had been placed on art more than 2000 years earlier by Plato and Aristotle. Not surprisingly, Bakhtin defined himself as an "anti-Aristotelian", and he created a space in which literary art, and adaptations in particular, could be more than mimesis, more than an always-inferior copy (Holquist and Liapunov 1990: xx). For Bakhtin the act of translation, understood broadly, plays a central role in the creative, artistic process.

DEFINING TRANSLATION

In order to explain the revolutionary implications of Bakhtin's ideas about translation I'd like to begin by outlining a more traditional understanding of the term. 'Translation' is an odd word that, over the years, has acquired, and in some cases lost, a broad range of meanings. The online version of the *Oxford English Dictionary* lists 15 different definitions, including the familiar ones that deal with "turning from one language into another" ('translation'). But the dictionary also lists some less familiar definitions that might help to reconceptualise the act of turning from one language into another. In classical physics, for instance, 'translation' can mean the transference of energy from one body to another, as when an object moving through space, full, as it were, of translational, kinetic energy, collides with another, relatively stationary object and 'translates' its energy to that object, causing it to move. As in all classical physics, however, the transfer is never perfect. Some of the energy is always lost, and the second object never travels quite as far or as fast as the first would have had the collision not taken place. This is, perhaps, a good metaphor for the way translation from one language to another has typically been viewed. In this understanding of translation, a word or a text is imagined to have a certain energy that may be transferred to a different word or text in another language. As with the objects in space, however, the transfer of energy is never perfect. The translated word or text is never quite as powerful or as meaningful, if you will, as the original.[6] Not coincidentally, adaptations have often been viewed in a similar manner.

This Newtonian understanding of 'translation', however, is utterly foreign to Bakhtin's way of thinking. In order to explain his ideas about translation I'd like to turn briefly to another writer. In 1922 Rainer Maria Rilke finished his *Duino Elegies*. The *Elegies* were soon being translated and published in several different languages. In 1925, Rilke received a letter from Witold Hulewicz, his Polish translator, with some questions regarding a specific passage in the text. In answer to these questions Rilke offered a suggestion that must have been frustrating for the translator. Rilke notes that the poems, like other elements of the world in general, were "transitory and frail", but argues that this imperfection, this fragility is not necessarily a bad thing. "Our task", he suggests, "is not to make all the things of life look bad and denigrate them" because they are impermanent (Norris and Keele 1993: viii). Instead the poet offers this philosophical advice, likely useless to someone looking for concrete answers about translating a passage:

> [P]recisely because of their transitoriness, which they share with us, we must comprehend, must grasp these phenomena, these things, more affectionately, more intimately, and transform them. Transform? Yes, our commission is to impress the transitory, frail world upon ourselves, that its very being is invisibly resurrected in us. (viii)[7]

Rilke equates the translation process with the writing of poetry in a way that must have been both liberating and perhaps a little frightening for his translator. He argues that translating poetry from one national language to another is analogous to the process of writing poetry in the first place, and that both enterprises amount to comprehending and then transforming the frail, transitory, ephemeral world into language. The poet 'translates' into language an image or an idea based on experience. The translator, in turn, translates into another language, an image or an idea based on a reading. Rilke insists that these are similar processes because comprehension must come first in both of these acts of translation. He does not assume that the meaning, either of what he sees in the world or of what readers understand when they read his poems, is obvious or given. In fact, Rilke ends his advice to the translator with the cheerful suggestion to "help yourself along further", explaining, "I'll tell you why: I don't know if I could ever say more" (viii). In short, he commissions the man as a poet, and sends him on his merry way. This attitude is certainly not limited to Rilke. Gentzler observes that "for writers such as Nicole Brossard . . . translation is not distinguished from 'original' writing. Brossard encourages her translators . . . to intervene, to write, to translate from within, and 'to go further'" (2008: 56). He also notes a similar attitude with some translators. "For Haroldo de Campos, the translation process is always creative, much like original writing. Translation reorganizes the signs, sounds, and images of the text, therefore leading to new insights and possibilities of thought" (86).

Translation for Rilke, and increasingly for others, is much more than simply turning from one language to another. As poets, translators of poetry, or readers of poetry our job begins, at least, in the same way; we must take the thing into our hearts and impress it upon ourselves. We must, to use the more familiar term, *comprehend* it. Only then can we translate or transform it so that "its very being is invisibly resurrected in us". This act of translation seems to be a necessary step in the process of understanding. Metaphysics aside, let us be clear that Rilke's 'transformation' is not the simple *transference* of energy defined by physics. To *comprehend* and *transform* implies a more profound and personal kind of change. These verbs largely reflect Bakhtin's understanding of translation, too.

A THEORY OF ADAPTATION

Before I return to Bakhtin it should be noted that understanding the nature of both translation and adaptation is more urgent than it has ever been. Twenty-first-century humans are constantly translating, but they are also literally surrounded by adaptations. Half the shows on Broadway or the West End are adaptations. More than half the films produced by Hollywood are adaptations. At least half the shows on television are either adaptations, or are based on a true story. The literature we read and the music to which we listen constantly adapts texts, as well as genre and style. Adaptation theory is only just catching up with the modern proliferation of adaptations. But despite the work of Bluestone, McFarlane, Naremore, Stam,

Cartmell, Whelehan, Hutcheon, Leitch and others, adaptation theory may still suffer from a lack of what might be termed 'grand theory'.[8]

In his 2004 keynote address to the American Folklore Society, the late Alan Dundes,[9] one of the central figures in the study of folklore throughout much of the 20th century, declared that folkloristics was languishing as a discipline largely because of a failure to establish a 'grand theory' of folklore. He argued that the lack of such theory was speeding the demise of folklore programs around the world, and pushing folklore into a "liminal" position in terms of other disciplines (2005: 387). He laments that without a guiding, principled, overall theory most Folklore Studies were little more than what he called "butterfly collecting", or the gathering of pretty or interesting tales, with no real purpose or end in mind (388). Although it's doubtful that he ever fully conceptualised it, it's clear that Bakhtin was constantly working towards what might be considered a grand theory of literature[10] in which the act of translation played a central role. He argued, for instance, that approaches to literary stylistics common in the first parts of the 20th century were inadequate to the task of explaining the relatively new literary genre of novels. For him these methods of study were, though he did not use the term, butterfly collecting. Most of these approaches he found either unprincipled, overly abstract, or both, and he labelled them "arbitrarily judgmental" (Holquist 1981: 260). He believed that critiques of literature, and of novels in particular, tended to be idiosyncratic and vague, and he wanted to develop a way of thinking and talking about novels that was both "principled and at the same time concrete" (260).

Scholars of Adaptation Studies have been working towards that same principled and concrete approach to adaptation, but, with respect to the scholars noted above, all of whom have recognised this problem, I'm not sure that we have found it. At least some of our work, including much of my own, amounts to little more than displays of adaptations arranged in an attractive manner. We might lament, as did Henry Adams more than 100 years ago as he searched the Paris Exposition for his own grand theory of history, "Where he saw sequence, other men saw something quite different, and no one saw the same unit of measure" (Adams 1918). Even when we discuss one of the most basic questions of Adaptation Studies, what is being adapted, we find ourselves in a confusing forest of terminology. Several early scholars, for instance, suggest that what is being adapted is the 'essence' of a text. This, unfortunately, is a term that many students of adaptation readily and unquestioningly accept. I write 'unfortunately' because any perceived 'essence' in a text is imaginary since every single reading of a text, even the author's, is at least somewhat idiosyncratic. Thus any 'spirit', 'geist' or 'essence' is really the result of a particular reading along with sometimes very subtle social negotiation.

Structuralist adaptation scholars have turned to Aristotelian or atomistic logic in their study of adaptation and suggested that all adapted texts should be dissected and understood as smaller bits like 'functions', 'kernels', 'catalysers' and 'indices'.[11] With deference for the painstaking work involved in analyses of this kind, and for the useful insights offered by these scholars, I find myself at odds with the basic premise of structuralism. Like the 'essence' noted above, structural models like this are both imaginary and insufficient. The intra- and intertextual relationships of adaptations are always more complex than even the most detailed models. That complexity has led some scholars, at the other extreme, to label adaptations simply as 'intertextual', and thus to wash their hands of the question of what is being adapted. This, as my mother used to say, is throwing out the baby with the bathwater, since it fails to explain how the general notion of intertextuality can offer useful tools for understanding the specific brand of intertextuality known as 'adaptation', or for exploring the particular relationships that exist between adapted texts and their antecedents.

Nevertheless, Bakhtin's ideas about intertextuality are applicable to Adaptation Studies. Bakhtin did not coin the term 'intertextuality', but his thoughts about how meaning is created clearly influenced what the word has come to mean. Although the idea of intertextuality has been applied in many complex and interesting ways, the basic concept is relatively simple. With reference to meaning at the word level, Bakhtin believed that contemporary linguistic theory was insufficient to explain how words mean. "As treated by traditional stylistic thought, the word acknowledges only itself (that is, its own context), its own object, its own direct expression and its own unitary and singular language" (1981: 276). He argued, however, that "[b]etween the word and its object", and "between the word and the speaking subject, there exists an elastic environment of other, alien words about the same object" through which the word is always forced to pass (276). Thus no word can relate solely to its object. Any utterance about the object in question is already lit, as it were, "by the 'light' of alien words that have already been spoken about it. It is entangled, shot through with shared thoughts, points of view, alien value judgments and accents" (276). Utterances, in short, are always influenced. Imagine, for instance, that I have a neighbour with a noisy dog and that I have angrily complained about the dog's barking several times. The neighbour has made an effort to keep his beloved pet a little quieter, but with little success. Now imagine that years later, in a completely different context, I mention to the neighbour that a co-worker 'dogs' my footsteps at work. Despite the very different subject matter, the new context and the new object, not to mention my intentions as the speaker, it's quite likely that the word 'dog' will inspire my neighbour to recall my earlier angry complaint, along with his feelings of frustration and perhaps guilt. His understanding of both my co-worker's actions and my role in the matter will almost certainly be influenced by the alien interrelationship of our earlier conflict. Bakhtin suggests that these often unintended and complicated webs of meaning surround every word we utter or hear, along with every image we see. All utterances are, so to speak, already in play.

The living utterance, having taken meaning and shape at a particular historical moment in a socially specific environment, cannot fail
to brush up against thousands of living dialogic threads, woven by
socio-ideological consciousness and around the given object of an
utterance; it cannot fail to become an active participant in social dialogue. After all, the utterance arises out of this dialogue as a continuation of it and as a rejoinder[12] to it—it does not approach the object
from the sidelines. (276–277)

Intertextuality would suggest that all meanings, including those generated
by adaptations, are negotiated in complex webs of intended and unintended
meanings like this.

But when we say that something is an adaptation what we are really
doing is identifying a specific kind of intertextuality. Certainly an understanding of intertextuality should be included in any Bakhtinian theory of
adaptation, but 'adaptation' implies that the influence of one word upon
another, or one text upon another, is both intentional on the part of the
speaker/performer/writer, and acknowledged by the listener/observer/
reader. Thus while suggesting that something is an adaptation does not
rule out either the intentional or unintentional interplay of texts in general
(intertextuality proper), it does indicate that at least some of the interplay
is by design and with a specific predecessor text (adaptation).[13] Some of the
meaning and even pleasure we derive from any adaptation is the result of
recognising this interplay between texts. The relationships, the simultaneous similarities and differences, between an adaptation and its source texts
tend to generate readings, the hallmark of literary thought, and, I would
argue, the central figure of a Bakhtinian notion of adaptation.

The necessity of multiple readings is one of the most basic and useful
ideas Bakhtin offers to the concept of literature and to Adaptation Studies. It is the result of the assumption that the meaning of literary texts is
always relative to other texts. Another way of saying this is that any literary text contains a plentitude of meanings. Recently a colleague suggested
that students are unable to understand (i.e., unable to generate readings
about) Shakespearian plays unless they first grasp the historical and social
facts surrounding the creation of the plays. But I find that my experience is
at odds with the primary assumption expressed by my colleague. Students
rarely suffer from a lack of understanding prior to grasping historical and
social contexts. In other words, even uninitiated students typically have no
problem generating readings about Shakespeare's plays or any other text,
for that matter. That is, apparently, not difficult at all. The plays have, if
you will, an overflowing "plentitude of meanings, some intended, others of
which [even the speaker is] unaware" (Holquist 1981: xx).

Laura Bohannan expressed this idea humorously and effectively back in
1966 in an essay titled 'Shakespeare in the Bush'. In this piece Bohannan,
an American anthropologist, describes a research trip she took to study

the Tiv peoples of West Africa in the early 1960s. Before she left, one of her British friends gave her a copy of *Hamlet*, with the hope that by "pro-longed meditation", she might "achieve the grace of correct interpretation". Months later, during a storytelling session in Africa, the elders of the group she was researching note that they had told her many stories, but that she has not shared any stories with them. They ask Bohannan to tell them a story from her culture. Having recently finished rereading *Hamlet*, Bohan-nan proceeds to tell them a story about the fated prince of Denmark. To her frustration, however, the elders stop her almost immediately to correct her 'mistakes' and to comment on the tale. Within moments the entire premise of *Hamlet*, as far as Bohannan is concerned, has been turned upside-down. The elders observe, for instance, that Claudius's quick marriage to Ger-trude is right and proper. After hearing about the marriage, one of the old men present "beamed and announced to the others, 'I told you that if we knew more about Europeans, we would find they really were very like us. In our country also,' he added to me, 'the younger brother marries the elder brother's widow and becomes the father of his children'".

Bohannan worries, like my colleague, that without a proper historical context the story she is telling will no longer make sense to her listeners, and the inappropriateness of the marriage is one of the central conceits of the story of Hamlet as she understands it. But her fears are ungrounded. The Tiv listeners understand the play quite well, though not at all as she does. No sooner has she recommenced her telling than they stop her again, this time to argue that the appearance of Hamlet senior is not the visit of a ghost at all, as Bohannan insists, but is rather an omen sent by a witch. Unable to convince them otherwise, Bohannan worries again that without this second foundational conflict the story will fail, but again she is wrong.

Hamlet's murder of Polonius is also transformed by Bohannan's audi-ence. After she describes the scene of Polonius's death, the elders

> looked at each other in supreme disgust. "That Polonius truly was a fool and a man who knew nothing! What child would not know enough to shout, 'It's me!'" With a pang, I remembered that these people are ardent hunters, always armed with bow, arrow, and machete; at the first rustle in the grass an arrow is aimed and ready, and the hunter shouts "Game!" If no human voice answers immediately, the arrow speeds on its way. Like a good hunter, Hamlet had shouted, "A rat!" (Bohannan 1966)

Polonius, however, had failed to shout, "It's me", and was thus killed in a way that the Tiv understood quite well. Ironically, they find Polonius to be a fool, as does Bohannan, but their reasons for this judgment are utterly different than hers. These listener-adaptations continue as the story goes on, and, just as Rilke had recommended to his translator, the Tiv elders comprehend the story of Hamlet by transforming or adapting it, if you will, upon themselves.[14]

Some parts of the story they find more difficult to comprehend or encompass than others. The elders are at first quite concerned about Hamlet's intention to take revenge upon his uncle. Since Claudius is an elder, the revenge represents a gross breech of protocol and potentially mars the story for them. But eventually they accept Hamlet's murder of Claudius as a fitting end for the tale. They conclude that it must have been Claudius who had sent the original ghostly omen to Hamlet in an attempt to bewitch the prince. Thus the king deserved what he got since he had caused the prince's madness in the first place. As Bohannan finishes the story the men praise her retelling, noting,

> "That was a very good story," added the old man, "and you told it with very few mistakes" . . ."Sometime," concluded the old man, gathering his ragged toga about him, "you must tell us some more stories of your country. We, who are elders, will instruct you in their true meaning, so that when you return to your own land your elders will see that you have not been sitting in the bush, but among those who know things and who have taught you wisdom." (1966)

The fact that tribesmen from West African can understand, or in other words generate, a perfectly sound reading of *Hamlet*, though in a manner utterly at odds with Bohannan's more traditional reading, is the perfect example of the "plentitude of meaning" Bakhtin described. In her essay Bohannan serves as both the interpreter and the translator of *Hamlet*. In these roles she must constantly negotiate the meaning of the tale in the new context her audience creates. That audience, however, is not passive. They, too, interpret and retranslate the story as she tells it. The implications of this dynamic for Adaptation Studies are game-changing. For Bakhtin literary texts are absolutely overflowing with meaning, and any interpretation and retelling or adaptation of a text, such as Bohannan's retelling of *Hamlet*, is liable to reveal or create even more new intended and unintended meanings. This is true in part because her audience members, themselves, interpret and retell the tale simultaneously with her. Bakhtin acknowledges this role of the audience, suggesting that "the reality reflected in the text, the authors creating the text, the performers of the text (if they exist) and finally the listeners or readers who recreate and in so doing renew the text— participate equally in the represented world in the text" (1981: 353). Thus the text, along with its meanings, are always negotiated.

This negotiation can be upsetting for someone who intends to communicate a specific message. Bohannan's frustration in this storytelling situation is familiar to anyone who has told a story, only to find that the audience has utterly missed the point. This potential for misunderstanding exists in part because any tale might supply a plentitude of meanings, and in part because "all transcription systems—including the speaking voice in a living utterance—are inadequate to the multiplicity of the meanings they seek to convey" (xx). Thus Bohannan's adaptation will never be able to convey all of *her* meanings, but at the same time it will offer many *more* meanings that she did not necessarily intend.

It is worth reiterating here that Bohannan was not only retelling *Hamlet* for an audience who had never heard it, she was also, and simultaneously, translating both the words and the concepts of the tale. This translation is a source of frustration for Bohannan, but serves as at least one of the springs of meaning for her audience. The movement between languages required Bohannan to do something that, while it is commonplace, is rather amazing. She had to hold a number of things in her mind at once. These include at least some of Shakespeare's words, her own conception of the play she had read, and the 'correct' interpretation mentioned by her British friend. She also had simultaneously to consider Tiv culture, the specific individuals to whom she was telling her tale, as well as the limitations and possibilities of the target language. All of this forced her to engage in a stunningly complex, multi-axis negotiation, or as Bakhtin would simply label it, a dialogue. The Tiv, for instance, have no concept of a ghost, and thus they assume that Hamlet the King's appearance is the result of witchcraft, an idea they do understand. Bohannan, however, recognising the central importance of this ghostly visitation to the story as she understands it, attempts to argue for the existence of ghosts. She finally gives up, though, and moves on to describe Hamlet's conversation with Horatio. She explains that Hamlet asks Horatio for help because he was "'a man who knew things'—the closest translation for scholar, but unfortunately it also meant witch". This mention of witches, of course, confirms what the listeners have suspected all along, that the ghostly omen is the result of witchcraft. The new reading they have generated, in other words, begins to be internally consistent.

As a reader of Bohannan's narrative, I recognise that the Tiv 'reading' of *Hamlet* is cohesive and perhaps even sensible. Although Bohannan ultimately fails to convey her intended meaning, the Tiv listeners are quite capable of finding a compelling and satisfying meaning in her translation. Bakhtin might have identified this act of translation as the key event in Bohannan's essay. Clearly translation here is much more than the transference of energy from one word to another. As Bohannan describes it, translation is a profoundly creative process both for the translator/teller and for the translator/listeners. The movement between languages becomes a moment of creation for all involved specifically because of (rather than in spite of) the impossibility of a perfect translation. Bakhtin argues that on a personal level "language lies at the border between oneself and the other" (1981: 293). It is what simultaneously divides and connects us. On a more global scale he suggests that as languages come into contact with each other, "the world becomes polyglot, once and for all and irreversibly", and thus gives rise to literature (12). *Hamlet* certainly existed in Bohannan's world prior to her trip to Africa, but

Bakhtin likely would have argued that it was not *literature* for her. It was closer to myth, a story with a single and self-evident meaning. Bohannan's act of translation transforms *Hamlet*, at least for her, from a monoglot text with at least an imaginable single 'correct' meaning, to a text with a plentitude of meanings. Her translation made it forever impossible for her to return to a world in which *Hamlet* could have only one meaning. By translating it she made *Hamlet*, in short, literature.

Bakhtin understands this creation of literature as a positive, even humanising thing, but of course, it comes at a price. He notes,

> This verbal-ideological decentering will occur only when a national culture loses its sealed-off and self-sufficient character, when it becomes conscious of itself as only one among other cultures and languages. It is this knowledge that will sap the roots of a mythological feeling for language, based as it is on an absolute fusion of ideological meaning with language; there will arise an acute feeling for language boundaries (social, national and semantic), and only then will language reveal its essential human character; from behind its words, forms, styles, nationally characteristic and socially typical faces begin to emerge, the images of speaking human beings. (1981: 370)

This approach to literature requires, in other words, that we give up an essentialist view of literary texts, and accept that notion that literary meaning is always negotiated and relative. Moreover, Bakhtin suggests that this relative perspective will lead to a more human or humane way of seeing the world.

Bakhtin's understanding of translation offers both a potential approach to adaptation pedagogy, and a theoretical foundation for adaptation theory. The approach to adaptation pedagogy I have written about elsewhere,[15] and I'll only briefly mention one of my classroom practices. I often begin courses in adaptation with a simple demonstration/experiment that illustrates both the value and importance of words to a literary text, as well as the relative nature of those words. Not surprisingly, it involves an act of translation. I ask two students who speak the same foreign language to volunteer, then ask one of them to leave the classroom. While the second volunteer is gone, I have the first translate and write on the board a short Emily Dickinson poem which I project on the overhead. I often use 'Apparently With No Surprise', which reads,

> Apparently with no surprise
> To any happy Flower
> The Frost beheads it at its play —
> In accidental power —
> The blonde Assassin passes on —
> The Sun proceeds unmoved
> To measure off another Day
> For an Approving God. (1960: 667–668)

Afterwards I switch off the overhead and ask the second volunteer to return to the classroom and translate the translation of the poem back into English. Then we compare the original with the translations. The results of this demonstration/experiment usually illustrate several of the principles expressed by Bakhtin. Student translators, for instance, must decide whether the Frost or the Flowers are at play, if the "blond assassin" is the frost or the sun, and what it means to "proceed unmoved". That phrase is particularly troublesome in Spanish, for instance, since 'to move' does not have the same double meaning that it does in English. Sometimes that line becomes "the Sun moves without moving," or "the Sun continues without emotion". Situations like this inevitably force negotiation, and much of this negotiation takes place publically as students observing the work of the translator suggest meanings they like better. Students inevitably recognise the way word play, sound, double meanings, rhythm and rhyme, all notoriously difficult to translate, add to the meaning of the original, but were largely invisible to them before the translation was attempted. Some elements of Dickinson's poem are inevitably lost in the translations, but students also find new meanings generated by the translations.

I call this both a demonstration and experiment because the readings created by the translations are never totally predictable. Personal experience, knowledge of the languages, familiarity with Dickinson, dialectical differences, and the reaction of the other students in the classroom all factor into the translation outcome. As Bakhtin foresees, the translation can't convey all of the intended meanings, but neither can it prevent the generation of new, unintended meanings. After this demonstration it's relatively easy to show the analogous relationships that are created as a novel is adapted to a radio drama, an amusement park ride is adapted to a film, a short story is adapted to a television show, or a video game is adapted to a novel and so on. In each of these cases a text is both translated and adapted, just as Bohannan's *Hamlet* was translated by her and adapted both by her and by her listeners.

More valuable than pedagogy, perhaps, is the potential foundation for adaptation theory suggested by Bakhtin's ideas about texts and translation. I have already mentioned that Bakhtin eschews essentialism. His answer to the question mentioned earlier, "What is being adapted", is found in his definition of an artistic text, which he sees as a subset of what he calls "cultural domains". Simply put, he argues that there is no "there" in a work of art, and thus avoids the question of "essence" altogether. A work of art, he writes, "should not be thought of as some kind of spatial whole, possessing not only boundaries but an inner territory. A cultural domain has no inner territory. It is located entirely upon boundaries, boundaries intersect it everywhere, passing through each of its constituent features" and thus defining and enlivening it (1990: 274). He continues: any artistic work "lives essentially on the boundaries, and it derives its seriousness and significance from this fact" (274). This concept suggests that what is being translated or adapted in any particular case could not be the text alone, or the essence of the text, since neither of these things exists. Rather what is adapted must be a particular understanding of the text that is dialogised, or constantly being negotiated along its boundaries. As Bohannan does with *Hamlet*, a film adaptor working with a literary text must simultaneously negotiate dozens of factors including particular readings that they or other creative colleagues might have, the conventions of both literature and cinema, the expectations of audiences (and that includes audiences who have read the original as well as audiences who have not) and, in the case of texts like *Hamlet*, *Pride and Prejudice*, the Sherlock Holmes tales, or *Frankenstein*, scholarly or popular readings that have become so common that they might be received as 'correct' readings. All of these boundaries help to create the thoroughly dialogised reading that is eventually adapted.

I note that the boundaries described above include those shared by the artistic work and the larger, practical world, as well as those boundaries it shares with other artistic works. Again, this suggests an important defining characteristic of adaptations. Contact at all of its boundaries gives any work, including an adaptation, its power or meaning. In Bakhtin's words, "a work is alive and possesses artistic validity in its intense and active interdetermination[16] with a reality that has been identified and evaluated by a performed action" (1990: 275). An artistic text's power, in short, comes from its interrelationship with reality. But Bakhtin's insistence that art maintain a relationship, an "interdetermination", with reality implies an element of particular importance to adaptation. I would suggest that one of the things that distinguishes adaptations is that in addition to their relationship with reality, they also tap a source of great power as they maintain an "intense and active interdetermination" with the *source texts* on their boundaries. Much of the power of an adaptation, in other words, derives from its interrelationship with source texts. On the other hand, some erstwhile adaptations, like the most recent film adaptation of Sherlock Holmes, *A Game of Shadows*, purposefully abandon engagement with specific Arthur Conan Doyle stories, and perhaps even with the Holmes character as Doyle depicted him. Thus they lose a potential source of power that would have come from the interdetermination of the new film with specific earlier texts. Audiences who watch *A Game of Shadows* expecting a brainy adventure film will likely enjoy it very much, but audiences who expect the film to share multiple boundaries with Doyle stories and characters may be less satisfied.

The converse may be illustrated by the first episode of the BBC series, *Sherlock* (2010) starring Benedict Cumberbatch and Martin Freeman. *A Study in Pink*, an adaptation of Doyle's first Holmes novel, *A Study in Scarlet*, is set in contemporary London. Near the beginning of the episode John Watson meets Holmes and, just as in the novel, Holmes correctly identifies Watson as a veteran of the war in Afghanistan. When I first watched the episode I can remember feeling a thrill of recognition as I remembered that Doyle's Watson was also an Afghan vet, but from a completely different war. Thus the situation is both the same, and yet quite different. Here, perhaps, we have found a working Bakhtinian definition of 'adaptation'. Adaptations are artistic works that share a significant degree of boundaries and interrelationships with other, previously known cultural domains. The more that meaning is generated in the adaptation by contact with one of these earlier domains, the more likely we are to identify it an adaptation. Thus I am inclined to classify the Jeremy Brett or Benedict Cumberbatch Sherlock Holmes films as 'adaptations' since these tend to be largely bounded by Doyle's stories and characters. I am less inclined to identify either of the Robert Downey Jr. Holmes films as adaptations of Doyle, since they have a much broader set of boundaries, including the James Bond films of the 1960s and '70s, steampunk novels, the *Mission Impossible* films and Downey's own colourful off-screen history.

IMPLICATIONS AND APPLICATIONS

This Bakhtinian understanding of adaptation points towards both methodology and subject matter for Adaptation Studies. Adaptation scholars are interested in the boundaries of any text, and the ways texts 'interdetermine' at those boundaries. We recognise adaptations as those texts that share boundaries with specific antecedent texts. Furthermore, the study of adaptations is most definitely the study of the interdetermination of languages. The meaning of a given element in an adaptation may very well exist only in the interplay of the languages, rather than in any one language itself. In fact, that gets at the heart of the adaptation project for scholars. We strive to understand not the text or the context, but the ways interrelated texts and contexts work together or against each other at their boundaries.

Another reference to Sherlock Holmes, this time 'The Hound of the Baskervilles', provides a good example of this approach. In the first chapter of Doyle's novella, Sherlock Holmes meets Dr. James Mortimer, an amateur phrenologist and the man who has requested his help in solving a mystery. After looking at Holmes for a moment, the doctor declares,

> You interest me very much, Mr. Holmes. I had hardly expected so dolichocephalic a skull or such well-marked supra-orbital development. Would you have any objection to my running my finger along your parietal fissure? A cast of your skull, sir, until the original is available, would be an ornament to any anthropological museum. It is not my intention to be fulsome, but I confess that I covet your skull. (Doyle 1901: 126)

In the mouth of Dr. Mortimer this declaration is humorous and suggests little more than the then current popularity of phrenology, Holmes's intelligence and Mortimer's lack of social grace.

In one of the many adaptations of this novella, the 2002 BBC version, however, these same lines have been taken away from Mortimer by the screenwriter and given instead to Jack Stapleton, who appears to be another bumbling amateur scientist. Later, however, we learn that Stapleton is actually the villain of the story. In that new context the lines Doyle had originally given to Mortimer take on a sinister meaning not present either in the novella or in earlier adaptations. The new meaning of the line, "I covet your skull", is particularly evident in the context of, and in contrast to, the novella. In other words, the new meaning is generated when, and only when, we view the film as an adaptation. In fact, it's unlikely that someone who did not have the novella in mind would even notice this new meaning.

This example of a comparison of two texts potentially leads to the sand trap of Adaptation Studies: fidelity criticism. Perhaps our constant circling back to fidelity should not be surprising. Bakhtin predicted it when he suggested that "a work is alive and possesses artistic validity in its intense and active interdetermination with a reality that has been identified and evaluated by a performed action" (1990: 275). In very early films this fidelity or interdetermination with reality was, in fact, the only criteria viewers were expected to use to judge the film. The Lumière brothers' 'Train Arriving in a Station' cannot be judged by anything other than its faithfulness to actuality. The more the film matches my experience of a train arriving at a station the more successful it is. In a fidelity approach to adaptation this fidelity to reality is simply replaced by fidelity to a source text: the closer the adaptation matches my experience with the original text the better it is.[17] But Bakhtin's ideas, again, complicate this simple equation, partly because he assumes that my experience with a text is not likely to be the same as anyone else's. Moreover, Bakhtin found in the moment of translation or adaptation not the loss of fidelity and the potential for damage, destruction or deformation of an original, but rather the possibility of creation of new art. Bakhtin does not argue against fidelity criticism directly, he simply sees infidelity as both inevitable and productive. The inability of any language to fully communicate intended meanings is one of the well-springs of art. "The decisive factor in this literary-language consciousness", he writes, is "above all the gap between language and its expressive material (on the one hand) and (on the other) the gap between this material and contemporary reality" (1981: 376). Moreover, the inevitable loss of meaning (infidelity) is overcompensated for by the power of language to generate unintended meanings, to fill, in fact, any text with a plentitude of meanings. Thus Bakhtin sees translation, and by extrapolation adaptation, as a creative event that generates literature, or more broadly, creates art.

HETEROGLOSSIA, POINT OF VIEW AND ADAPTATION

Several times in the course of this chapter I have mentioned Bakhtin's conception of language, but it's worth taking a few moments to describe his notions about this subject more fully. There are several places where we might start, but perhaps most useful in terms of translation and adaptation is his idea of the relativity of languages. Bakhtin argues that "[l]anguages throw light on each other: one language can, after all, see itself only in the light of another language" (1981: 12). Bakhtin suggests that we can come to understand our own language only in the context of other languages, in dialogue with them, if you will. I would argue that this applies to the 'languages' of adaptation, as well. Although I am a teacher of literature, I learned fully to appreciate novels like *The Great Gatsby* and *For Whom the Bell Tolls* as literature only after I had experienced them as adaptations. For me, at least, the 'literariness' of these novels was created by their translation/adaptation from the language of a novel to the 'language' of another novel or to the language of a film.

I am not, by the way, inclined to argue that there is a single language of cinema any more than there is a single language of novels. It's not clear to me, for instance, how much information in a film is communicated linguistically. Certainly there is 'cinematic language', and my students recognise every year that they know a great deal about the language of film, even if they don't realise that they do. They have been watching films since they were born, and they are, most definitely, cinema natives. They automatically recognise that when scenes from two different locations are intercut it typically means that the events are happening at the same time, that a slow crossfade often indicates the passage of time, or that a close-up on a character's face suggests that the character is thinking deeply about something. But some information communicated in a film is not really linguistic. The use of the colour red in *The Sixth Sense* certainly communicates information via cinematography, but the information it communicates is idiosyncratic to this particular film. Perhaps this image approaches what Roland Barthes called the "third meaning" in film. Barthes suggested that the point of a character's beard, the shape of an eye or mouth, or the tilt of a head could communicate, but that it was impossible to reduce these elements to any kind of linguistic code (1977: 53).

For Bakhtin, however, language was more than a system for coding and decoding information. He believed that language played a much more central role in our lives. He believed in language "not as a system of abstract grammatical categories, but rather language conceived as ideologically saturated, language as a world view" (1981: 271). He believed, in other words, that our way of perceiving and understanding the world was inextricably associated with our language. Of course this is not news for linguists, but it suggests something important for adaptation theorists. Years ago I learned the Italian word *boh*, a word for which there is no direct translation in English.[18] It is the rough linguistic equivalent of a shrug of one's shoulders, and might be translated as, 'I'm not sure', 'I don't know', 'Who knows?' or even 'Who cares?' As with most bits of language, the context in which the word is spoken and the facial and body language associated with a particular iteration are very important to understanding its meaning. More important to this discussion, however, is the notion that, along with lexical information, even this small word conveys a piece of Italian worldview. As I translate the word into English, then, I am up against more than a simple problem of linguistics. To translate a word like *boh* I must begin by recognising that the very idea of *boh* may be culturally foreign at least to some members of an English-speaking audience.

Once we admit that language is closely associated with worldview the consequences for literature, and any adaptations associated with literature seem logical. For Bakhtin any work of art created with language cannot help but reflect worldview. Since different characters in a novel or play, for instance, speak different languages, or in other words sound different, they bring to the work different worldviews. Hamlet sounds different from the gravediggers, who sound different from Rosencrantz or Guildenstern, who sound different from Claudius and so on. And for Bakhtin, to *sound* different, at least in a work of literature, is to *be* different. "All languages of heteroglossia", he writes, "whatever the principle underlying them and making each unique, are specific points of view on the world, forms for conceptualizing the world in words, specific world views, each characterized by its own objects, meanings, and values" (1981: 291–292).

This multiplicity of languages/worldviews potentially found within works of art leads us to one of Bakhtin's most well-known and interesting literary concepts. Bakhtin called the interplay of languages/worldviews within a single text *heteroglossia*, and he believed that the correlation between language and worldview was inevitable (1981: 315). To the extent that an author successfully created or mimicked a language, he or she could not help but represent worldview. In fact, Bakhtin argued that because of heteroglossia a text might mean something quite different from what an author intended: "The language used by characters in the novel, how they speak, is verbally and semantically autonomous, each character's speech possesses its own belief system, since each is the speech of another in another's language, thus it may also refract authorial intentions" (315). This *intra*textual dialogic is distinct from the *inter*textual dynamic discussed earlier. Here characters within the text function in the same way as the texts themselves do in the larger world. The author's voice within the text becomes only one voice among many that potentially mean. The various characters in a work of fiction are placed "in a zone of potential conversation with the author, in a zone of dialogical contact", if you will (45). The author then "polemicizes with this language, argues with it, agrees with it (although with conditions), interrogates it, eavesdrops on it, but also ridicules it, paradoxically exaggerates it and so forth" (46). "Even in those places where the author's voice seems at first glance to be unitary and consistent, direct and unmediatedly intentional", Bakhtin argues, "beneath that smooth single-languaged surface we can nevertheless uncover prose's three-dimensionality, its profound speech diversity" (315). This explains how a character like Huckleberry Finn can mean one thing when he says, "All right, then, I'll go to hell", and yet Twain mean something completely different. Speeches like this are double-voiced. They serve "simultaneously two different intentions: the direct intention of the character who is speaking, and the refracted intention of the author" (324).[19] Bakhtin suggested that heteroglossia is a defining characteristic of novels, but certainly other works of art, including plays, films, radio dramas and so on, seem to function in a similar manner. Any text in which language is successfully created inevitably contains heteroglossia and thus intratextual dialogue. For Adaptation Studies that means any adaptation of a text that incorporates heteroglossia must find, or fail to find, ways to handle this dimension of the text, often blithely labelled 'point of view'.

Most of us are more or less familiar with the standard distinctions we have been taught to make concerning point of view. We recognise examples of first, second and third person points of view, as well as levels of omniscience. Moreover, most of us have been taught to view an inconsistent or shifting point of view as a literary flaw. This scheme and these assumptions, however, are typically rendered obsolete the first time we read complex works like those of Henry James. Even James's most straightforward early works, novellas like *Daisy Miller* or *Washington Square*, are far too complex for the simple minded system of point of view students learned in high school.[20] Although I can only briefly sketch it, a Bakhtinian approach to adaptation would suggest that point of view is not a peripheral element, but perhaps the central feature in any adaptation. Unfortunately, studying point of view in a text by a writer like Henry James, or even Mark Twain with the tools most of us have learned in high school or college is like trying to fix a pocket watch with a ball peen hammer. First, second, and third person, along with the qualifier 'omniscient' or 'limited omniscient', simply does not provide a tool fine enough to work with some texts.

In *Washington Square* (1880), James tells the story of Dr. Austin Sloper and his adult daughter Catherine. Sloper's infant son had died some years before Catherine's birth, and his wife had also died only days after Catherine was born. Sloper feels that Catherine was poor compensation for his losses. In an early chapter the ostensible third person narrator describes Catherine's maturation:

> When it had been duly impressed upon her that she was a young lady—it was a good while before she could believe it—she suddenly developed a lively taste for dress: a lively taste is quite the expression to use. I feel as if I ought to write it very small, her judgement in this matter was by no means infallible; it was liable to confusions and embarrassments. Her great indulgence of it was really the desire of a rather inarticulate nature to manifest itself; she sought to be eloquent in her garments, and to make up for her diffidence of speech by a fine frankness of costume.

Despite the third person *form* of this narration, the narrator is clearly not the kind of objective third person narrator most readers are used to. This note, for instance, that "it was a good while before she could believe it", suggests that the narrator is a distinct individual, and an opinionated one at that. Again, the observation that "a lively taste is quite the expression to use. I feel as if I ought to write it small", along with the first person "I", suggests strong opinion as well as sarcastic wit. Continuing to discuss Catherine's wardrobe preferences, the narrator notes of Sloper,

> It simply appeared to him proper and reasonable that a well-bred young woman should not carry half her fortune on her back. Catherine's back was a broad one, and would have carried a good deal; but to the weight of the paternal displeasure she never ventured to expose it.

Again, this passage has the appearance of third person narrative, but the words "proper" and "reasonable", along with the joke about Catherine's broad back, again seems to be coming from Sloper himself. The more one reads the novel and becomes exposed to the directly quoted speech of Dr. Sloper the more one may come to identify the narrator with Sloper, though speeches like the ones quoted above are clearly not first person.

This complicated narration leads directly to what may be considered one of the novel's central conceits. Sloper consistently misjudges his daughter, and since the narrator seems intimately associated with Sloper, readers, unless they are very careful indeed, will commit the same mistake. Part of the drama in the novel is created as a more accurate idea of Catherine's character is revealed in the teeth of what Sloper and the narrator, and perhaps the reader, believe her to be.[21]

Any adaptation of this novel must deal with this distinctly literary element of the novel. A film, for instance, that adapted James's plot and characters, but failed to find an analog for this complicated point of view that simultaneously reveals and hides Catherine's character would miss a potential source of power and meaning. William Wyler, in his 1949 film adaptation of the novel, *The Heiress*, creates a situation similar to that found in the novel by limiting our views of Catherine outside of the presence of her father and keeping her largely silent, for the first third of the film.[22] Thus he allows the judgments of Dr. Sloper, played by the wonderfully dry Ralph Richardson, to be the only ones the audience hears. Since we have no evidence to the contrary, we must assume that Sloper is correct in his low esteem of Catherine's intelligence and will. As the film goes on we get to see and hear Catherine out of her father's context. In one scene she makes a clever comment to her aunt, in another she seems to politely acknowledge, though not accept, her father's opinion of her. I've taken the time to discuss this particular text because it highlights heteroglossia and one of the problems faced by adaptors and by those who would study adaptations. Point of view in this novel is not simply the means of narration. It is often one of the important ways that information is being communicated. Without a relatively nuanced understanding of point of view, a good deal of the meaning of this particular novel would be lost. In other words, a dimension of the text would be invisible. A reader of the novel would certainly be handicapped if he or she were unable to access this dimension of meaning, but this weakness is compounded when one studies the novel in the context of an adaptation. If one does not have the vocabulary or the concepts to discuss or understand the point of view in a literary text, how can one hope to understand an adapted point of view? Perhaps more to the point, a translator or an adaptor who fails to recognise this dimension of the text would be at a definite disadvantage when attempting to translate or adapt it.

Bakhtin potentially offers concepts that make a more nuanced notion of point of view possible. This, in turn, makes the recognition and analysis of devices such as the ones described above more likely. Bakhtin was intrigued with point of view. In fact, much of his work found in *The Dialogic Imagination* may be considered an attempt to create a more refined notion of point of view. Using the idea of heteroglossia as a foundation, Bakhtin argues, for instance, that authors might create "character zones" in otherwise neutral, third person narration. He identifies these as "invasions into authorial speech of others expressive indicators" (1981: 316). The passages cited above provide a good example of Sloper's expressive indicators invading and colouring or shadowing the narratorial voice.

THE CHRONOTOPE

Another potentially useful tool Bakhtin offers to scholars of adaptation is the notion of the 'chronotope'.[23] 'Chronotope', an invented word that may be roughly translated as 'time/space', is Bakhtin's elegant solution to a vexing problem, the apparently unlimited subjectivity of art. Bakhtin notes the central importance of the 'language' of mathematics in expressing and handling abstract ideas about the real world. I might use a mathematical abstraction derived from a survey, for instance, to discuss public opinion about a political candidate, even though the opinions have "no intrinsic spatial and temporal determinations" (1981: 257). They are, in other words, imaginary. Mathematics, nevertheless, provides a language that allows me to manipulate these abstract ideas in a useful manner. Bakhtin suggests that artistic thought, also abstract, faces a similar problem. "Meanings", he argues, "exist not only in abstract cognition, they exist in artistic thought as well", and like mathematical abstractions, "these artistic meanings are likewise not subject to temporal and spatial determinations" (257). Nevertheless, artistic ideas still seem to have meaning. In order for us to understand the "meanings" of a work of art, he argues, these meanings "must take on the form of a sign" in the way mathematics becomes the sign for other kinds of abstract thought. That sign, whatever it is, Bakhtin calls the chronotope.

The idea of the chronotope is important to Bakhtin because it is the mechanism by which reality is assimilated into art, as well as the way that more or less abstract thought is made into a sign, a 'language', if you will, which will allow it to be communicated and understood. In short, Bakhtin argues that we can't understand artistic ideas until they are given time and place. In fiction, characters, events, locations, and so on all might give time and place to an artistic idea, and thus function as chronotopes. Polonius, for instance, embodies a specific worldview, as we have already discussed. Whether in print or on stage, Polonius becomes a chronotope of the abstract ideas that make up his worldview. He is, for instance, servile to those he considers superior, bullying to his daughter and anxious for his son. He is learned, but not clever, and nearly always careful to observe protocol and appearance. He becomes the way that these abstract, artistic ideas may be handled and manipulated within the work of art. As he comes into contact and conflict with Claudius, Laertes, Ophelia and Hamlet those ideas he represents come into contact/conflict with the ideas these other characters represent, many of which are radically different. As readers/viewers we may find ourselves judging not only Polonius to be a fool, but his ideas, his worldview, to be foolish. As illustrated by Bohannan's narrative, however, the chronotope is not carved in stone. It is always subject to both intratextual and intertextual dialogue and negotiation.

This constant dialogue becomes one of the humanising elements of Bakhtin's work. It prevents him ever from falling into a reductionist way of thinking. The text, he writes, "never appears as a dead thing", with a meaning that may be assumed, because "beginning with any text—and sometimes passing through a lengthy series of mediating links—we always arrive, in the final analysis, at the human voice, which is to say we come up against the human being" (1981: 252–253). The inevitable dialogue, the fact that no work of art is able to stand alone in its meaning, is for Bakhtin the best, the most human part of any work of art. As did Rilke, Bakhtin suggests that complicated ideas must be both comprehended and made concrete, or perhaps 'corporeal' is a better term, before they can be understood. The creation of these chronotopes is part of the work of translation, and I would add, the work of adaptation. "It is precisely the chronotope", Bakhtin writes, "that provides the ground essential for the showing forth, the representability of events" and makes literary and cinematic art, at least, possible (250).

CONCLUSIONS

What is outlined here is not a grand or even a comprehensive theory of adaptation. I have only briefly sketched Bakhtin's concepts of translation, language, point of view, heteroglossia and chronotopes, and I have not even mentioned his ideas concerning parody, influence or the carnivalesque.

Nevertheless, even in the abbreviated form found here, Bakhtin's ideas frame the study of adaptations in a productive manner. First, Bakhtin's suggestion that there is no 'inside' to a text, but that texts gain their meaning and relevance through the contact they make with other texts along their boarders potentially defines adaptation and at the same time avoids the traps of essentialism and fidelity. Knowing that adaptations are texts that share boarders and 'interdeterminations' with other, previous texts helps to explain the pleasure or frustration we may receive from an adaptation. The more these boarders are shared the more likely a text is to be identified as an adaptation. Shared boarders between texts also generate readings through the similarities and differences (or similarities within differences) along those boarders. And literary texts, for Bakhtin, by their very definition retain a plentitude of both intentional and unintentional meanings. Adaptations may or may not adopt these meanings, but the very act of adaptation inevitably creates even more meanings for which future participants with the text must account.

Bakhtin's concept of heteroglossia, and his insistence that language, even the language of fictional characters, conveys worldview speaks to Adaptation Studies. Not only does it focus adaptation scholars on the central role of point of view, but it also obligates us to pay close attention to language as it is adapted. Bakhtin asks us to study both the intertextual as well as the intratextual dialogues constantly taking place.

Finally, Bakhtin's broad conception of language and translation easily brings adaptation within the umbrella of translation. That makes it possible to discuss adaptation as a kind of translation, and this is worthwhile because of the central role translation plays in Bakhtin's literary scheme. As the source of 'literary consciousness' it would be difficult to overstate the importance of translation for Bakhtin. And this central role translation play for him suggests the potential prominence of Adaptation Studies. As it is outlined here, the study of adaptations is not a peripheral branch of literary or film theory, but rather the exploration of a central part of all artistic endeavours.

ACKNOWLEDGMENTS

Thanks to Raissa Vulfovna Solovieva for her invaluable help translating and explaining some of Bakhtin's terminology, as well as her careful and insightful reading.

NOTES

1. Bakhtin uses the Russian word "stanovlenie" here to indicate a kind of language that is unfinished, growing or in the process of becoming.
2. I note here that Bakhtin's ideas about translation were definitely not static or simplistic. He imagined, for instance, both "literal translation", *doslovnyi perevod*, and "artistic translation", *khudozhestvennyi perevod* (Solovieva, Personal interview, 28 September 2012).

3. Translators have often used the English word 'text', where Bakhtin used the Russian word, *vyskazyvanie* or 'utterance'. A literal English translation of 'utterance', however, implies little more than a word or short statement. The Russian *vyskazyvanie*, on the other hand, suggests a statement that is personal, perhaps emotional, and that may be intended to elicit a reaction from an audience. There is most definitely an anticipation of audience implied in *vyskazyvanie* (Solovieva, Personal interview, 28 September 2012).

4. Edwin Gentzler takes this notion one step further by arguing that translation is one of the creators of culture, too. "Translation in the Americas is less something that happens between separate and distinct cultures and more something that is constitutive of those cultures" (2008: 5).

5. Gentzler argues that "monolingualism cannot exist without the 'Other,' in this case multilingualism" (2008: 9–10). I agree in principle, and thus tend to treat Bakhtin's assertions about monolinguistic culture as a kind of thought-experiment.

6. Thanks to Physicist Dr. Scott Bergeson for his help explaining this concept.

7. Oddly enough, this advice to 'resurrect' the transitory and frail world upon ourselves reflects something like the biblical use of the word 'translate'. John Wycliffe, in his 1382 translation of the New Testament, uses the word 'translation' to mean to "remove from earth to heaven without death" ('translation').

8. Leitch and Hutcheon have both penned what may eventually be considered successful grand theories of adaptation.

9. Dundes died less than a year after delivering this speech.

10. I use the term 'theory' here, and throughout this essay, advisedly. Michael Holquist and Vadim Liapunov have noted that Bakhtin's work is "militantly opposed to most conceptions of—precisely—theory. His achievement can be called theoretical only in the sense that all grand *anti*-theories are inevitably implicated in what they oppose" (1990: xx).

11. See Brian McFarlane.

12. Bakhtin uses the Russian *replika* here, suggesting an answer or response, akin to the response one actor gives to another.

13. Linda Hutcheon has suggested something similar in her groundbreaking *A Theory of Adaptation*.

14. Gentzler cites a similar situation surrounding Michel Garneau's 1978 French Canadian translation of Shakespeare's *Macbeth*. He writes, "Garneau's translation hauntingly evokes both a similar social situation—Quebec's relationship to Canada recalls Scotland's to England—and a geographic national presence—the heath of Scotland/England evokes the association with the brûlé, the desolate land of northern Quebec, logged out and burned by the colonizing French. The working-class farmers, hunters, loggers, and fishermen who live in that vast rural expanse of Quebec comprising over 80 percent of the province, identified only too well with the play, which evoked especially their feelings of marginalization and exile" (2008: 49).

15. See *The Pedagogy of Adaptation*.

16. Bakhtin combines the Russian words *vzaimo* and *opredelenie* to indicate a simultaneous reciprocal definition. In other words, 'interdetermination' suggests that the texts and contexts in question simultaneously define each other.

17. Translation Studies has increasingly come to reject the notion of fidelity. Gentzler writes, "Over the past two decades, Translation Studies research also demonstrates that fidelity is an impossible standard; all translators make choices, favoring one artistic or ideological feature over another, and their translations reflect such preferences" (2008: 111). Emily Apter notes,

however, that "translations are always trying to disguise the impossibility of fidelity to the original tongue" (2006: 211).
18. Since penning this sentence I have come to believe that the recently coined English word, 'meh' might come close to a direct translation.
19. I note here that 'intention' always implies audience, and Huck's audience may or may not be the same as Twain's audience or Clemons's audience.
20. See David Jauss's 'From Long Shots to X-Rays: Distance and Point of View in Fiction Writing' for an excellent, if not Bakhtinian, approach to this subject.
21. I have discussed a similar situation in terms of Daisy Buchannan in Fitzgerald's *The Great Gatsby*. See 'Adaptations in the Classroom: Using Film to "Read" *The Great Gatsby*'.
22. The situation with this film is complicated by the fact that Wyler was not adapting the novel as he created his film, but was rather adapting an adaptation, the stage play produced two years earlier and written by Ruth and Augustus Goetz.
23. I have purposefully ignored the structuralist or morphological implications of Bakhtin's use of the word 'chronotope' in favour of the more basic concept of chronotope as the textual embodiment of an abstract concept. Like his colleague Vladimir Propp, Bakhtin hoped that a careful analysis of texts, in Bakhtin's case novels or romances, might create a useful list of 'functions', or what Stith Thompson would later call 'motifs', that would be widely applicable to other texts. But Bakhtin's list of these motifs was never exhaustive or even lengthy.

WORKS CITED

Adams, Henry. 1918. *The Education of Henry Adams*. New York: Houghton & Mifflin Company. http://xroads.virginia.edu/~HYPER/HADAMS/ha_home.html (accessed 14 March 2012).
Apter, Emily. 2006. *The Translation Zone*. Princeton, NJ: Princeton University Press.
Bakhtin, Mikhail Mikhailovich. 1981. *The Dialogic Imagination*. Trans. Caryl Emerson and Michael Holquist. Ed Michael Holquist. Austin: University of Texas Press.
Bakhtin, Mikhail Mikhailovich. 1990. *Art and Answerability: Early Philosophical Essays by M. M. Bakhtin*. Trans. Vadim Liapunov. Ed. Michael Holquist and Vadim Liapunov. Austin: University of Texas Press.
Barthes, Roland. 1977. *Image, Music, Text*. Trans. Stephen Heath. New York: Noonday Press.
Bohannan, Laura. 1966. 'Shakespeare in the Bush'. *Natural History Magazine*, August–September. http://www.naturalhistorymag.com/editors_pick/1966_08–09_pick.html (accessed 14 March 2012).
Clark, Katerina and Michael Holquist. 1984. *Mikhail Bakhtin*. Cambridge, MA: Harvard University Press.
Cutchins, Dennis. 2003. 'Adaptations in the Classroom: Using Film to 'Read' *The Great Gatsby*'. *Literature Film Quarterly*, 31:4, pp. 295–303.
Cutchins, Dennis, Laurence Raw and James Welsh (eds.). 2010. *The Pedagogy of Adaptation*. Lanham, MD: Scarecrow Press.
Dickinson, Emily. 1890. 'Death and Life'. *Poems of Emily Dickinson*. Wikisource, 17 March 2010. http://en.wikisource.org/w/index.php?title=Death_and_Life&oldid=1807049 (accessed 15 January 2013).

Doyle, Arthur Conan. 1901. 'The Hound of the Baskervilles'. *The Strand Magazine*, August 1901–April 1902. Electronic Text Center, University of Virginia Library. http://etext.lib.virginia.edu/toc/modeng/public/DoyHoun.html (accessed 14 March 2012).

Dundes, Alan. 2005. 'Folkloristics in the Twenty-First Century'. *Journal of American Folklore*, 118, pp. 385–408.

Gentzler, Edwin. 2008. *Translation and Identity in the Americas: New Directions in Translation Theory*. New York: Routledge.

Heiress, The. 1949. Dir. William Wyler The Heiress. Perf. Olivia de Havilland, Ralph Richardson, and Montgomery Cliff. Paramount.

Holquist, Michael. 1981. 'Introduction'. In: Michael Holquist (ed.), *The Dialogic Imagination*. Trans. Caryl Emerson and Michael Holquist. Austin: University of Texas Press, pp xv-xxxiii.

Holquist, Michael and Vadim Liapunov. 1990. 'Introduction'. In: Michael Holquist and Vadim Liapunov (eds.), *Art and Answerability: Early Philosophical Essays by M. M. Bakhtin*. Trans. Vadim Liapunov. Austin: University of Texas Press, pp. pp. ix-xix

Hound of the Baskervilles, The. 2002. Dir. David Attwood. Perf. Richard Roxburgh, Ian Hart, Richard E. Grant. London: BBC.

Hutcheon, Linda. 2006. *A Theory of Adaptation*. New York: Routledge.

James, Henry. 1880. *Washington Square*. Project Gutenberg. http://www.gutenberg.org/ebooks/2870 (accessed 14 March 2012).

Jauss, David. 2000. 'From Long Shots to X-Rays: Distance and Point of View in Fiction Writing'. *The Writer's Chronicle*, 33:1, pp. 5–12.

McFarlane, Brian. 1996. *Novel to Film: An Introduction to the Theory of Adaptation*. New York: Oxford University Press.

Norris, Leslie, and Alan Keele. 1993. 'Foreword'. In: Rainer Maria Rilke, *The Duino Elegies*. Trans. Leslie Norris and Alan Keele. Columbia, SC: Camden House, pp. v–ix.

Sherlock Holmes: A Game of Shadows. 2011. Dir. Guy Ritchie. Perf. Robert Downey Jr., Jude Law. Warner Brothers.

'Study in Pink, A'. *Sherlock*. 2010. Dir. Paul McGuigan, Written by Steven Moffat. BBC.

4 Anti-Essentialist Versions of Aggregate Alice

A Grin Without a Cat

Eckart Voigts-Virchow

VERSIONS: POLYTEXT AND POLYPROCESS

This chapter delves into the intertextual realm of adaptation, franchise serialization and transmedia storytelling, adaptation and translation—and the Derridean terms 'citability' and 'iterability' that it is going to introduce to the field. It argues that transmedia polytexting renders any sense of a transportable essence irrelevant. Lewis Carroll's character Alice, from *Alice's Adventures in Wonderland* and *Through the Looking Glass*, will be a useful test case because—as has been thoroughly documented by Leach (1999), Brooker (2004), McHale (n.d.) and others—Alice rewritings have been ubiquitous in recent years. The first part will discuss the terminological unease around the terms 'serialization', 'transmedia storytelling', 'translation' and 'adaptation'. Even if we accept intertextuality and intermediality as umbrella terms, the cultural analysis of proliferating textualities or polytextualities seems to be increasingly riddled with terminological mayhem, which may be one of the reasons for Brian McHale to recently dismiss many of the existing terms and settle on a very broad 'pseudo-quantitative' category of 'version': "If *version* may be defined as a later text standing in a relationship of *partial similarity* or *partial repetition* to some earlier text, then one way of constructing a typology of versions would be in terms of differing *dosages* of similarity and difference" (n. pg.).

But there are more terms available: New Media Studies have left a decisive mark on the field. Bolter and Grusin's term 'remediation' has been used synonymously with 'intermediality', addressing the refashioning or transcoding of an older medium in a new one. Following Gitelman, Moore has suggested the term 'protocol' to account for media-related adaptive changes, which is reminiscent of Foucault's more politicized use of the terms 'dispositif/apparatus': "The protocols of media refer to 'a vast clutter of normative rules and default conditions' of media use" (2010: 180).

One sign of the increasing unhappiness with existing models is the trend to apply further metaphors (adaptation as murder, phantom, vampire, theatre, mimicry) to textual diversification. Marsh takes the idea of 'murder' to represent "a metaphor for the process of adaptation itself" (2011: 178):

in adaptations of a murder case, the 'essential' story is killed in proliferating adaptations. Simone Murray has addressed 'phantom' adaptations (i.e.,
adaptations that never or almost never materialize) to remind Adaptation
Studies of the necessity to move beyond textual analyses (2008: 6). Graham
Ley sees theatrical work as an example of what he calls 'primary' processes
of adaptation: "[T]he adaptation of non-theatrical material into theatre"
(2009: 206). Emig brings postcolonial theory, namely the terms 'mimicry'
and 'third space', to bear on Adaptation Studies (2012: 20–21). Finally, the
metaphors of vampiristic and haunting adaptations suggest precisely the
idea that I am going to discuss below in further detail. Kamilla Elliott has
shown that Adaptation Studies has been 'haunted' by 'ghostly' metaphors
(2003: 133f.). Invoking a Derridean 'hauntology', Pietrzak-Franger hijacks
the metaphor as productive, arguing that adaptations are ghosts as "transformations conjured up in the present" (2012: 79). Thomas Leitch argues
for insubstantiality of cultural products and cultural energy, in his metaphor of 'vampire adaptation':

> Just as adaptations may be argued to feed like vampires off their source
> texts, those texts themselves assume the defining characteristic of vam-
> pires—the status of undead spirits whose unnaturally prolonged life
> depends on the sustenance they derive from younger, fresher blood—
> through the process of adaptation, which allows them to extend their
> life through a series of updated avatars. (2011: 6)

As metaphors are always attempts to escape from a terminological conun-
drum, we might conclude that no single term has so far captured the essence
of the field. This essay argues that terminological multiplicity should be a
welcome effect of researching Adaptation Studies, as it is a field without an
essence; it is—crucially—anti-essentialist, and the chapter will make this
case by borrowing both its examples and its guiding metaphor from one of
the most important polytexts in recent years—'aggregate' Alice narratives.
The term 'polytext' is taken from revisionist textual scholars who argue
that any text is merely apparent in a variety of manifestations ('textualter-
ity', Grigely 1991: 176–177). Adaptation Studies, as hardly any introduction to the field fails to point out, is not just engaged with poly-*texts*, but
also with poly-*processes*: 'to aggregate' signifies movement in time. Hence,
the field of Adaptation Studies is by nature anti-essentialist as the study of
processes precludes the study of essences.

ADAPTATION AND ESSENTIALISM

Let us stay briefly with the question of essentialism and discuss the processes of adaptation in their biological applications. It is worth mentioning
that Charles Darwin's *The Origin of Species*—contrary to what the title

suggests—was not at all concerned with origins. Leaving this question to the creationists, Darwin usefully focused on the perpetual processes of change to which organisms were subjected in nature. In philosophy, essentialism holds that for a kind of entity one may define a set of characteristics that this entity necessarily must possess—the entity's essential features. The consensus in the philosophy of biology, however, holds that essentialism is dead: no members of a species share a distinctive set of properties (Okasha 2002: 191). In fact, Darwinian concepts of evolutionary change preclude any essentialist concept of a species, as traits are subject to constant evolutionary change and variation. As Sterelny and Griffiths point out, "no intrinsic genotypic or phenotypic property is essential to being a member of a species" (1999: 186). Entities in biology are, therefore, relational and historical.

It is intriguing to apply this biological consensus, which has recently come under attack (Devitt 2008), to apply to the analysis of cultural adaptation. These attempts are legion, and I have been critical of the awkwardly named 'literary Darwinism', which I polemically designated 'droso-philology' (Voigts-Virchow 2006: 256–261). Infamously, Dawkins analogised genetic and cultural reproduction in 1989, applying genetic theory via the term 'meme' ("a unit of cultural inheritance", "a unit of cultural transmission, or a unit of *imitation*", Dawkins 1989: 192) to "tunes, ideas, catchphrases, clothes, fashions, ways of making pots or of building arches": "Just as genes propagate themselves in the gene pool by leaping from body to body via sperms and eggs, so memes propagate themselves in the meme pool by leaping from brain to brain " (192). Distin (2005) and others have pointed out that this is a mere analogy or metaphor, but scholars such as Elliott (2012) have insisted on the applicability of biological terminologies to cultural adaptation. Elliott argues that a shift towards models of co-operation and diversity makes evolutionary approaches to cultural production more palatable—and probably more productive (153–154). I would like to add that, above all, it must be anti-essentialist. Species are not constant, but have evolved. As a brief look at the dogs in the neighbourhood will make clear, traits within species vary immensely and species distinctions are often unclear; I designate my pet dog to the species *canis familiaris* in a relational way, by way of comparison to other species rather than by maintaining essential features. Likewise, the Burton Alice is a relational member of the species 'Blockbuster Hollywood' or 'Disney' and of the species 'adaptations of the Carroll Alice'. Cultural genres are relational, as the career of Wittgenstein's term 'family resemblance' in genre theory suggests (Fishelov 1991). Carroll's Alice has bred a wide variety of versions, often around kernel of core features. These necessary conditions (128) that make them a part of the 'genre' of 'Alice adaptations' are, however, relational and mutable.

The anti-adaptational affect that prevailed in Adaptation Studies for so long, with tell-tale phrases such as betrayal, deformation and deviation, is based on essentialist notions of art and culture and does not accept art as inconstant, evolving and variational. One of the consequences of transmedia polytexting is that any sense of a transportable essence (character, place, plot, etc.) must be negligible. This chapter, then, refutes essential notions both with respect to an essence of medium (media specificity) and with reference to narrative (fidelity). It takes the view that if an essence does exist, it can only be of the black box kind (without access to its characteristics, only in terms of appearance). It follows that observing adaptational change and intertextual proliferation renders notions of essence untenable in the arts and culture.

In fact, rather than searching for essences, Literary, Media and Cultural studies must continue to investigate the processes involved in artistic and cultural productivity—a radical focus not on the products, but the processes of adaptation. It is clearly no surprise that the grandmother of New Adaptation Studies, Linda Hutcheon, was also keenly interested in other processual literary genres (irony, parody) and that Siobhan O'Flynn's afterword to the new edition of her seminal book addresses transmedia practices (Hutcheon with O'Flynn 2012). Whereas evolutionary psychologists and sociobiologists address culture with a set of universal norms ("human nature"), one must insist with Roland Barthes and the general drift of Cultural Studies that we only have access to "human naturalizations": there is no universal essence, not even in Shakespeare or Austen, but there is meaning bestowed upon a work by a specific audience at a specific cultural moment in a given code and medium. This is the paradoxical 'essence' of years of research into intertextuality and intermediality, and it is evident even in early versions of cultural hermeneutics (creative misreading, etc.). As I have argued elsewhere, the study of meta-adaptation, namely the observation of adaptational observation, or the dialogue with adaptational dialogue, or the attempt to see adaptations as adaptations, is the best way to make adaptational processes explicit (Voigts-Virchow 2009).

At the core of this chapter, then, is a discussion about substance, or rather, the paradoxical presence without substance. In a way, Lewis Carroll himself has given an intriguing analogy to the transmedial, intertextual, vampiristic overkill of proliferating polytexts in the Cheshire Cat, who vanishes slowly until only the grin remains: "Well! I've often seen a cat without a grin,' thought Alice; 'but a grin without a cat! It's the most curious thing I ever saw in my life" (Carroll 1970: 91). In his famous annotations (another polytext Alice), Martin Gardner glosses that Carroll might be referring to pure mathematics (as the grin, completely removed from the empirical world). I would like to suggest adaptation and serialization as referents of the cat's grin: if the cat continues to grin, it is a trace—citability without essence or substance, even in the absence of the body, or, we might say, the signifier. In Alice adaptations, Carroll's inventions are an *absence présente* (Paul Valéry). The idea of the *absence présente* has had a remarkable career in symbolist and modernist aesthetics as a gesture of denial—Beckett's and Pinter's pauses and silences—and in postmodernist theory (Derrida's trace). The resistance to adaptations can always be linked to the denial of 'original' pleasure. Alice later on becomes aware of the insubstantiality (and playfulness) at the heart of her entire experience, when, prior to waking up, she discovers the Wonderland character to be "nothing but a pack of cards!" (Carroll 1970: 161).

Can Alice, a serialized, adapted, multimodal, ghostly text, be a presence ("grin") even if the body ("cat"), that is, substance, of Alice is not present? In the subsequent sections, I would like to address both the 'external' or macro-serialization and the 'internal' seriality of the Alice aggregate and discuss it as templates for transmedia storytelling and translation. Finally, with terms such as 'citability' and 'iterability', I will describe its lack of substance as an anti-essentialist 'grin without a cat'.

SERIALIZATION WRITES AGAIN I: FRANCHISES

In current popular culture, the "polycentrist" and "neo-Baroque" (Angela Ndalianis, 2000, 2004) franchise is the most obvious and certainly the most viable mode of serialization. Franchises encourage serialization as they create a great demand for "aggregate texts" (Arnett 2009), text clusters or text "remixes" (Lessig 2008) that operate in transmedial storyworlds and create a sustained and intensified experience of fictional worlds on the part of the consumers. On the other hand, aggregate texts necessitate long-term narrative co-ordination on the part of the producers which they undertake with the prospect of the long-term revenues that might be described as the prime attraction of franchise serialization. As a result, various characters and spaces, from film-based or literature-derived franchises, take on a permanent presence which is frequently syndicated in dozens of countries, often in adaptations and translations across different languages and ethnicities (film franchises such as *James Bond*, *Harry Potter*, *The Lord of the Rings* and *Star Wars*; television shows in a variety of genres, such as dramedy: *Sex and the City* and *Desperate Housewives*; drama: *Mad Men* and *The Sopranos*; fantasy: *Lost*; cop shows: *CSI*, *The Wire*, *Law & Order* and *24*).

We might want to argue that in the wide field of intertextualities, translations and serializations are closely linked to ideas of temporality. The serializer writes again, with a different or continuing story. Serialization is, by nature, temporal in the sense that a narrative is extended into a future (sequel) or a previously unwritten past (prequel). Its aim is to keep a coherent audience across media boundaries. Unfolding along a temporal axis of narrative, the prequel and the sequel may be addressed as relatively uncontroversial genres of serialization that may require degrees of adaptation. Leitch (2007: 120) designs them "adaptations of a character . . . with the ability to generate continuing adventures", often along similar narrative formulae. The character, or a set of characters, or a location, or a character and location in transformation, function as anchors that keep the unfolding narratives 'rooted' to a semantic or narrative basis. This is why I speak of 'Alice narratives' or 'aggregate Alice'.

The fact that Alice (the character) has undergone so many transformations—from the dark bobtail in Dodgson's drawings, via the blonde Victorian child in Tenniell's illustrations, to the even blonder and blander Disney Alice (1951), to a cipher for the junkie in Grace Slick's "White Rabbit" or the mad, vorpal blade-carrying adolescent Alice in the computer game *Alice: Madness Returns* or the aged Lady Fairchild in Alan Moore/Melinda Gebbie's pornographic comic *Lost Girls* (1991–1992)[1]—makes it important for adaptations and serializations to root these proliferating narratives in a character (Alice), a place (Wonderland) or a language (the neologisms of Jabberwocky). Often, these supposed 'roots' turn out to be quite meaningless—so much so that the consensus on characters called 'Alice' might be little more than suggesting 'femininity', 'curiosity', 'singularity' or young age (even the latter criterion is now rather flexible).

Not every adaptation is a serialization. Leitch declared adaptation a genre (albeit on too narrow notions such as costumes, period settings, focus on authors, book, words, intertitles) by making it a special case in the wider intertextual field. He argues that

> reading any book, attending any play, looking at any painting, or watching any film allows an audience to test assumptions formed by earlier experiences of books or plays or paintings or films against a new set of norms and values. The distinctiveness of adaptation as a genre is that it foregrounds this possibility and makes it more active, more exigent, more indispensable. (2008b: 117)

This would also apply to some (if not all) forms of serialization, where assumptions created form earlier textual experience may be mandatory for textual enjoyment. Serialized adaptation of narratives occurs if text aggregates suggest a sustained adaptive mode that creates a narrative potentially without closure. As in the case discussed here, Alice adaptations are 'serial' in the sense that they have become a sustained and permanent presence. This presence must be immediately recognizable (as opposed to translation, when it remains hidden, or adaptation, when it is perceived as altered). Often, the sustained narrative modes are guaranteed by the serializers, for instance, when we speak of the Disney Alice or the Burton Alice (which is also, of course, a Disney Alice, so, strictly speaking, a Disney Burton Alice).

SERIALIZATION WRITES AGAIN II: INTERNAL SERIALIZATION

One might, however, also look at the internal seriality of Alice or microserialization and address Carroll's narrative itself as a serial-series hybrid. We enter a dreamworld constituted by a series of relatively self-contained episodical encounters linked by the presence of Alice and, to some extent, other characters such as the white rabbit. The aleatory, random and disjunct nature of these encounters may prefigure narratively the modernist encounter with a meaningless world and Carroll's nonsense poetry may lead towards the formalization of the dream in the surrealists. Thus, the inconclusiveness and lacking substance of characters found and lost—even if couched within a kind of closure of falling asleep and waking up, may suggest a narrative 'flow', a modernist seriality. That is the internal or micro-seriality of Alice.

Franchises, however, offer transmedial seriality in the sense that they may originate in a specific medium or format, but are subsequently distributed as aggregates across a great variety of media outlets. Some internal aspects of the Alice books may contribute to its transmedialization. Once in Wonderland, Alice's attempts to follow the White Rabbit are repeatedly hindered by some new obstacle, particularly in the hall of (locked) doors. Small wonder, then, that this structure of episodical obstacles made the Alice books an ideal template for computer games—replicating the spatial design even of the early text adventure games: rooms with level-specific obstacles and an inventory of objects or devices: for example, a bottle with the sign, "Drink me!". Contrary to Elliott's complaints[2] I think that the entire *Alice's Adventures in Wonderland* adheres to the episodic structural logic of a computer game—the solving of riddles and the performing of tasks to reach (episodically) the next space or level.

The link between Alice and visual culture has also frequently been noted. One might claim a 'natural' affinity of the Alice books' obsession with shapes, bodies and change to the ability of the 'cinema of attractions' to achieve just that—maybe via Carroll's fascination for the shape-changing, framing and appearing/disappearing technologies of photography. Tim Burton's Alice is clearly a neo-Baroque sequel reminiscent of Angela Ndalianis' experience of *The Matrix*:

> During my first viewing of *The Matrix* . . . I found my senses bombarded by imagery, movements, and sounds that plunged me into a state of disorientation and overstimulation. Not only was an array of framing effects and camera movements employed (from high-velocity pans, tracks, and fast-paced edits to 360-degree camera somersaults), but there was motion, and there was lots of it! Bodies, cameras, sound, and visual effects—everything moved and moved fast. (2004: 155)

The Alice books themselves are iconotexts and, for instance, in the framing and size variations the books reflect at least metaphorically the processes of new visual technologies. Whenever the iconotext uses forms that are specific to writing, such as the visual (or pattern) poetry of the mouse's tail/tale, this generates interesting problems in cross-media transposition. The linguistic playfulness of puns, a major feature of Alice, is a source of difficulties in verbal transposition—in translation. When looking at transmedia aggregates focused on the narratives and character of *Alice,* one must bear in mind that the book appeared in the heyday of literary serialization and—in *Through the Looking Glass* as a sequel to *Alice's Adventures in Wonderland*—produced its first sequel by its original author, Lewis Carroll.

Now, the Alice books have transformed into a multimodal transmedia storytelling franchise that uses platforms such as computer games, comics, TV animation, 3D CGI movies and rock songs. Alice is everywhere, and, as Kali Israel notes, "no one can keep their hands off Alice" (2000: 280). Interestingly, Alice is a typically 'serial' character in the sense that she is static enough to remain recognizable, iterable, citable, but also able to change considerably—she is by no means 'essential'. In fact, the very name Alice now seems to be almost a 'brand'—a term that nicely illustrates the conventionality of the 'actualized', 'given' features and a term that almost automatically conjures up certain cultural assumptions no matter whether they are or are not realized.

A citable core element in the design of a franchise, then, seems to be the brand (Grainge 2008). It is the 'citability', that is the immediately recognizable presentability of titles, images, names, characters, typeface and so on, of a franchise that is at the core of any franchise marketing strategy. A case in point is the cover of the recent *Alice in Zombieland*: in a kind of assonance, the title exchanges "Zombie" for "wonder", but the pattern is recognizably Carrollian. The Hatter and Alice are still recognizably there and constitute the 'branding' of the franchise, but at the same time they are different enough to re-contextualize Alice, different enough to be seen as a citation. They are a trace, an *absence présente*.

TRANSMEDIA STORYTELLING WRITES AGAIN

To the extent that Alice narratives are multimodal and cross boundaries of distinct media or integrate them, they are excellent examples of 'transmedia storytelling'. The term 'transmedia storytelling' is often conflated with either serialization or adaptation. In its narrow sense, however, it would address the media base of given texts or the media-specific aspects of media change. Transmedia storytelling writes again—but in a different medium. In a perfect transmedia storytelling world,

> each medium does what it does best—so that a story might be introduced in a film, expanded through television, novels, and comics, and its world might be explored and experienced through game play. Each franchise entry needs to be self-contained enough to enable autonomous consumption. That is, you don't need to have seen the film to enjoy the game and vice-versa. (Jenkins, 2003: 3)

Jenkins deliberately excludes the knowing joys of recognizing adaptations, but he forgets that, even in traditional adaptations, knowledge of the prior text may afford merely additional pleasures, but is by no means a necessary precondition of enjoying a text. One should also point out that the process of variation—the polyprocess—does not begin with a first 'adaptation'. The Alice narrative has been multimodal (Kress and van Leeuwen 1998: 197) from its very beginning. It began as an oral story, told to Alice on a boat trip by Dodgson; it then became an iconotext, written down and drawn in the green manuscript book given to Alice, while at the same time Dodgson expanded it for publication. Since then, it has circulated globally in a great variety of media.

Jenkins developed his theory of transmedia storytelling to account for globally circulated media narratives, such as *The Matrix*. Media proliferation often corresponds to cultural standardization—the current circulation of proliferating superhero narratives is a case in point. The activities of fans as participating 'pro-sumers' are a possible answer to this standardization and speak for the need to 'acquire' and 'inhabit' texts. Discussions of transmedia storytelling often focus on 'vernacular' activities—and the 'vernacular' genesis of *Alice* as the everyday, recreational pastime of an Oxford Maths Don is a welcome reminder. A perfect example of a transmedia-told Alice—and in particular the 'vernacular' aspects of this storytelling is *Inanimate Alice*, a web-based interactive 'novel' originated by novelist Kate Pullinger and digital artist Chris Joseph.[3] The first-person narrative uses web-based technologies to create, via sound, images and writing, the story of a growing Alice. In the four episodes published to date the links to Carroll are tenuous—such as the youthful, curious female character, the episodical task—and problem-solving structure, and the recurringly bewildering environments (mainly generated via disorientating visual and sonic effects). Alice's father, who appears as the 'white rabbit', leads her into wonderland but subsequently dis- and reappears, and 'Brad', her imaginary companion as sketch on her hand-held device, may be seen as a variant of the Cheshire Cat. The makers of the four, increasingly long and complex stories of *Inanimate Alice* (to date, set in China, Italy, Russia and the Midlands, UK) have found a receptive audience among teachers. The project is clearly intent on spreading the 'digital novel', focused on the global experience of Alice as 'Everygirl', via tapping into the 'vernacular' resources of their global audience, that is, mash-ups and other kinds of 'pro-sumer' intertextuality. The texts continue as an 'educationalized' transmedia package, invoking the ideals of transmedia storytelling as they insist that the growth of Alice is paralleled by the growth of Alice narratives through the multimodal activities of the intertextually active aggregates which continue re-creating it. The makers of *Inanimate Alice* clearly hope that via Facebook, via new user-generated offshoots and versions, audiences will continue to 'acquire' and 'sustain' the textual universe. All of these texts—whether they contain marked or unmarked references to Alice—are going to supply more traces of the absent Carrollian narratives.

TRANSLATION WRITES AGAIN

The acquisition and sustenance of texts may be seen as the result of processes of adaptation and translation, and translation is an intriguing case of an *absence présente*, coming tangentially close to a text, but resisting the accomplishment of transporting essence. Even the standardized texts of corporate digitization will vary and be accompanied with translations (captions, or, in some countries, dubbed versions) readily available from a 'menu'. The concept of 'translation' marks the need for cultural and linguistic adaptation.

The translator writes again, albeit in a different language. As a textual camouflage, it tends, unlike adaptations, to see the masking of the source text (i.e., the source language) as a cherished quality. In the sense that translations are a mask, they are even resisting and denying the inevitable traces they bear of the source text. Leitch concludes somewhat bluntly that the term 'translation' is too narrow for the scope of adaptation: "Adaptations engage in a wider variety of cultural tasks than the metaphor of translation can explain" (2008a: 71). After all, as John Milton reminds us, translators still have to sign contracts that include statements along these lines: "I promise to produce an accurate version of the original with no alterations, omissions or additions" (2009: 48). Translations aim to expand (not just to keep) the audience for a text, by removing linguistic and cultural obstacles. André Lefevere's term "refraction", however, usefully links translations to other intertextual practices. Lefevere starts from the assumption that translations have to adjust text according to the availability of conceptual or cultural grids. Any encounter with texts is likely to be with a refracted text of a larger textual universe (1992). When a first encounter with Alice is via Grace Slick's 'White Rabbit', this song clearly refracts other Alice narratives—and this is true down to the very tenuous level of allusion. Even a translation does not just reflect the translated text, but may be seen as one refraction of it.

Let us look at the 'translatability' of Alice first, taking the well-researched example of the 'Jabberwocky' *Looking Glass* poem as our prime example. Alice discovers the poem only after she realizes that she has to supply a mirror in order to read it—and after reading it, comments bemusedly: "It seems very pretty. . . . But it is *rather* hard to understand!" (1970: 197). Here, it is the very absence of meaning (presence without substance), or, to be more precise, the reduced semantic referentiality, that becomes a clear asset and chief attraction of the text:

> Twas brillig, and the slithy toves
> Did gyre and gimble in the wabe: (191)

The phonology, morphology and syntax of the first stanza are very clearly English and grammatically unproblematic. As Hofstadter noted in *Gödel, Escher, Bach*, there is no semantic correspondent for 'slithy' in any language, but "in the brain of a native speaker of English, 'slithy' probably activates such symbols as 'slimy', 'slither', 'slippery', 'lithe', and 'sly', to varying extents" (1999: 366). Would 'bubricilleux' or 'huilasse' in French, 'schlichte', or 'glaße' in German, 'fleximiloso' in Spanish or 'slidaj' in Esperanto 'work' as well—that is evoke a similar network of associations? As there is no or little semantic 'substance' to Jabberwocky, the 'same thing' which is present both in the text and, ideally, in its adaptation becomes fluid. Unsurprisingly, translations of 'nonsense' indicate the aesthetic potential of anti-essentialist insubstantiality. Play replaces meaning.

THE CITABILITY AND ITERABILITY OF ALICE AGGREGATES

The words 'citable' and 'iterable' have sneaked into this essay and are in need of a short introduction. Citability is a word that was of particular importance for Walter Benjamin in his discussion of epic theatre. As Samuel Weber has noted, the term suggests a kind of movement: "[I]ts Latin root, *citare*, to set in movement. In English this resonance is buried in verbs such as 'incite' and 'excite'. And yet, setting-into movement is only half the story here" (2004: 45). A serialized, adapted or translated text, thus, is a text brought into movement. It is also Derrida's term for the capacity for projection into multiple contexts (in his rejection of the idea of a literal meaning). For Derrida, the transferability and endless potential for recontextualization of writing is central: "Every sign, linguistic or non linguistic, spoken or written . . . can be cited, put between quotation marks; thereby it can break every given context" (1982: 320). The iterability of signs constitutes their endless, instable play. In the words of Balkin,

> Iterability is the capacity of signs (and texts) to be repeated in new situations and grafted onto new contexts. Derrida's aphorism 'iterability alters' . . . means that the insertion of texts into new contexts continually produces new meanings that are both partly different from and partly similar to previous understandings. (Thus, there is a nested opposition between them.). The term 'play' is sometimes used to describe the resulting instability in meaning produced by iterability. (1996)

Serializations, as we have seen in the case of *Inanimate Alice*, share this aspect of being potentially unrestricted. Henry Jenkins, however, has noted that franchises are subject to constraints: "There has to be a breaking point beyond which franchises cannot be stretched, subplots can't be added, secondary characters can't be identified, and references can't be fully realized. We just don't know where it is yet" (2006: 127).

Alice may be not so much constrained by the first Alice narrative provided by Lewis Carroll, but by narrative fatigue—an exhaustion of viable spin-offs. She, however, (1) has become a permanent presence due to frequent adaptation, and (2) does in fact frequently change her shape. Brian McHale recently argued that 1966 was a turnaround year in Alice re-writings. Coinciding with McHale's periodisation of the beginning of postmodernism, 1966 marks for him the turning point at which adaptations cease to engage primarily with the original Alice texts and spin off into a "new and transformative understanding": "We might say that, post-1966, in the aftermath of 'White Rabbit,' *Alice goes viral*" (2011). In other words, she has become citable, iterable, an ex-cited, refracted polytext. McHale also, usefully, notes that Alice advances in age and that her ability to cross cultural fields—which McHale explains in part with narrative traits (such as the episodic structure and low levels of narrativity)—has made her highly marketable. For McHale, the shape-changing Alice is thus a quintessentially postmodern 'Plurabelle'.

From the start, Alice has been a children's book that has had a double address, that has appealed to adults not just children, and now, having crystallized and thus become recognizable and citable, she has become an Alice of all trades. Among other things, Alice is a meta-narrative, and dangerously so, because it implies a non-teleological world "where it is always 6 o'clock", "where you keep moving around" and "things get used up" (Carroll 1970: 99) as the Mad Hatter says: in other words, an exhausted world without meaning, in spite of all the narratives. In several ways (exhaustion, *absence présente*), Lewis Carroll was in fact a kind of Samuel Beckett.

The most recent, high-profile adaptation of Alice was Tim Burton's *Alice in Wonderland*. Kamilla Elliott's review (2010) made a lot of interesting points about it, arguing (1) that it is a compendium text that adapts a wide set of texts, some within and some without the Alice polytext canon, and (2) that the attempt to flesh out the text as narrative and as visual performance (CGI, 3D) harms the text's fundamental anti-authoritative and pro-nonsense, pro-imagination attitudes. Is this the cat without the grin (the Las Vegas version of a theme-park Alice) or the grin without the cat—in other words, where is, for us, the relational substance of Alice that may or may not be lost in serialization?

A mix of live-action, motion capture and computer-generated imagery (CGI), Burton's adaptation of *Alice* utilises cutting-edge, hybridised animation techniques, as well as stereoscopic 3-D technology. The film was shown on IMAX screens, as well as in traditional theatres, to tremendous international response. During its 12-week theatrical run, the film grossed an impressive $1 billion worldwide.

On the one hand, Burton's Alice is a recognisably Lewis Carroll's Alice that still has the pre-sixties Alice in it. More crucially, however, it has embedded preceding Alice rewritings. It is both animation and live action, invoking both traditions of Alice movies. Alice is now 19 years old and needs to be rescued from a marriage proposal—representing the much-beloved post-pubescent, more openly sexualized, complexified post-1966 Alice. Wonderland is now called "Underland"—alluding to the vertical logic that is crucial to all psychoanalytical readings of Alice: the Carroll myth.

During the Mad Tea Party in Carroll's first *Alice* book, the Dormouse tells Alice about the three sisters of the treacle-well, who learned to draw everything "'that begins with an M, such as mouse-traps, and the moon, and memory, and muchness'" (Carroll 1970: 103). This notion of "muchness" returns in Burton's film as an attribute that the Hatter (Johnny Depp) claims Alice has lost and must reclaim. Especially in this unreal city devoted to ubiquitous entertainment one may wax cynical about a Hollywood movie claiming to restore, via a neo-Baroque cinema-of-attractions adaptation, the 'muchness', that is, the power of imagination to create life from narrative, to Alice. Clearly, Hollywood must mistake "the drawing of a muchness" for 'too-muchness', for neo-Baroque overstimulation. But then, a muchness cannot be drawn, it is not in an individual movie, but in the very citability and iterability of a narrative. However, the character of the Hatter, here as performed by Johnny Depp, is an interesting example of a citable, iterable core element of Alice—he still is to some extent the Mad Hatter of Carroll and Tenniel, but at the same time he carries the clout of the dominant Hollywood actor in fantasy and children's narratives and becomes the spokesman for the power of imagination.

A coherent and recognisable look is thus at the heart of the transmedia franchise, and *Alice*—crucially visual from the illustrations of Carroll and Tenniel onwards—is a text that can be usefully connected to dominant franchise genres such as children's fiction, fantasy and so on. Non-narrative, performative elements such as design or clothing and narrative elements, such as characters, settings and so forth, emerge as the dominant categories (I may want to adapt the terminology of kernels and satellites here) for the packaging of the franchise.

On a very simple narrative level, the fact that Alice follows the white rabbit and falls down a hole is part of the immediately citable core qualities of any Alice narrative—so much so that one finds it in wildly different versions, from the very first film of Alice in 1903 to K3, the pre-teen-directed Dutch girl group's song and musical 'Alice in Wonderland' (2011). Ensuring the citability of Alice, this narrative verticality ("underland") and the underlying attitude of curiosity have been used in products that are only tenuously linked to Alice (such as Grace Slick's 'White Rabbit'), but may (and must, as this kind of iterability may become mandatory) be used in any future Alice franchises.

As, however, the CGI works hard to render the imagination real and as the fantasy world is presented as a cinematic flashback, the surface nod to the power of dreaming may be compromised. Elliott concludes,

In the altered states of madness, dreaming, and CGI, the impossible is possible and seems real. 3D makes it seem more so. At the end of the film, Alice not only abandons the film-as-dream metaphor in favour of the film-as-memory flashback, she also comes down squarely on the side of reality: "It wasn't a dream at all. It was a memory. *This place is real*". Alice's didactic declaration of Underland's reality, however, ruptures rather than affirms tensions between impossibility and possibility, and reality and fantasy. (2010: 199)

Current franchises make the iterable, citable Alice look coherent and recognisable, but that fantastic Wonderland also looks, increasingly, real.

A different kind of reality, a pure, demystified Lewis Carroll, is currently the main concern of the Lewis Carroll Society, but this would be also an Alice and a Lewis Carroll who are no longer citable, transferable. It is the cat without the grin and it is the grin, however much deprived of substance, that remains. The author is part of the polytext citability and the Lewis Carroll Society should see the very fact that Carroll is a classic, out-of-copyright author—and an author shrouded in gossip, rumour and myth—as an asset. Alice is in desperate need of recontextualisation. However frightening and uncomfortable it is, she needs to change her shape. In the sense of Derrida, the Lewis Carroll Society tries to suppress meanings, whereas adaptors such as Jonathan Miller, Dennis Potter, Kate Pullinger, Jan Svankmajer, Marilyn Manson or Tim Burton are deconstructing a citable, iterable Alice. This is an important aspect of the increasing citability of the shapeshifting *Alice*.[4]

Kali Israel even argues that the name 'Alice' might be addressed as a cipher for desire—both sexual and narrative longing—indicating

how modern Alice-invoking works by novelists and are repeatedly crossed by questions about knowledge and sexuality. The texts I read grapple with the tensions of knowing about and wondering about Alice; they thematize stories as much as sex. . . . We recall stories of Alice Liddell's requests that Charles Dodgson tell and write stories for her. Alice is a name for wanting stories to have, stories to keep, and stories to continue (2000: 257–258)

This sounds almost like a cue for the digital proliferation of *Inanimate Alice*. The citability and iterability of narratives, texts and performances is a quality that does not solely reside within themselves, but in their continuing serialization, in the citability and iterability that drives their serial reproduction. This review of the polytext realm of Alice narratives shows that the anti-essentialist terms such as 'citability' and 'iterability' are productive for the analysis of transmedia franchise storytelling. It is precisely the anti-essentialist thrust of Adaptation Studies that will ensure its continuing relevance in cultural analysis—a continuation that invites the analogy of a grin without a cat.

NOTES

1. As the last examples illustrate, these revisions presuppose a sexualised undercurrent, as evinced for instance in Marilyn Manson's (currently abandoned) 2006 film project *Phantasmagoria: The Visions of Lewis Carroll*. See Brooker (2004: 53–55) for the recontextualization of Alice. A classic 'adult' Alice movie is Bill Osco's musical porn spoof of 1976, a new hardcore porn version—obviously attempting to cash in on the Tim Burton version, is Cal Vista's *Alice* (2010). See also Melinda Gebbie/Alan Moore's *Lost Girls*. There is a growing tendency in academia to metacritically review and debunk this sexualisation of Carroll. For a more thorough discussion, see my forthcoming paper '"No One Can Keep Their Hands Off Alice": Alice, the "Carroll Myth" and Bio-fiction' in: Sissy Helff (ed.) *Tantalizing Alice*.
2. Kamilla Elliott argues that the Burton movie imposes the computer game aesthetics she finds only in Chapter IV ("tasks, levels, spaces, problem solving, and battles") on the entire text (2010: 195).
3. For a full analysis see Stewart (2011). I would like to thank the anonymous reader at Routledge for directing my attention to *Inanimate Alice*.
4. Her variable appearance has been a key interest in research on Alice; for an exploration of that theme in Burton's *Alice* and in Adaptation Studies, see Primorac (forthcoming).

WORKS CITED

Alice in Wonderland. 2010. Writ. Linda Woolverton. Dir. Tim Burton.

Arnett, Robert P. 2009. '*Casino Royale* and Franchise Remix: James Bond as Superhero'. *Film Criticism*, 33, pp. 1–16.

Balkin, Jack M. 1996. 'Deconstruction'. In: D. Patterson (ed.), *A Companion to the Philosophy of Law and Legal Theory*. Oxford: Blackwell. http://www.yale.edu/lawweb/jbalkin/articles/deconessay.pdf (accessed 24 March 2013).

Bolter, Jay David and Richard Grusin. 1999. *Remediation: Understanding New Media*. Cambridge, MA: MIT Press.

Brooker, Will. 2004. *Alice's Adventures. Lewis Carroll in Popular Culture*. New York: Continuum.

Carroll, Lewis. 1970. *The Annotated Alice*. [*Alice's Adventures in Wonderland and Through the Looking Glass*]. Ed. Martin Gardner. Harmondsworth, England: Penguin/Puffin Books.

Davis, Richard Brian (ed.). 2010. *Alice in Wonderland and Philosophy*. Hoboken, NJ: Wiley.

Derrida, Jacques. 1982. *Margins of Philosophy*. Chicago: University of Chicago Press.

Devitt, Michael. 2008. 'Resurrecting Biological Essentialism'. *Philosophy of Science*, 75, pp. 344–382.

Elliott, Kamilla. 2003. *Rethinking the Novel / Film Debate*. Cambridge: Cambridge University Press.

Elliott, Kamilla. 2010. 'Adaptation as Compendium: Tim Burton's *Alice in Wonderland*'. *Adaptation*, 3:2, pp.193–201.

Elliott, Kamilla. 2012. 'The Adaptation of Adaptation'. In: Pascal Nicklas and Oliver Lindner (eds.), *Adaptation and Cultural Appropriation*. Berlin: De Gruyter, pp. 145–161.

Emig, Rainer. 2012. 'Adaptation in Theory''. In: Pascal Nicklas and Oliver Lindner (eds.), *Adaptation and Cultural Appropriation*. Berlin: De Gruyter, pp. 14–24.

Fishelov, David. 1991. 'Genre Theory and Family Resemblance—Revisited'. *Poetics*, 20, pp. 123–138.

Grainge, Paul. 2008. *Brand Hollywood: Selling Entertainment in a Global Media Age*. London: Routledge.

Grigeley, Joseph. 1991. 'The Textual Event'. In: Philip Cohen (ed.), *Devils and Angels: Textual Editing and Literary Theory*. Charlottesville: University of Virginia Press, pp. 167–194.

Hofstadter, Douglas R. 1999. *Gödel, Escher, Bach: An Eternal Golden Braid*. New York: Basic Books.

Hollingsworth, Christopher (ed.). 2009. *Alice Beyond Wonderland: Essays for the Twenty-First Century*. Iowa City: University of Iowa Press.

Hutcheon, Linda with Siobhan O'Flynn. 2012. *A Theory of Adaptation*. 2nd ed. New York and London: Routledge.

Israel, Kali. 2000. 'Asking Alice: Victorian and Other Alices in Contemporary Culture'. In: John Kucich and Dianne F. Sadoff (eds.), *Victorian Afterlife: Postmodern Culture Rewrites the Nineteenth Century*. Minneapolis: University of Minnesota Press, pp. 252–287.

Jenkins, Henry. 2003. 'Transmedia Storytelling'. In: *MIT Technology Review*. 15 January, pp. 1–3. http://www.technologyreview.com/biomedicine/13052/ (accessed 31 May 2012).

Jenkins, Henry. 2006. *Convergence Culture: Where Old and New Media Collide*. New York: New York University Press.

Jones, Jo Elwyn and J. Francis Gladstone (eds.). 1998. *The 'Alice' Companion: A Guide to Lewis Carroll's 'Alice' Books*. Basingstoke, England: Macmillan.

Kress, Gunther and Theo van Leeuwen (eds.). 1998. 'Front Pages: (The Critical) Analysis of Newspaper Layout'. In: Allan Bell and Peter Garrett (eds.), *Approaches to Media Discourse*. Oxford: Blackwell, pp. 186–219.

Leach, Karoline. 1999. *In The Shadow of the Dreamchild*. London: Peter Owen.

Lefevere, André. 1992. *Translation, Rewriting and the Manipulation of Literary Fame*. London: Routledge.

Leitch, Thomas. 2007. *Film Adaptation and Its Discontents: From* Gone With the Wind *to* The Passion of the Christ. Baltimore: The Johns Hopkins University Press.

Leitch, Thomas. 2008a. 'Adaptation at the Crossroads'. *Adaptation*, 1:1, pp. 63–77.

Leitch, Thomas. 2008b. 'Adaptation: The Genre'. *Adaptation*, 1:2, pp. 106–120.

Lessig, Lawrence. 2008. *Remix*. New York: Penguin Press.

Ley, Graham. 2009. '"Discursive Embodiment": The Theatre as Adaptation'. *Journal of Adaptation in Film and Performance*, 2:3, pp. 201–209.

Marsh, Huw. 2011. "Adaptation of a Murder/Murder as Adaptation: The Parker-Hulme Case in Angela Carter's "The Christchurch Murder" and Peter Jackson's *Heavenly Creatures*'. *Adaptation*, 4:2, pp. 167–179.

McHale, Brian. n.d. '"Things then did not delay in turning curious": Some Version of Alice, 1966–2010'. Project Narrative, the Ohio State University. https://projectnarrative.osu.edu/about/current-research/lectures-and-presentations/mchale (accessed 31 May 2012).

Meier, Franz. 2009. 'Photographic Wonderland: Intermediality and Identity in Lewis Carroll's *Alice* Books'. In: Christopher Hollingsworth (ed.), *Alice beyond Wonderland: Essays for the Twenty-first Century*. Iowa City: University of Iowa Press, pp. 117–133.

Milton, John. 2009. *Agents of Translation*. Amsterdam: John Benjamins.Moore, Michael Ryan. 2010. 'Adaptation and New Media'. *Adaptation*, 3.2, pp. 179–192.

Murray, Simone. 2008. 'Phantom Adaptations: Eucalyptus, the Adaptation Industry and the Film that Never Was'. *Adaptation*, 1:1, pp. 5–23.

Ndalianis, Angela. 2000. 'The Frenzy of the Visible: Spectacle and Motion in the Era of the Digital'. *Senses of Cinema*. http://sensesofcinema.com/2000/feature-articles/matrix-2/ (accessed 31 May 2012).

Ndalianis, Angela. 2004. *Neo-Baroque Aesthetics and Contemporary Entertainment*. Cambridge, MA: MIT Press.

Nicklas, Pascal, and Oliver Lindner. 2012. *Adaptation and Cultural Appropriation*. Berlin: De Gruyter.

Okasha, Samir. 2002. 'Darwinian Metaphysics: Species and the Question of Essentialism'. *Synthese*, 131, pp. 191–213.

Phillips, Robert. 1974. *Aspects of Alice: Lewis Carroll's Dreamchild as Seen Through the Critic's Looking Glasses*. Hardmondsworth, England: Penguin.

Pietrzak-Franger, Monika. 2012. 'Conversing With Ghosts: Or, the Ethics of Adaptation'. In: Pascal Nicklas and Oliver Lindner (eds.), *Adaptation and Cultural Appropriation*. Berlin: De Gruyter, pp. 70–88.

Primorac, Antonija. Forthcoming. 'Fashioning a Neo-Victorian Heroine: Adaptation and Appropriation as Tailoring and Shape-Shifting in Tim Burton's *Alice in Wonderland*'.

Sterelny, Kim and Paul E. Griffiths (eds.). 1999. *Sex & Death: An Introduction to Philosophy of Biology*. Chicago: University of Chicago Press.

Stewart, Gavin. 2010. 'The Paratexts of Inanimate Alice: Thresholds, Genre Expectations and Status'. *Convergence*, 16:1, pp. 57–74.

Voigts-Virchow, Eckart. 2006. 'Adaptation, *Adaptation* and Drosophilology, or Hollywood, Bio-Poetics and Literary Darwinism'. In: Christoph Houswitschka, Gabriele Knappe and Anja Müller (eds.), *Proceedings Anglistentag 2005*. Trier: Wissenschaftlicher Verlag Trier, pp. 247–263.

Voigts-Virchow, Eckart. 2009. '"MetAdaptation": Adaptation and Intermediality—Cock and Bull'. *Journal of Adaptation in Film and Performance*, 2:2, pp. 137–152.

Waxman, Lori. 2011. 'Through the Looking Glass With Heart-Shaped Sunglasses: Searching for Lolita and Alice in Contemporary Representations of Girls'. In: Lori Waxman and Catherine Grant (eds.), *Girls! Girls! Girls! In Contemporary Art*. Bristol, England: Intellect, pp. 17–44.

Weber, Samuel. 2004. *Theatricality as Medium*. New York: Fordham University Press.

Part II
Merging Ideas

5   Theorising *Omkara*

John Milton

ADAPTING *OTHELLO*

Othello has been one of the most adapted plays by Shakespeare. There have been two opera adaptations. The first is *Otello*, a three act opera with an Italian libretto by Francesco Maria Berio di Salsi and music by Gioachino Rossini (1816). The opera deviates from Shakespeare's original in a number of aspects: Jago is less diabolical than his Shakespearean counterpart, the setting is Venice rather than Cyprus, and the composer and librettist provided an alternative happy ending to the work, a common practice with drama and opera from the late seventeenth century to the early nineteenth century, as in the case of Nahum Tate's *The History of King Lear* (1681), with its happy ending, with Edgar marrying Cordelia. Today the opera is rarely performed. The famous opera adaptation is that of Giuseppe Verdi and librettist Arrigo Boito, who adapted Shakespeare's play to *Otello* (1887), frequently considered Verdi's greatest opera. A film version was made by Franco Zeffirelli in1986 starring Plácido Domingo as Othello.

A number of dance versions have also been made: John Neumeier's ballet *Othello* (1985) for the Hamburg Ballet; Lar Lubovitch's *Othello* (2002) for the San Francisco Ballet; *Prologue*, choreographed by Jacques d'Amboise for the New York City Ballet in 1967 as a prequel to Shakespeare's play; *Othello*, choreographed by John Butler to the music of Dvořák for Carla Fracci; the La Scala Ballet verson of 1976; and a version choreographed by Jean-Pierre Bonnefous for the Louisville Ballet in the 1980s.

In addition a number of well-known film versions have been made. Amongst them are Orson Welles's *The Tragedy of Othello: The Moor of Venice* (1952); Laurence Olivier's *Othello* (1965), based on John Dexter's National Theatre Company's production; and Trevor Nunn's 1989 version filmed at Stratford, with black opera singer Willard White in the leading role, opposite Ian McKellen's Iago.

The first major screen production casting a black actor as Othello only came in 1995 with Laurence Fishburne playing opposite Kenneth Branagh's Iago. This film was made during the O. J. Simpson murder trial, inviting obvious parallels.

Among filmed adaptations we can mention the 1962 British *All Night Long*, in which Othello is Rex, a jazz bandleader; the 1974 *Catch My Soul*, adapted from Jack Good's rock musical, directed by Patrick McGoohan; the 1982 *Othello, the Black Commando* written by and starring Max H. Boulois with Tony Curtis as Colonel Iago and Joanna Pettet as Desdemona; the more recent *O*, a modern update, set in an American high school, starring Mekhi Phifer as Odin (Othello), Julia Stiles as Desi (Desdemona) and Josh Hartnett as Hugo (Iago); and the 2008 *Jarum Halus*, a modern updated Malaysian version, in English and Malay by Mark Tan.

On television, in addition to the 1981 BBC version, and the 1990 TV filming of the 1989 Stratford version, we can highlight the 2001 UK ITV *Othello*, in which Othello is the first black Commissioner of London's Metropolitan Police.

OTHELLO IN INDIA

Much recent writing on *Othello* in India seems to take either a postcolonialist approach or is critical of such an approach by valuing native Indian art and stage forms which have produced adaptations of *Othello* which may not fit into a postcolonial agenda. In '"Local-manufacture made-in-India Othello fellows": Issues of Race, Hybridity and Location in Post-Colonial Shakespeares', Ania Loomba compares Salman Rushdie's *The Moor's Last Sigh* (1995), "the product of a sophisticated English-speaking intellectual hankering for a remembered home", with Rushdie, "the high priest of diasporic postcoloniality, and master of the hybrid tongue . . . at pains to delineate the long and intricate history of racial intermingling in this region [the Malabar coast]" (1998: 153), with the traditional dance form Sadanam Balakrishnan's Kathakali *Othello* (1996), which appropriates Shakespeare's tragedy to this highly stylised art form but "skirts all questions and histories of difference . . . to craft a vocabulary that will allow it to experiment with plays like *Othello* without violating its own specific cades of signification" (153).

However, this somewhat disparaging view of the traditional Kathakali *Othello* view is contested by Poonam Trivedi in her article 'Folk Shakespeare', which rejects Loomba's critique that Balakrishnan's Kathakali *Othello* ignores racism and stereotypes the idea of 'blackness' by portraying Iago as a vicious *katti*, a black-bearded, red-nosed character dressed in black. Trivedi stresses that in Kathakali the colour black does not "signify evil so singularly in a culture of predominantly dark-skinned people whose major deities and demons are both dark-colored. The issue of Othello's blackness, therefore, becomes more than a mere black/white evil/good dichotomy" (2004: 187), and Trivedi accuses Loomba of a lack of engagement with the traditional art forms and accuses her of seeing the problems of *Othello* through western dialectics.

As an example of a successful adaptation of *Othello*, she mentions Jayaraaj's 1998 film of *Kaliyattam*, based on *Othello*, which she finds as "the most acute postcolonial reworking of Shakespeare into folk theater forms", but one where the transposition of Othello into caste and communal politics and discriminations "more pernicious in Indian society, form a more apt equivalent of Othello's 'blackness' than an imported notion of race, which remains largely a Western postcolonial dilemma" (2004: 187).

In 'Different Othello(s) and Contentious Spectators: Changing Responses in India', Nandi Bhatia compares Trivedi's views on Balakrishnan's Kathakali *Othello* with other *Othellos* in India. She begins with James Barry's 1848 production at the Sans Souci Theatre in Calcutta, in which a Bengali actor, Baishnava Charan Adhya, was cast in the role of Othello. Chatterjee and Singh analyse the reception of Othello in the context of the "disciplining gaze of surveillance" of racialised spaces and attribute the commotion it caused amongst colonial officials with their hidden racial anxieties at a time when colonial relations were beginning to get tense. The opening performance of Barry's *Othello*, despite being well advertised ahead of time, was "abruptly aborted due to the opposition of a local military commanding officer, who refused permission for his men to play extras in the production" (Chatterjee and Singh, in Bhatia 2007: 157).

She then moves to regional theatre groups, as from the 1950s, mentioning Utpal Dutt, who trained under Geoffrey and Laura Kendal, organised through his Little Theatre Group the plays of Shakespeare for primarily urban audiences, but who then turned to the use of folk techniques of the Jatra to perform plays such as Macbeth for village audiences. Mr. Buckingham's construction of the Indian audience in the Merchant-Ivory film *The Shakespeare Wallah* (1965) is based on the memoirs of Geoffrey Kendal, in which he recalls the enormous popularity of Shakespearean plays performed by his troupe to Indian audiences between 1953 and 1956. This is the 'universal' and 'timeless' bard.

Bhatia also mentions the 1969 Urdu *Othello* by Ebrahim Alkazi, a celebrated director of the National School of Drama in Delhi, and Roysten Abel's 1990s *Othello, a Play in Black and White*, produced by the United Players Guild, a Delhi-based theatre company that Abel and Lushin Dubey set up in 1995, which became known for its experimental Shakespearean plays; Abel's play was performed in different parts of India, and won the Fringe Award at the Edinburgh Festival in 1999. Abel's play shows an Indian troupe rehearsing Othello under an Italian director, in which the actor playing Othello was a traditional *kathakali* actor coming from a lower caste.

In her introduction to *India's Shakespeare: Translation, Interpretation and Performance*, Poonan Trivedi outlines the history of productions of Shakespeare in India, which begins with productions of *Hamlet* and *Richard II* aboard the ships of the East India Company in 1607. The Calcutta Theatre (1775–1808) was set up with the help of David Garrick. Indians participated actively in the establishment of theatres like the Chowringee Theatre in Calcutta (1813) and the Grant Road Theatre in Bombay (1846). After the 1835 Education Act, when English was established as the colonial language, "Shakespeare was moved from the fashionable and cultural to the imperial and ideological axis" (2006: 15).

Trivedi strongly criticises the lack of research into sources which she feels is typical of much postcolonial writing on Shakespeare in India, as in Loomba. The valorisation of the theoretical over the textual leads to "a cavalier approach, where no need is felt to consult or track down original sources—translations, recordings or production files" (2006: 23). Greater effort should be made to research into the multifarious influences that the plays of Shakespeare have had in the very different aspects of Indian life, languages and cultures instead of pigeonholing Indian versions of Shakespeare into postcolonial clichés.

Trivedi stresses the beginning of two very different ideological streams: first, an academised literary Shakespeare when appealed to Anglicised Indians, and second, a popular Shakespeare translated and transformed on stage. Translations were made into the different Indian languages, with *The Merchant of Venice* in Bengali and *The Taming of the Shrew* in Gujarati both in 1852. The Parsi Theatre in Bombay was particularly instrumental in touring with adapted versions of Shakespeare "and it would not be an exaggeration to say that Shakespeare was popularized, commercialized and insinuated into the psyche of these audiences—without their knowing that it was Shakespeare—through the transformations effected by the Parsi theatre" (2006: 15–16).

Many translations were carried out into the major Indian languages between 1900 and 1930, with *The Merchant of Venice* being the most popular play, followed by *The Comedy of Errors*, but with the independence movement, there was a considerable fall in the number of productions, and after independence in 1947 "there was now a greater sensitivity toward the complexity of Shakespeare and a corresponding maturity of response" (Trivedi 2006: 16–17), with a number of new faithful translations, especially into Hindi.

Trivedi describes the emergence of a threefold process on the Indian stage. First, versions in translation without indianisations or transformations, interested more in the ideas of the play, and often called essentialising, and illustrated by the Urdu *Raja Lear* in western dress (1964). The "second, indigenizing stream was to assimilate Shakespeare not just into the traditional performative but also into the philosophic fabric of India" (2006: 17), exemplified by B. V. Karanth's Macbeth performed in *yakshagana* (1979), and K. N. Panikkar presenting *The Tempest* (2000) in the form of traditional Sanskrit drama and *kudiattam*. A more recent trend is the "assertion of playful freedom and postcolonial confidence to cut, critique and rewrite" (2006: 17), as in the already mentioned case of Royston Abel's bilingual *Othello, a Play in Black and White* (1999).

Where does *Omkara* fit into Trivedi's tripartite division? It is respectful to Shakespeare, with the trailer emphasising and the opening credits clearly stating that it is a version of Shakespeare updated to contemporary India. Yet, at the same time, *Omkara* is a very Indian film, fitting into the contemporary Bollywood fashion for gangster movies, as does Bhardwaj's earlier *Maqbool* (2003), based on *Macbeth*, and rather than underlining elements such as cast and race, drawing attention to "other kinds of urgencies that mark the contemporary postcolonial milieu in India: problems and crime related to caste warfare and the violence against women that remains at the center of these crimes, along with lawlessness, clan rivalry and political deceit" (2003: 170).

OTHELLO AND OMKARA

Omkara, a 2006 Bollywood production, is directed by Vishal Bhardwaj, who also composed the entire musical score for the film, with song lyrics by Gulzar. It is part of a series of film interpretations of literary works by Bhardwaj, made after *Maqbool* (2003) based on Shakespeare's *Macbeth* and *Chatri Chor* (English title: *The Blue Umbrella*, 2007) based on Ruskin Bond's *The Blue Umbrella*.

The plot of *Omkara* is as follows: Omkara Shukla or Omi (Ajay Devgan) is a *baahubali*, a political enforcer, leader of a gang which carries out political crimes for the local politician Tiwari Bhaisaab (Naseeruddin Shah), who is initially conducting his business from inside prison. Ishwar 'Langda' Tyagi (Saif Ali Khan) and Keshav 'Kesu Firangi' Upadhyay (Vivek Oberoi) are his closest lieutenants.

The film starts with Langda Tyagi hijacking a *baraat*, the marriage procession of the bridegroom, and sending Rajju (Deepak Dobriyal), the bridegroom, to try and stop Omkara from abducting the bride, Dolly Mishra (Kareena Kapoor). Rajju fails, and the wedding never takes place.

Dolly's father, Advocate Ragunath Mishra (Kamal Tiwari), mostly referred in the movie as 'Vakeel Saab' (Lawyer Sir), is furious and confronts Omi. He puts a gun to Omi's head and demands the return of his daughter. A telephone call comes from Bhaisaab, who intervenes and resolves the conflict by mentioning the current political conditions and prevents bloodshed. Still unconvinced, Vakeel Saab grieves to Bhaisaab the next day. To bring a final solution to this issue, Dolly is made to appear in front of her father and clarify that she eloped with Omi rather than being abducted forcefully. She also tells the events of how she fell in love with Omkara. The father leaves feeling betrayed and ashamed.

After some crafty political arm-twisting, involving an MMS sex scandal, Omkara eliminates a powerful electoral rival. Bhaisaab is elected for Parliament, and Omkara is promoted from 'bahubali' to the candidate for the upcoming state elections. Omkara appoints Kesu over Langda as his successor once he enters politics himself as Kesu will be able to get out the student vote. Langda, disappointed with Omkara's poor judgment and jealous of Kesu, his younger and less-experienced superior, hatches a plot to revenge both his offenders. At the celebration when Billo dances and sings the well-known Beedi song, Langda eggs Kesu on, taking advantage of Kesu's low threshold for alcohol. Kesu sings and dances with Billo, and then Langda causes a violent brawl between Kesu and Rajju, Dolly's original suitor. Such irresponsible behaviour of Kesu infuriates Omi, who now starts becoming unsure about his own decision.

Langda plays the role of a concerned friend and convinces Kesu to appeal to Dolly, in order to mollify Omi. On the other he starts to disrepute Dolly by implicating Kesu's visits to ask Dolly for her help as meetings in an illicit love affair between the two. A *kamarbandh* (kumerband), a piece of traditional jewellery worn around the waist, carelessly dropped by Dolly and stolen by Langda's wife Indu (Konkona Sen Sharma), which eventually reaches Billo Chamanbahar (Bipasha Basu) as a gift from Kesu, plays an important part in the plot, as evidence of Dolly's infidelity.

By the time of the climax, the night of their wedding, Omi is convinced that Dolly and Kesu have been having an affair behind his back. In utter rage, he smothers his new wife to death. Langda shoots Kesu with a silent approval from Omi. Kesu doesn't die but gets hit with a bullet in his arm. Hearing gunshots and in shock Indu enters the room where Omi is sitting next to Dolly's corpse in remorse. Indu notices the *kamarbandh* and mentions stealing it, they both understand the fatal misunderstanding and Langda as its root cause. In retribution, Indu slashes Langda's throat and Omi commits suicide. The movie closes with Omi lying dead of the floor and Dolly's dead body swinging above his, while Kesu is looking on.

Omkara was shown at the 2006 Cannes Film Festival and the Cairo International Film Festival, where Bhardwaj was awarded for Best Artistic Contribution in Cinema of a Director, and the film won three awards at the Kara Film Festival, an award at the Asian Festival of First Films, three National Film Awards and seven Filmfare Awards.

Omkara grossed $16,466,144 worldwide in its total run at the box office, ten times more than it cost to make. It had a fairly good performance at the box office in India but earned greater accolade outside India and was especially popular in the UK, where it entered the UK Top Ten and also did very well in Australia, South Africa and the United States.

Film critics have been mostly positive, especially on the performance of Saif Ali Khan (Langda/Iago). Naman Ramachandran praises Khan's transition from boy actor to mature actor, specialising in the role of the villain: "The limping Khan, with shorn tresses, yellowed teeth and resolutely non-designer stubble, inhabits the part completely, spitting venom and chewing any available scenery" (2006). By contrast, he is less enthusiastic about Ajay Devgan as Omkara, whose "performance is so understated that his character's innate jealousy and possessiveness are visible only sporadically. This is Othello as wallpaper".

The *Guardian* film critic Peter Bradshaw commented, "Vishal Bhardwaj's *Omkara* is a flawed but worthwhile attempt to transfer *Othello* to the modern setting of Uttar Pradesh in India and to render the story in a Bollywood style". Bradshaw also finds parallels between Bollywood and Shakespeare, because Bollywood, he added, "with its liking for ingenious fantasy and romance, has often seemed to me to resemble in style, nothing so much as a late Shakespearean play" (in Bhatia 2007: 170). Philip French in *The Observer* was more enthusiastic, calling *Omkara* "ingenious" and making the Shakespeare parallel: "Mobile phones are used where Shakespeare employed eaves dropping; an erotic, bejeweled waistband replaces the handkerchief as a compromising device" (170).

ANALYSING *OMKARA*

In one of the few attempts at structuring a theory of adaptation, Lawrence Venuti criticises the lack of a theoretical basis of much work on Film Adaptation, where he finds the idea of intertextuality far too vague. There is also a tendency for an uncritical bias either in favour or against the film version. Using Patrick Catrysse's concept of semiotic and pragmatic norms, and Gideon Toury's theories on translational acceptability and adequacy as a means of defining equivalence, he develops the wider concept of the *interpretant*, developing Charles Sanders Pierce's term (Venuti 2007: 31).

Venuti describes two kinds of interpretants. Formal interpretants show a structural correspondence between the adapted and the original material. These may be the plot details, the particular style of director or studio, or concept of genre that necessitates a manipulation or revision of the adapted materials (2007: 33).

Second, thematic interpretants are codes, values, ideologies. They may include an interpretation of the adapted materials that has been formulated elsewhere, a morality or cultural taste shared by the filmmakers and used to appeal to a particular audience, or a political position that reflects the interests of a specific social group (Venuti 2007: 33).

In previously published work I have been critical of the lack of attention Adaptation Studies has given to language transfer (Milton 2009), and suggest that Adaptation Studies should borrow from Translation Studies. I criticise the monolingualism of much work in Adaptation Studies, giving an example of an article which shows a totally uncritical use of a subtitled version of Wim Wenders' 'Wings of Desire' for a Newcastle-upon-Tyne stage version of the German film. Apparently, the subtitled version would give a totally transparent view of the original, and the article failed to show any awareness of possible omissions, additions and/or distortions which the subtitled version might contain.

Thus I suggest a third interpretant, that of 'linguistic interpretant', which could be defined as: changes in linguistic material from one language to another or within the same language: additions, omissions, distortions, updatings, modifications, cultural changes.

FORMAL INTERPRETANTS

From the above it can clearly be seen that the plot and characters in *Omkara* are very similar, though the film is set in contemporary gangster India, more precisely in Uttar Pradesh, and the characters speak Hindi with accents from the region. Each of Shakespeare's main characters has its equivalent in *Omkara*: Othello is Omkara (Omi) Shukla; the Duke of Venice is Tiwari Bhaisaab; Iago is Langda Tyagi; Michael Cassio is Kesu Firangi (*firangi* = foreigner, possible because of his knowledge of English); Desdemona is Dolly Mishra, daughter of Advocate Raghunath Mishra (Brabantio), employed by Bhaisaab. Emilia is the feisty Indu; and Bianca is singer and dancer, a *nachnewaali*, Billo Chamanbahar. Rodrigo is Dolly's jilted fiancé Rajju.

The one major plot change, which could even be called a tightening of the Shakespeare plot, is that Rajju is about to marry Dolly at the beginning of the film. In *Othello* Rodrigo is no more than a pretender from a similar social class to Desdemona. Other smaller changes are made: Indu (Emilia) becomes Omkara's sister, thus Langda (Iago) is Omkara's brother-in-law. Indu befriends Dolly, her future sister-in-law, but who does not act as a waiting-maid to her, and Langda (Iago), now and Indu are given an eight-year-old son, Golu. At the end of the play Indu kills Langda by slashing his throat, whereas in Othello Iago is taken away to be judged and almost certainly killed.

Another change is that it is the Rodrigo character, Rajju, who first encourages Langda to take revenge on Omi by pretending that Dolly is having an affair with Kesu: "That pretender Kesu comes out of nowhere and seizes the bone out of your mouth. Where did your guts go walking then?"[1] A number of key, or perhaps, signature, moments in the plot are replicated in *Omkara*. The "Keep up your bright swords, for the dew will rust them" speech, made by Othello in I.ii, has its equivalent in a showdown between the followers of Omi and Advocate Mishra, Dolly's father, who accuses Omi of having abducted Dolly. The imposing Omkara enters and does not flinch when the Advocate holds a gun to his head. The scene is only interrupted when Bhaisaab calls and persuades the Advocate not to kill Omi for the time being. Later Dolly is called to testify that she has not been kidnapped by Omi. They seem to be very happy together, emphasised by the background music and songs. Dolly is looking after Omkara after he has been wounded in the shoulder, and we see Omkara recovering and their taking walks together. Dolly says, "I remember feeling like a blind bird plunging down an empty well". She thinks about suicide and says: "Rajju will marry me dead". Thus their courtship seems to contain none of visits made by Shakespeare's Othello to Brabantio's house where he entertained (and won) Desdemona by the stories of his life.

Cassio's getting drunk in Cyprus has its equivalent in the celebration scene of victory over the enemy gang, where the sexually provocative Billo (Bianca) sings the Beedi song. Langda dances with Kesu, cajoles him to drink, then Kesu takes the stage with Billo. Rajan's smoking then upsets Billo, and this is sufficient reason for the drunken Kesu to set about Rajju. The handkerchief becomes a *kamarbandh*, a family heirloom of all the brides in Omkara's family, but its function is retained as Langda leads Omi into seeing it on Billo. The final murder and suicide follow Othello somewhat closely, though the bedroom scene is considerably shorter, and the difference that Indu (Emilia) kills Langda (Iago) by slashing his throat.

Further elements of the plot that are omitted include Othello's epilepsy and the Willow Song sung by Desdemona. By contrast, the plot adds details in the battle between the political gangs. A thug belonging to the rival gang, Kichlu, attempts to kill Bhaisaab, who is hospitalised, and then Kichlu is killed when watching the seductive Billo dance. A change that is made is that while Othello and Desdemona have already eloped and married at the beginning of the play, Omi and Dolly elope but do not marry until near the end of the play "on an auspicious day". This, it seems, would be the correct behavior in Omkara's village.

THEMATIC INTERPRETANTS

The central motives of jealousy and betrayal remain intact, as does the purity of Desdemona. Dolly Mishra seems to have led a protected life and is being sexually awoken by Omi, although she has always been good friends with Kesu, who attended the same school and who acted as a go-between, fetching and taking her and Omi's letters.

The one thematic interpretant which contemporary productions of Othello almost never follow is that of the age difference between Desdemona, sixteen years old in the Shakespearean text, and Othello, whose exact age we never know, but who must be between forty and fifty. Kareena Kapoor (Dolly) was twenty-six when she made the film, and Ajay Devgan (Omkara) thirty-seven, and this is the apparent difference we see on the screen.

The "proto-feminist" speech of Emilia in IV.iii, in which she puts forwards the view that women should betray their unfaithful husbands, is omitted in *Omkara*. This is softened to a comment on women's power in sexual relations with their husbands: "My grandmother always told me to keep these men slightly hungry, else the day they satisfied they'll puke you out like nobody's business". Indu also becomes something of an advisor to her brother, Omi, maybe also adding to his doubts about Desdemona:

When the scriptures themselves have sullied women, who can blame mere mortals like you. We renounce our homes and walk into your lives with bare empty hands. But even after the holy fires approve us. We're regarded disloyal sooner than loyal. But if you have the slightest of doubts do not stoop to attend the marriage.

An attempt is made to replicate the elements of racial difference and of Omi being an outsider as his humble origins are emphasised. He is the illegitimate child of a higher caste Brahmin man and a lower caste woman, and this is mentioned on occasions, particularly by Dolly's father, Advocate Ragunath Mishra. His skin colour is also slightly darker than that of the rest of the cast. Indeed, a "Granny" inside Omkara's village asks where Omkara obtained such a "fair" bride. By contrast, Dolly, Bhaisaab, Kesu and Langda all fully fledged Brahmins. However, as previously mentioned, this never becomes a contentious point in the film.

As mentioned, the gang rivalry and gang violence replaces the war between Venice and the Ottoman Empire. This, however, would seem to bear little importance on the details of the plot or central themes. Othello is very much a personal domestic tragedy, and the battle in Cyprus only acts as a background.

It is a norm of that Bollywood films must contain music and dance scenes. Music is important to the film. Kesu plays the guitar and teaches Dolly Stevie Wonder's 'I Just Called to Say I Love You'. The lullaby, sung by Suresh Wadkar, is used both for the tender scene of Omkara and Dolly resting after apparently having made love, and Omkara singing over Dolly's lifeless body. Director Bhardwaj, who actually began his Bollywood career as musical director on films such as *Maachis* (1996) and *Satya* (1998), also composed the music.

There are two dances, the first at the celebration when the rival gang is defeated, the equivalent of the Cyprus commemoration. Billo (Bianca) gyrates and sings to an all-male audience the Beedi song with its strong sexual insinuations: "Light your fags with the heat of my bosom/ It's burning up inside me/ Light your stoves with the heat of my bosom/ Burn your coals with the heat of my bosom". As mentioned, this results in Kesu roughing up Rajju.

The second dance routine takes place when Billo's performance is used to entrap Kichlu, a member of the opposing gang, who has, in a murder attempt, wounded Bhaisaab. All the participants in the plot are disguised as policemen, and Omkara and Langda enter also disguised as policemen. Billo sings the Namak number, "My tongue longs to taste the spice", Omkara and Langda kill Kichlu, but what is more important for the plot is that Billo is wearing Dolly's *kamarbandh*. Langda has told Omkara about Kesu telling him that he and Billo making love at night when all she was wearing was the *kamarbandh*. Omkara finds himself pointing his gun at Kesu, but of course does not fire.

LINGUISTIC INTERPRETANTS

This section will deal with issues of language in *Omkara*. Unfortunately here I am dependent on the comments of others and the English subtitles of the Hindi dialogue. Hopefully a future study will examine the accuracy of the subtitles. Unlike the great majority of Bollywood films, Omkara contains a number of expletives, mostly coming from Langda (Singh 2007) in the Khariboli dialect of Uttar Pradesh (Adarsh 2006). To this reviewer the language of the film is at times too strong: "The director and his team of writers [Vishal Bhardwal, Robin Bhatt, Abhishek Chaubey] could've toned down the expletives in the film", and may have been a reason for its relative lack of success in conservative India when compared to the UK.

Some of the strong language manages to come through in the subtitles, as in this exchange between Langda and Indu rendered into very British slang:

Indu: I've been toiling away at these chapattis and nobody cares a shit
Langda: Have you ever fed me with half this love?
Indu: Bugger off.

An analysis of the linguistic interpretants will show that language is the one area where *Omkara* differs most from *Othello*. Shakespeare's Othello is voluble, and uses a pompous and excessively formal language, often to disguise his insecurity. Omi is much more of the strong silent type, familiar to us from Hollywood characters such as Marshall Will Kane (Cary Grant) in *High Noon* (1952) who fails to make a single long speech. Langda's language is often nearer that of Iago, though a large amount of the dialogue in which Iago persuades Othello that Cassio is having an affair is missing. Furthermore, none of Iago's soliloquies remain.

However, there remain certain moments when Langda's speeches are similar to those of Iago. First, when Langda and Omi return unexpectedly, Kesu has been teaching Dolly how to sing Stevie Wonder's song, 'I Just called to Say I Love You', and he rushes off, not wishing for a further confrontation with his boss:

Omkara: Wasn't that Kesu?
Langda: Leave the poor boy alone. Why in the world would he come to see Dolly in your absence?
Omkara: But it did look like his bike
Langda: Como on bro, Kesu's our own. Why would he run like a thief on seeing you?

He then unsuccessfully tries to phone Kesu.

Langda: Can't believe that was Kesu
Omkara: What in the world could he be up with Dolly at this hour?

The insinuations are similar to those in *Othello*:

Iago: Ha! I like not that.
Othello: What dost thou say?
Iago: Nothing my lord; or if—I know not what.
Iago: Cassio, my lord? No, sure, I cannot think it That he would sneak away so guilty-like, Seeing you coming. (III.iii)

And later:

Omkara: Dolly is happier with the forgiving than the wedding
Langda: Our Dolly dotes on Kesu. They've known each other for a long time. They both went to the same college. No wonder.
Omkara: No wonder what?
Langda: Me and my filthy mind
Omkara: Langda, tell me what's on your mind.
Langda: Dolly is such a stunner, and Kesu such a flirt. Just wondering if he has ever had any designs on her. Kesu is a sweet soul but he strays around too much . . . bloody slut. It won't be a bad idea if we keep an eye on her till the wedding. The world is full of big bad wolves and our Dolly is too naïve.

Then, when Omi is demanding proof:

Langda: May my tongue fall out before I utter another word
          . . .
          No, that's what you wanted to hear. Do you have the courage to hear the truth? When I stayed at Kesu's house, I heard him mutter in his sleep: "Dolly, if our love has to love, we'll have to hide it from the entire world".

We can compare this to *Othello* III.iii.407–423:

Iago: I do not like the office.
             But sith I am entered in the cause so far-
             Pricked to't by foolish honesty and love-
             I will go on. I lay with Cassio lately,
             And being troubled with a raging tooth
             I could not sleep.
             . . .
             In sleep I heard him say: 'Sweet Desdemona,
             Let us be wary, let us hide our loves';
             And then cry 'O sweet creature!' and kiss me hard
             As if he plucked up kissed by the roots,
             That grew upon my lips; then laid his leg

Over my thigh, and sighed and kissed, and then
Cried 'cursèd fate that gave thee to the Moor!'

Shakespeare's Othello wins Desdemona through the story of his life he
tells her on his many visits to her home, described by Iago as "bragging
and telling her fantastical lies" (II.i.216). Omi courts her in a very different way. As mentioned above, we see Dolly nursing Omkara back to
health after being wounded in the shoulder. The scene has no dialogue,
but we hear the plaintive *O Saathi Re* song to signify the beginning of
their romance. Then, at what seems to be the engagement party between
Rajan and Dolly, looks pass across the room between Omkara and Dolly.
This 'Othello' does not win his Desdemona through his stories but rather
by his quiet powerful masculinity.

A thematic line is, "She who can dupe her own father will never be
anyone's to claim", originally made by Dolly's father, the Advocate, and
repeated twice by Omkara. This is a rewriting of Brabantio's lines, "Look
to her, moor, if thou hast eyes to see./ She has deceived her father, and may
thee" (I.iii. 289–290). This idea is repeated by Iago, "She did deceive her
father, marrying you,/ And when she seemed to shake, and fear your looks,/
She loved them most" (III.iii. 205–208). And before his suicide there is no
bombastic speech from Omkara. He merely utters, "Forget how I pasted
the army guy in court. And our friend Indore Singh?" He then shoots himself in the heart with the same courage.

I believe that *Omkara* is typical of adaptations of Shakespeare in losing
much of the original language. Generally, this will be the first element to
disappear, and the adaptation may do little more than reflect a number of
the key images such as "the green-eyed monster" (III.iii), "Keep up your
bright swords, for the dew will rust them" (I.ii.) and "an old black ram
is tupping your white ewe" (I.i.). It is not difficult to see why Shakespeare's language gives difficulties to adaptors: it is, after all, more than
400 years old, but contains many more difficulties for the contemporary
spectator than the language of his near contemporaries in France, Molière,
Racine and Corneille, with his archaisms, use of unusual dialect words,
neologisms, puns, innuendo, classical references, images of subjects we
know little about today such as falconry and alchemy, and a frequent long-
windedness, all resulting in much of the text being cut both for unadapted
stage versions and rewritten for adaptations. Basically, Shakespeare's language is very difficult!

By contrast, the central themes of Shakespeare's most famous plays:
love, passion, jealousy, betrayal, revenge, senility, ambition, procrastina-
tion, a domineering wife, are much easier for us to understand and connect
with, and, as seen in the analysis of the linguistic and formal interpretants,
are, in *Omkara*, maintained to a great extent. The fact that Shakespeare's
plays can successfully exist without language can be illustrated by referring to the Synectic Theater, a group based in Washington, DC, who have

produced very successful wordless productions of "Silent Shakespeare", with absolutely no text, speech or songs, the plays being narrated through action, mime, dance, music and use of props. In 2011 and 2012 the group produced *Macbeth*, *Othello*, *Romeo and Juliet* and *Taming of the Shrew*.

CONCLUDING REMARKS

The *Omkara* film adaptation of *Othello* accurately follows the formal and thematic elements of Othello, departing from Othello only at certain moments. Indeed the official film poster emphasises that *Omkara* is "[a] Vishal Bhardwaj Adaptation of Shakespeare's *Othello*", and the trailer declares it "[a] timeless tale of trust, seduction and betrayal" "based on William Shakespeare's Othello". However, it is much less closer in linguistic terms, only occasionally reflecting the Shakespeare original. I suggested that this is a characteristic of contemporary adaptations of Shakespeare. In the case of *Othello*, adaptations tend to follow the formal elements of plot, characters and structure—the formal interpretants—and the central themes of betrayal and jealousy—the thematic interpretants; however, many of the linguistic interpretants—such as the bombast of Othello's speeches, Iago's soliloquies, the repetition of linguistic signifiers such as Iago continually being referred to as "honest", and Shakespeare's continual punning and (over)loaded metaphors, multiple references, use of dialects, neologisms and so on—are the elements which adapters, as in the case of *Omkara*, tend to eliminate, and the language of *Omkara* is much nearer that of a contemporary Bollywood gangster movie than that of Shakespeare. The themes are many of Shakespeare's plays are relatively straightforward to us; the way in which Shakespeare uses language much less so.

To conclude, and further illustrate this point by one other example of a classic work, which, in adaptation, loses much of its original language, the linguistic interpretant. The ideas and themes (thematic interpretant) and characters and plot development (formal interpretant) of *Don Quijote* remain: Don Quixote himself, Sancho Panza, Dulcinea, Rocinante, the well-known episodes such as Don Quixote's belief that the inn is a castle, and his attack on the windmills that he takes for ferocious giants. Little is remembered of the actual language of the original (linguistic interpretant) except maybe for the opening, "En un lugar de la Mancha". We could likewise think of the central images of Dickens' *A Christmas Carol* or *Oliver Twist*, and *David Copperfield*, Defoe's *Robinson Crusoe* and Swift's *Gulliver's Travels*.

My study on the adapted translations of the Brazilian book club, the Clube do Livro (Milton 2001, 2002) showed that these works, aimed at a mass market, pasteurised the stylistic characteristics of the original language, obliterating the linguistic interpretant. Examining the standardisation of the translated language in the Clube do Livro's translations of

Rabelais's *Gargantua*, Dickens' *Hard Times*, and Charlotte Brontë's *The Professor*, I concluded,

> It is through standardization of language that the homogenous, inoffensive text approved of by schools and the Church is produced. Stylistic differences and the idiosyncrasies of experimental authors are erased, with the result that such authors end up by using the 'correct' standard register of the target language irrespective of the nature of the original. (2001: 59)

In 'Vampire Adaptations' Thomas Leitch develops the image of adaptations as vampires "one of the hoariest clichés in the field of Adaptation Studies . . . that adaptations act like vampires in sucking the life out of the passive, helpless progenitor texts who enable their existence" (2011: 5). This "life" seems to consist of the central themes, images, tropes, while it is the language element, the linguistic interpretant, which remains in the original and is not sucked out.

NOTES

1. All quotations from *Omkara* are taken from the English subtitles.

WORKS CITED

Maqbool. 2003. Writ. Abbas Tyrewala and Vishal Bhardwaj. Dir. Vishal Bhardwaj.

Adarsh, Taran. 2006. 'Omkara'. *Bollywood Hungama*. http://www.bollywood-hungama.com/movies/review/12773/index.html (accessed 31 December 2010).

Bhatia, Nandi. 2007. 'Different Othello(s) and Contentious Spectators: Changing Responses in India'. *Gramma: Journal of Theory and Criticism*, 15, pp. 155–174.

Chatterjee, Sudipto and Jyotsna Singh. 1999. 'Moor or Less? The Surveillance of Othello, Calcutta 1848'. In: Christy Desmet and Robert Sawyer (eds.), *Shakespeare and Appropriation*. London: Routledge, pp. 65–82.

Leitch, Thomas. 2011. 'Vampire Adaptation'. *Journal of Adaptation in Film and Performance*, 4:1, pp. 5–16.

Loomba, Ania. 1998. '"Local-manufacture made-in-India Othello fellows": Issues of Race, Hybridity and Location in Post-Colonial Shakespeares'. In: Ania Loomba and Martin Orkin (eds.), *Post-Colonial Shakespeares*. London: Routledge, pp. 143–163.

Milton, John. 2001. 'The Translation of Classic Fiction for Mass Markets: The Case of a Brazilian Book Club, the Clube do Livro'. *The Translator*, 7:1, pp. 43–69.

Milton, John. 2002. *O Clube do Livro e a Tradução*. Bauru: Editora da Universidade do Sagrado Coração (EDUSC).

Milton, John. 2009. 'Between the Cat and the Devil: Adaptation Studies and Translation Studies'. *Journal of Adaptation in Film & Performance*, 2:1, pp. 47–64.

Ramachandran, Naman. 2006. 'Omkara'. *Sight & Sound*, 16:10, p. 76.

Singh, Amardeep. 2007. '"Omkara", "Othello", and the Dirty Business of Politics (a Film Review)'. http://www.lehigh.edu/~amsp/2006/07/omkara-othello-and-dirty-business-of.html (accessed 31 December 2010).

Trivedi, Poonam. 2004. '"Folk Shakespeare": The Performance of Shakespeare in Traditional Indian Theater Forms'. In: Poonam Trivedi and Dennis Bartholomeusz (eds.), *India's Shakespeare: Translation, Interpretation and Performance*. Newark: University of Delaware Press, pp. 171–192.

Trivedi, Poonam, and Dennis Bartholomeusz (eds.). 2006. *Shakespeare: Translation, Interpretation and Performance*. Delhi: Dorling Kindersley.

Venuti, Lawrence. 2007. 'Adaptation, Translation, Critique'. *Journal of Visual Culture*, 6:1, pp. 2–43. http://vcu.sagepub.com/cgi/content/abstract/6/1/25 (accessed 31 December 2010).

6 *The Thief of Bagdad*
Foreignising Adaptations

Jessica Wiest

INTRODUCTION

In 1991, when American troops invaded Iraq, the western world got first-hand television coverage of a Middle East unlike anything they had been taught to imagine. The televised images of the 'real' Baghdad clashed with Hollywood's white-domed, snake-charmer, magic carpet world of the Arabian Nights. This sharp contrast between perceived reality, and Hollywood fantasy redoubled the investigation into the western cultural appropriation of the Middle East begun by Edward Said in the 1970s. The US invasion of Iraq led to a renewed burst of scholarship, and the past two to three decades have seen new analyses of the culture, historiography, imperialism, anthropology, literature and—especially—the film adaptations that created and perpetuated the stereotypes of a fictionalised Middle East.

Edward Said gives important and useful context for examining such eastern stereotypes with his seminal work *Orientalism*, and any analysis of the relationship of west and east is incomplete without acknowledging his groundwork. But, as Susan Nance argues in her 2009 publication, *How the Arabian Nights Inspired the American Dream*, scholars need to use Said's ideas as a springboard rather than the final word. She actually chastises those who are hesitant to push his scholarship further:

> [T]hese writers pay lip service to "Orientalism" but do not actually engage with the full theoretical implications of Said's arguments with respect to *how* subconscious discursive power has supposedly worked through cultural texts and *how*, precisely, this is connected to the formulation of foreign policy and military or diplomatic action. Instead common scholarly interpretation sees a predatory inevitability in American engagement with the Muslim world because authors tend to focus analysis on cultural "texts" in isolation from the moment of production or live display. (Nance 2009: 7)

An analysis of what Nance calls "the moment of production" potentially sheds light on the proximate rather than the overarching motivation behind

Orientalist stereotypes. What, for example, were the specific cultural and political environments in which a text was produced? How do the history and personality of the author or translator perpetuate cultural stereotypes? If one is to understand a text that crosses language and culture borders, then it is essential to recognise these specific and often personal contexts. Intercultural works typically have translators, and these translators are situated in their own cultural and historical contexts. Translation Studies, therefore, provides a fitting dimension for examining the relationships between east and west, even in terms of film adaptation, because in understanding more about the translation process we recognise that the translator (or adaptor) heavily influences how a text is represented.

TRANSLATION THEORY

As any translator can attest, there are no exact translations. Unlike mathmatics, the process of translation is contextual, not formulaic. *Respondez-vous s'il vous plaît* does not translate directly into "please let me know if you will be attending," just as *adios* doesn't simply mean 'goodbye'. The words *'a dios'* represent a phrase with deep religious and historical meaning very different from the American phrase 'see you later'. In the translator's preface to Derrida's *Of Grammatology*, Gayatri Spivak gives an important point of view on the translation process. She discusses the common situation of a word being *under erasure* during translation. She defines this as "to write a word, cross it out, and then print both word and deletion. . . . In examining familiar things we come to such unfamiliar conclusions that our very language is twisted and bent even as it guides us. Writing 'under erasure' is the mark of this contortion" (in Niranjana 1992: 48). Spivak suggests that the work of a translator is agonising, since any given word might have dozens of simultaneous meanings. The simultaneity of these meanings gives language its nuance and richness, but it also makes the process of translation more difficult, especially for the knowledgeable translator.

Because language is ambiguous, the process of translation occasionally results in cultural casualties. According to Tejaswini Niranjana, translation often acts as a colonising influence, particularly when languages are not on 'equal' socio-political footing. "In creating coherent and transparent texts and subjects", she argues, "translation participates—across a range of discourses—in the *fixing* of colonized cultures, making them seem static and unchanging rather than historically constructed" (1992: 3). This is precisely the problem with the English translation of *adios*. The cultural, historical and religious contexts of this one word are all but lost when it is translated as "goodbye". The richness of *adios* is lost, flattened into one dimension in which the new meaning belongs to the translator rather than to the author or the source language.

The complexity of translating thus creates two related problems. First, readers tend to ignore the role of the translator and imagine that the translated text is the original text. Second, readers usually fail to recognise that translation always involves multiple acts of interpretation, even with a single word. As Niranjana puts it, translation often functions in our society as a seemingly "transparent presentation of something that already exists" (1992: 3). She is quick to point out, however, that "the 'original' is actually brought into being through translation" (3). Thus when we read the English translation of Derrida's work, we are not reading Derrida. We are instead reading a new 'original' created by Spivak. Translation scholar Lawrence Venuti has, for over a decade now, led the discourse on these translation problems. "By producing the illusion of transparency", he claims, "a fluent translation masquerades as a true semantic equivalence when it in fact inscribes the foreign text with a partial interpretation, partial to English-language values, reducing if not simply excluding the very differences that translation is called on to convey" (2008: 16). In other words, what Venuti calls "domesticating translation" assumes that the target language—often the colonising language of English—can effectively communicate exactly and precisely what the original did. It assumes that the word 'goodbye' is a perfectly adequate equivalent to *adios*. Not only is this assumption presumptuous, it's "ethnocentric violence", according to Venuti (16). Venuti argues that domesticating translation can and ought to be replaced with a very different strategy that he calls "foreignizing translation". While the former, he argues, is an "ethnocentric reduction of the foreign text to receiving cultural values, bringing the author back home", the latter is "an ethnodeviant pressure on those values to register the linguistic and cultural differences of the foreign text, sending the reader abroad" (2008: 15). Thus, instead of translating *adios* into 'goodbye', it might instead be translated into the distinctly foreign-sounding phrase, 'I commend you to God'. Such a phrase is slightly jarring in English, because it is not a typical English phrase. This translation, although arguably not an exact literal translation of *adios*, attempts to capture some of the religious and syntactical uniqueness of the original phrase, and in doing so foreignises by privileging the Spanish source language over the English target language.

Wenfen Yang, in his 2010 article 'Brief Study on Domestication and Foreignization in Translation', has called for the dispute between these two translation strategies to be "viewed from a brand new perspective—social, cultural and historical". He claims that the "conflict between domestication and foreignization as opposite translation strategies can be regarded as the cultural and political rather than linguistic extension of the time-worn controversy over free translation and literal translation" (2010: 77). In other words, Yang advocates defining both domesticating and foreignising translations more broadly to include cultural and political contexts. My analysis uses Yang's broader definitions to deal with the complicated situation in which a foreignising work goes beyond simply privileging the source text and instead serves the political purposes of the translator. Such biased translations occur when translators promote, enlarge or in any way change the meaning or nuance of particular passages in order to create more colourful, more interesting or more politically charged works based on their foreign status. Foreignising translations occasionally include calculated differences from their source texts in order to meet political or social agendas, a fact that problematises Venuti's assertion that foreignising translations commit less violence to a source culture than do domesticating translations. But even Venuti admits that the translation of a foreign text must be read "as an interpretation that imitates yet varies foreign textual features in accordance with the translator's cultural situation and historical moment" (2008: 124). Understanding the translator's situation, then, illuminates the process of manipulation and stereotyping.

In *The Translator's Invisibility: A History of Translation*, Venuti spends a chapter analysing the translation projects of Italian writer Iginio Ugo Tarchetti (1839–1869). Tarchetti belonged to a dissident political group during his day: the Milanese movement *scapigliatura*, "a loosely associated group of artists, composers, and writers who contested bourgeois values . . . [and] were at variance with the highly conservative realism that had dominated Italian fiction since . . . 1827" (2008: 125–126). As a member of this group, Tarchetti actively did political work with his writing and translating. According to Venuti, Tarchetti was not above tweaking his translated works in order to produce social change in nineteenth century Italy. He "adapted fantastic motifs, reproduced scenes, translated, even plagiarized—yet each discursive practice served the political function of interrogating ideologies and addressing hierarchical social relations in Italy" (126). One of the texts that Tarchetti used in this manner was *The Arabian Nights*. He rebelled against the dominant political ideal of conservative realism by using the backdrop of 'Arabia' to create his own alternate social vision.

Venuti claims that "[d]iscourse produces concrete social effects: the novel can alter subjectivity and motor social change" (2008: 128). Through his translated texts Tarchetti felt that he could produce such social change, "transforming foreign texts to function in a different cultural formation" and molding them to fit his political agenda (126). Venuti translates a passage from Tarchetti's work *Tutte le opere* to illustrate:

> The Persians and the Arabs drew from the variety of their nomad life, and from their virgin nature, and from their burning sky the first novelistic narratives, hence the laws and customs of the Arabs' social and domestic community have been well-known and familiar to us for a long time, and Strabo lamented that love for the marvelous rendered uncertain the histories of these nations. (in Venuti 2008: 132)

According to Venuti, "the passage shows him [Tarchetti] actively rewriting his cultural materials so as to transform the Orient into a vehicle for his democratic social vision" (2008: 132). The construction of this "virgin nature" ostensibly contrasts a weak eastern femininity with the dominating western culture. This representation of Arabic culture, again according to Venuti, has two different facets—a utopian image, as well as picture of the exotic and phantasmagorical, but both representations "aim to make Persia and Arabia perform a European function, the regeneration of Italian fiction and society" (132), creating a new foundation on which to construct conversations about literature. And really, though this translation may be performing a "European function", as Venuti claims, it is more overtly serving Tarchetti's personal political agenda.

Niranjana's and Venuti's ideas about translation and the role of the translator offer a useful metaphor for exploring transnational film adaptations. As Cutchins and Albrecht-Crane argue in their introduction to *New Beginnings for Adaptation Studies*,

> Rather than seeing adaptations as taking one thing (a novel's imagined 'essence') and placing it into another context, we should recognize that the 'essence' is neither knowable, nor directly representable. A novel's imagined essence remains elusive and ambiguous; what one does achieve in reading, or in adapting a text, is thus always more, less, or other than what the novel or the author wanted to express. (2010: 17)

Thus, just as the process of translation showcases the difficulty of language parameters (think Spivak's contortions), film adaptations demonstrate the complexity of the word-into-film process, as well as the potential for foreignising or domesticating translations. The similarities between literary translation and film adaptation in this process revolve around the idea that the intermediary (either translator or adaptor) plays a key role in the balance between source and target texts. Yang gives a good context for this idea: "In his famous lecture *On the Different Ways of Translation*, Friedrich Schleiermacher demanded that translations from different languages into German should read and sound different: the reader should be able to guess the Spanish behind a translation from Spanish, and the Greek behind a translation from Greek" (2010: 78). This notion, one of the roots of the idea of foreignising translation, is completely compatible with adaptation theory. Assuming that adaptations should be foreignised, then a movie based on a video game (e.g., *The Prince of Persia*, 2010) should have a different feel from a movie based on a novel (*Pride and Prejudice*, 2005) which in turn should have a slightly different feel from a movie based on a play (*Chicago*, 2002) or a movie based on a theme park ride (*Pirates of the Caribbean*, 2003). The idea of foreignising translation provides valuable context for discussing films—not in terms of their fidelity to a source text but in terms of their dissonance to films from other sources. As Yang puts it, "[F]oreignization advocated by Venuti and his followers is a non-fluent or estranging translation style designed to make visible the presence

of the translator by highlighting the foreign identity of the ST [source text]"
(2010: 78). Taking a cue from the translation theories of Venuti, Niranjana
and Yang, I want to examine the role of the producer of the 1940 film
The Thief of Bagdad. Alexander Korda, I argue, was a translator of sorts,
remaking the tale of Aladdin as well as the 1924 American film *The Thief
of Bagdad* into a distinctly British film. In so doing he was "maintaining a
refusal of the dominant" language of early twentieth-century cinema—that
of Hollywood—by "developing affiliations with marginal cultural values",
in this case British values (Venuti 2008: 125).

This was not the first time that the *Arabian Nights* had been used in
this manner. Like Tarchetti's translations, the early literary translations
(and ensuing film adaptations) of the *Arabian Nights* were often political
vehicles for translators, with the adapted culture having little say about
its own representation. As John Eisele argues, "At the beginning of the
twentieth century, Arabs were not regarded as a threat to the interests of
the United States" (2002: 72), and thus had little means of defending themselves against the onslaught of western stereotypes or of offering effective
counter-narratives. Middle Easterners were essentially defenceless against
the western translation of their culture. And *The Arabian Nights* were
certainly at the centre of many of these cultural translations. It is difficult to trace the genealogy of the western retellings of these stories, for
they went through their own series of both domesticating and foreignising
translations. Richard Francis Burton (1821–1890), one of the preeminent
translators of the *Nights*, candidly admitted he had an agenda with his
translations. Burton decried the earlier "unsexed and unsouled" translated
versions (which were themselves a product of their era), claiming he wanted
to present English readers with a "full, complete, unvarnished, uncastrated
copy of the great original" (in Shamma 2005: 54). He made it very clear that
his text was translated from the original Arabic rather than from Antoine
Galland's French interpretation, which was the first widely circulated western translation and the source text for many successive translations. With
this cry for authenticity, however, came a subversive social agenda: that of
using *The Arabian Nights* to reform what Burton saw as Victorian sexual
hypocrisy. "The England of our day would fain bring up both sexes and
keep all ages in profound ignorance of sexual and intersexual relations;
and the consequences of that imbecility are peculiarly cruel and afflicting",
he said. "I proposed to supply the want in these pages" (in Shamma 2005:
54). Though his work wasn't as politically charged as Tarchetti's, Burton's
version of the tales nonetheless had a definite social agenda that fuelled his
translation, and the stereotype of the passionate Arab provided a useful
vehicle for the social reform Burton wanted to accomplish. According to
Venuti, "Burton's Orientalism was deployed in an effort to upset the hierarchy of moral values in Victorian Britain. In this respect, especially when
set against Lane's domesticating version, Burton's translation can be called
foreignizing in intention" (2008: 269).

THE THIEF OF BAGDAD (1924)

Because *The Arabian Nights* were a popular source text for film adaptation as well, it wasn't too surprising when in 1924, Douglas Fairbanks, a member of Hollywood's elite, decided he wanted to produce a silent film version of the *Nights* called *The Thief of Bagdad*. This film, though it claims to be an adaptation of the *Nights*, straddles an interesting line between the fantasy world of the Middle East and the dusty streets of the Old West. As director Raoul Walsh candidly admits, he had only made American Western films up until that point: "[M]ost of the productions I had directed dealt with cowboys and gangsters and pimps and prostitutes and the dregs of the American West" (1974: 163). Consequently, Walsh's notions of 'authenticity' to the original tales are questionable. He claims that his plot is true to the "general themes of *A Thousand and One Nights*" and that the artistic sets were "great enough to convince me that I was walking the streets of old Bagdad" (163). But it is doubtful that Walsh had ever visited Bagdad or even read the *Nights*. His claims for authenticity rest on already established Orientalisations of Middle Eastern culture. This is especially exemplified in his comment that the place to find extras for his film was "[i]n Mexican town", because "[a] dark-faced Mexican with a head-rag hiding everything except his eyes and nose and mouth will pass for an Arab any time" (164).

While Walsh may have been somewhat haphazard in his approach to the tale, Douglas Fairbanks, as the producer and star actor, had a concrete agenda for his film. According to an unnamed scenario writer, Fairbanks said, "Our hero must be Every Young Man—of this age or any age—who believes that happiness is a quality that can be stolen; who is selfish—at odds with the world—rebellious toward conventions on which comfortable human relations are based" (in Cooperson 2006: 271). This same writer claimed that the entire foundation for the film came from one sole quatrain of Burton's translated *Nights*:

> Seek not thy happiness to steal,
> 'Tis work alone will win thee weal.
> Who seeketh bliss sans toil and strife,
> The impossible seeketh and wasteth life. (Cooperson 2006: 271)

From this single quatrain comes the rather rigidly enforced moral of the movie, a phrase that appears literally written in the stars on screen at the beginning and end of the film: "Happiness must be earned".

The plot embodies a typical moral rags-to-riches tale. Fairbanks plays the thief, a young man who lives on the streets and steals whatever he fancies, running from soldiers and rejecting religious reformation. He undergoes a transformation, however, when he sees the beautiful princess and decides to undergo a quest of bravery in order to beat out all the other suitors to win her love, marry her and take her away on a fantastic flying carpet. According to Michael Cooperson, "Fairbanks' *Thief* recuperates the anarchic foreigner by casting him as a convert to the rule of law and the Puritan work ethic. 'By toil the sweets of human life are found,' the holy man cries, reforming the thief and familiarizing the exotic characters as players in a Horatio Alger success story" (2006: 271). Thus, Fairbanks' film is a classic example of a domesticating adaptation. It had an agenda that catered to the rugged individualistic and prohibitionist mentality of early twentieth-century America, and it adjusted the source text accordingly.

Despite its domesticating socio-political agenda, however, Fairbanks' movie, by all accounts, represented a breakthrough in technology and in sheer size. The number of extras and the extraordinary sets were unprecedented. *Guinness Film: Facts and Feats* recognises it as the most expensive film produced up to that point, with a record $2,000,000 in production costs at a time when the average Hollywood film cost $300,000 (Robertson 1985: 38). In 1996, the National Film Registry assumed protection of Fairbanks' movie, thus ensuring the film's preservation for all time as one of the culturally, historically or aesthetically important films safeguarded by the National Film Preservation Act. Admittedly, these films "are not selected as the 'best' American films of all time, but rather as works of enduring importance to American culture" (Anonym. 2009). The 1924 *The Thief of Bagdad* thus became a kind of icon, *The Arabian Nights* fantasy film after which all successive ones were patterned.

Ironically enough, John Eisele claims that this film "did not make the grade" because "unlike *The Sheik*, it did not lead to a spate of look-alike films. In fact, it may have actually slowed down the production of Arabian nights films for more than a decade" (2009: 79). Although Eisele's facts are correct, I disagree with his conclusion that *The Thief* didn't make the grade. In fact, the opposite is true: Fairbanks's *Thief* was so big and so expensive that later producers shied away from attempting to compete with it. They knew that they could not muster the kind of financial backing that Douglas Fairbanks brought to the 1924 film. Any remake or look-alike would betray the disparity in budget.

As discussed earlier with the example of Tarchetti, "Foreignizing translation is a dissident cultural practice, maintaining a refusal of the dominant by developing affiliations with marginal linguistic and cultural values in the receiving situation" (Venuti 2008: 125). Thus, in an analysis of the 1940 British remake of *The Thief of Bagdad*, it's important to understand the dominant Hollywood film culture of the 1930s in order to analyse how producer Alexander Korda acted as a foreignising translator. Korda provided the cultural dissidence that Venuti advocates with translation, a politically calculated dissidence that required American audiences to re-evaluate their movie expectations. The impetus behind the 1940 version of *The Thief of Bagdad* began two decades before the film, with a floundering British film industry. In the 1920s, in an effort to jumpstart the industry, the British government passed the Cinematograph Films Act of 1927, requiring cinema owners to show a certain number of British-made films. Known as the 'quota', this act resulted in a demand for British-made films, something that Nicholas Pronay claims "proved to be a remarkably successful exercise in government intervention" (1983: 381). It increased the production of British-made major feature films from virtually nothing to making Britain, in 1936, "the second largest film-producer in the world, only exceeded by the United States, with 212 British-made feature films being registered in that year" (381). Nevertheless, in 1931, when Alexander Korda arrived in Britain, the industry was still struggling. The films produced to fill the quota were vastly unpopular with audiences and producers alike, who saw them as mass-produced, bland films that had to be churned out on a regular basis. These 'quota quickies' were generally produced on a government subsidy of £4,000–6,000 (in contrast to the £30,000 it usually took to make a feature film production in the 1930s) (Kulik 1975: 71). To make matters worse, the original intention of the law was soon subverted. American film companies quickly realised that they could simply set up shop in Britain and churn out films that fit the quota regulations, since technically they were produced on British soil. As a result, the British film industry in 1931 was suffering from not only Hollywood oppression, but also from its own government's clumsy attempts to fix the matter.

ALEXANDER KORDA

Another key to understanding the foreignising of the 1940 *Thief* are the social and cultural contexts of the adaptor. Just as translation "imitates yet varies foreign textual features in accordance with the translator's cultural situation and historical moment" (Venuti 2008: 124), foreignised adaptation similarly imitates yet varies the film features based on the adaptor's situation and historical context. Thus, an understanding of the foreignised elements of Korda's

1940 *Thief* requires extensive background on the man himself in order to effectively situate his work. Alexander Korda had begun his movie-making career in his native Hungary, where he became a pioneer in film production in a country that was just beginning to enter the world of cinema. He was appointed Commissioner of Film in Count Mihaly Karolyi's liberal government in 1918. When the Hungarian Communist Party took over one year later, Korda was apparently persuasive enough to keep his powerful position, though under a different title, as a member of the Communist Directory for the Arts. When the Communists lost power several months later, however, it was a little too much to ask that he successfully switch sympathies once again. Korda found himself in a rather sticky situation, because as a Jew, a liberal and a filmmaker, he was a prime target for persecution in the new government. He fled to Vienna for a few years and from there went on to Hollywood.

Korda's experience as a Hollywood director reveals a good deal about his personality. He insisted, for instance, on having his first contract translated into Hungarian before he would agree to sign it, but after it was translated he simply stated, "All right then, I'll sign. If they don't let me do what I want over there, I'll simply come back" (in Kulik 1975: 42). Arriving in Hollywood in 1927, Korda started with First National Studios at $350 a week, where he established himself as a director, successfully producing a handful of films (mostly silent), including *The Stolen Bride* (1927) and *The Private Life of Helen of Troy* (1927). He rose quickly in the ranks and in 1930 signed a contract with Fox studios at $100,000 a year. Though he was making more money than ever and establishing himself more firmly in Hollywood, Korda was also becoming increasingly disgruntled with the movies that Fox assigned him to make and the rigid corporate film hierarchy. His frustration finally came to a head in 1930 when he was assigned to make *The Princess and the Plumber*, a movie that he claims he "hated". When the film was almost finished, the top executives of Fox screened it and weren't completely satisfied. They claimed it needed some "menace" (Kulik 1975: 54–55). Korda refused to reshoot, and the result was unpleasant.

He was summoned to the executive office and offered a quiet exit from his contract with a severance package of $25,000. This was rather short of the $45,000 remaining on his contract, so he refused. This refusal resulted in the studio writing him out a new contract that removed him from his nice office with its private bathroom and garden. The new contract stipulated that he sit in his new cubicle every day for nine hours with a one-hour lunch break. There were also strict rules about where he could and could not smoke. Korda had discovered Hollywood's infamous "demotion ploy", or "dog house" (Kulik 1975: 55–56). After two weeks of sitting it out, Korda returned to the studio heads and finally agreed to leave. The severance package, however, had dropped to $15,000. Humiliated, Korda took the money and left, only to find that his name had been blacklisted at every major Hollywood studio (56). Infuriated, Korda expressed his sentiments about Hollywood in a letter to his friend and scriptwriter Lajos Biro: "I am fed up to the teeth with Hollywood. I'm working very seriously on a plan—i.e. to get some money together ($250,000) and start in Europe. I'm convinced that the European market is a good one and is going to get better" (in Stockham 1992: 12). Korda specifically wanted to be in England. In early 1930, while at a luncheon with Lajos Biro and British actor George Grossmith, he is reported to have claimed that "England ought to be making the best pictures in the world", to which Grossmith replied, "Well, why can't we three—you and Biro and I—go to England and make them?" (in Kulik 1975: 54). Korda's disillusionment with Hollywood, the dominant film culture of the time, was foundational for his dissident work later on.

After leaving America, Korda ended up in Paris. He was just barely getting settled in his new environment when a call came from Paramount British; Paramount executives did not like their local manager, and they asked

Korda if he would like the job. Korda literally dropped everything he was working on in Paris (which included a series of three films) and left straight-away for Britain. In February of 1932, shortly after his arrival, a journalist for *Film Weekly* commented on the influx of foreign directors:

> We should welcome American and Continental directors as long as they justify themselves by helping to make better and more widely accept-able British pictures. Men like Alexander Korda, Paul Stein, Mervyn Le Rooy, and Rowland V. Lee should not be regarded with jealousy and suspicion simply because they do not happen to be British-born. Their skill and experience are their passports. (cited in Kulik 1975: 70)

In Korda's own eyes, he was the potential saviour of the British national film movement. Not only did he have the talent, but given his past expe-rience in America, he was incredibly motivated to produce films that could rival Hollywood's best. His biographer Karol Kulik says, "Both the man and his film became the foundations of British hopes for waging a successful campaign against Hollywood's domination of world markets . . . 'audacity' and 'imagination' were the two qualities which British film people lacked and which Alex Korda had in seemingly inexhaustible abundance " (1975: 69–70).

When he decided to produce *The Thief of Bagdad* in 1939, Korda was at a political crossroads in his career. He had established himself in Britain and proved that he could make really excellent films—he'd gotten rave reviews for *The Private Life of Henry VIII* (1933) and *The Rise of Catherine the Great* (1934). The *Dallas News* said, "It is no longer possible to dispar-age the technical method of British pictures. *Henry VIII* is extraordinary in photographic beauty and lavishness of investiture" (in Stockham 1992: 53). The *San Diego Sun* clamoured that it "is an English picture which can be linked with the best American productions" (54). The following year's release of *The Rise of Catherine the Great* was a similar success. "Another ace from England and out of the same deck, Korda", claimed *Variety* (55). The *Baltimore Sun* noted, "In the field of historical pictures it is evident that England is able to beat Hollywood at its own game. *Christina* [*Queen Christina* (1933)] is the best American made costumer turned out in Cali-fornia since the talkies and *Catherine* is superior in every respect" (55).

This praise was extremely significant because it came from American critics. Korda was so intent on proving himself against Hollywood that the American critics were the ones he wanted to please. So the positive reception that he got with his early British feature films was certainly significant. But Korda was not satisfied. He didn't want to just beat Hollywood's 'histori-cal pictures'—he wanted to dominate the very finest that Hollywood had to offer. Choosing to remake Fairbanks' 1924 *The Thief of Bagdad* was a very calculated decision: for a producer interested in flexing his cinematic mus-cles, what better film to remake than *The Thief of Bagdad*, a film that had become so iconic that it had defied sequels or remakes? And Korda's version was not going to be just any remake. His idea of an effective film was similar to that of an effective foreignised translation, one that is so distinct that it "'cannot be confused with either the source-language text or a text written originally in the target language'" (Albrecht, in Yang 2010: 78). This idea of taking a film and making it distinctly British parallels Albrecht's notion of producing a translation that is not limited to either the source-language or the target language. Thus, though Korda was taking a film and making another film (same 'language'), he took it from an American source and gave it a British makeover, intending to send it right back to America. The American film market, then, can represent both the source and the target, with Korda the translator acting as the intermediary and using 'Britishness' to foreignise Hollywood's dominant film culture. In a kind of parallel to Tarchetti's foreignising, *The Thief of Bagdad* (1940) used the *Nights* text as a vague backdrop for the British nationalistic film movement.

Although it is a distinctly British film, there are some problems intrinsic to the assertion that Korda's film was nationalistic. Venuti argues that nationalistic agendas are associated with domesticating translations. At face value, Korda seems to be simply domesticating an adaptation of the tales *The Arabian Nights* by translating it into a British film that privileges British actors and British accents. While this domestication is undeniably present in the form of Orientalist stereotypes, a more in-depth analysis reveals that Korda's main goal was to make a foreignised adaptation of the 1924 film, one that created dissidence for American audiences by exposing them to values other than their own. Venuti claims that "without such practices as foreignizing translations to test its limits a culture can lapse into an exclusionary or narcissistic complacency and become a fertile ground for ideological developments such as nationalisms and fundamentalisms" (2008: 20). Fairbanks' 1924 version of *The Thief of Bagdad* may be seen as a domesticating translation of the text *The Arabian Nights* because it created an Americanised translation of Middle Eastern culture made palatable for American audiences. Korda's work, on the other hand, though nationalistic for the British audience, is an example of a foreignising translation rather than a domesticating one because of his treatment of the source text and the target audiences. The 1940 version of *The Thief of Bagdad* was calculated to revitalise British cinema, but it was not directed solely at British audiences. In fact, based on Korda's history and agenda, I would argue that this film was actually aimed primarily at American audiences. Thus, rather than "an ethnocentric reduction of the foreign text to receiving cultural values", this film represents "an ethnodeviant pressure on those values to register the . . . cultural differences of the foreign text" (15). The foreign elements, in this case, being the British stylistic and plot elements, which were calculated to provide dissidence to the Hollywood-dominated film style.

Sarah Street, in her 2009 work *British National Cinema*, claims that current

> ideas about national cinemas have developed to such an extent that for many critics we are now living in a 'post-national' period which acknowledges the need to examine cinema from perspectives that celebrate pluralities and the blurring of boundaries instead of seeking to locate an essentialised notion of national identity. (2009: 2)

That being said, however, I feel that it is valuable to examine this 1940 film in the context of just such an "essentialized notion of national identity" that Street wants us to move away from because that's how Korda would have treated it. Korda, in fact, argued in 1933 in defence of the nationalistic film as a method for creating an awareness of difference. "[T]he phrase 'international film' is a little ambiguous", he said. "I do not mean that a film must try to suit the psychology and manners of every country in which it is going to be shown. On the contrary, to be really international a film must first of all be truly and intensely national" (in Kulik 1975: 97). Thus, for Korda, a film that had definitively British qualities was one that was worth sending into the international, and particularly the American, market. He gives the example of American gangster films, which, he claims "are essentially American in every detail. . . . If a gangster in an American film is depicted drawing a gun from his hip-pocket, nobody in Britain is likely to object on the grounds that it is not a common practice for Englishmen to carry guns" (97). Korda wanted qualities of 'Britishness' to be just as widely and unmistakably recognised. Arguably, Korda intended for such British elements to become as iconic as Hollywood's portrayal of American gangsters. And, he claims, he—a Hungarian—was the man to produce such an intensely nationalistic film:

> An outsider often makes the best job of a national film. He is not cumbered with excessively detailed knowledge and associations. He gets a fresh slant on things. For instance, I should hate to try to make a Hungarian film, while I would love to make one about the highlands that would be a really national Scottish film—and indeed I plan to do so. . . . I know there are people who think it odd that a Hungarian from Hollywood should direct an English historical film, but I can't see their argument. (97–98)

Korda's claim gives voice to the idea that in order to effectively provide dissidence in the film industry, he had to give it a little push. His work was to take the "narcissistic complacency" (Venuti 2008: 20) of American cinema and test its limits by foreignising one of Hollywood's iconic films and sending American moviegoers abroad.

The first image that audiences see when watching one of Alexander Korda's productions is his name in large print and the symbol of Big Ben as the trademark for the company (see Figure 6.1). Stockham claims that by the time he had settled in Britain, Korda was a "committed Anglophile", and he wanted his movies to open with "a symbol that would be the embodiment of British films" (1992: 20). Though he spoke with a Hungarian accent all his life, Korda was determined to make films that claimed Britishness right from the opening credits. With competition that included a lion (MGM) and a globe (Universal), Korda's Big Ben logo instantly localised his films: rather than an animal or planet, both of which are fairly generic and universal, his image distinctly claimed British authenticity. Just north of the Palace of Westminster in London, the tower that houses Big Ben is at the heart of the English capital, and has come to be the icon of London just as the Eiffel Tower is the symbol of Paris. The bell, the clock and the tower have all come to be represented by the name Big Ben, tolling the time for all of London and, by extension, the entire British Empire. As an icon for a film production company, this tower also very conveniently speaks to the era of the British nationalised film industry. Though his appropriation of such a monument might be questionable, one of Korda's contemporaries, British filmmaker Ian Dalrymple, gave his stamp of approval to Korda's trademark based on the quality of his movies: "[T]he sort of films to which the infant Big Ben boomed forth its first introductions bore small resemblance to the worthless pound-a-footers [quota films] pumped out by upstart self-styled producers" (1957: 297–298).

Figure 6.1 The opening credits of Korda's 1940 *The Thief of Bagdad*.

THE THIEF OF BAGDAD (1940)

The 1940 film *The Thief of Bagdad* is the story of young Prince Ahmed who is deceived by his trusted advisor Jafar into going among his people in the guise of a commoner, at which point Jafar has him apprehended and put into prison for some small matter. Ahmed escapes from the prison with the help of a young thief named Abu, and together the two go on an adventure that involves Ahmed falling in love with a princess and having to outwit Jafar to regain his throne. Korda uses his plot structure to create nationalistic dissidence in contrast to its American predecessor. While the 1924 American film starts with a young thief who aspires to become a prince by using his clever wit to eventually win the heart of the princess, the 1940 plot divides the one character into two—a prince and a thief. The American version deals with themes of social mobility because Fairbanks' rise from thief to prince represents the potential of any ambitious dreamer. Korda's version, on the other hand, begins with a prince who is betrayed by his royal advisor and has to work his way back up to his rightful place on the throne. The action of the British film focuses on Ahmed's struggle to regain his kingdom and win the princess, while the thief Abu, played by child actor Sabu, takes a secondary position as more of a comic relief character. The American film is about meritocracy—the British film, about aristocracy. While both films have a thief and are titled *The Thief of Bagdad*, Korda's film relegates the role of the thief to a juvenile one, emphasising its difference from the 1924 rags-to-riches, 'American dream' story where happiness can be earned, and where every thief is a potential prince. In Fairbanks' film, the thief can earn a fortune, get a change of clothes and then become a prince. In reaction to this, Korda deliberately keeps his social classes more rigid. His film deals with the nuances of monarchical rule, the political balance of power, and the danger of corrupt advisors.

Another element of nationalistic dissidence is the ship imagery of the 1940 film. Following the opening credits, the first image of Korda's *Thief* is a giant ship (see Figure 6.2), an image that is referenced continually throughout the movie. This is in stark contrast to the 1924 film, which, true to its cowboy heritage, deals almost exclusively with more what could be considered the more American horseback transportation (see Figure 6.3). Thus, when Korda creates a naval reference right at the beginning of his film he's citing an image that almost can't get any more iconically British, particularly in its opposition to Fairbanks' film. The American film is completely landlocked, and while it does have a scene with an underwater search for treasure, it is done on a sound stage with Fairbanks 'swimming' through the air supported by cables. Korda's version, in contrast, deals with ocean and ship imagery much more concretely: the princess is taken away against her will in Jafar's ship, the prince and the thief Abu travel the Arabic world by boat (see Figure 6.4), Abu dreams of becoming a sailor someday (complete with his own musical number 'I Want to Be

Figure 6.2   The opening shot of the 1940 *Thief*.

Figure 6.3   Douglas Fairbanks on horseback in the 1924 *Thief*.

Figure 6.4   Prince Ahmed and Abu travel to Basra by boat in the 1940 *Thief*.

a Sailor'). The seafaring prowess of the Middle Easterners in this story is apparently second only to that of Great Britain itself, and is a decidedly foreignised element. The ship imagery, as one of the main focuses of Korda's adaptation, becomes a very ostentatious reminder of Britain's historical maritime dominance in contrast to the horseback-riding Western feel of the American version.

Another major element of scenic difference that Korda emphasises is that of the garden imagery. Britain is well known for its gardens, and the British garden is an iconic part of the culture. Thus Korda jumped on the chance to create a gorgeous garden for his film. The garden setting of the American 1924 film has a few sparse bushes and one large rose tree (see Figure 6.5), but Korda's garden distinguishes itself with dark green foliage, large sweeping trees, a vast pool and a classical columned structure. The 1940 film can almost be heard to scoff at its 1924 predecessor, 'You call *that* a garden? We'll show you a garden', one complete with flamingos, bright flowers and lush greenery. Because Walsh had only directed American Western films up until this point, presumably the garden wouldn't have had very high priority in his mind. Furthermore, American film had frequently associated itself with the cowboy image, and, by extension, the deserts of California and Kanab, Utah. Because the setting for the American cowboy film was most often the desert, Korda could easily highlight the difference between the lush, verdant England and the desert image of America popularised by cowboy movies. Because it was a weak point in the American film, it was easy to exploit in the British foreignisation.

Figure 6.5 The garden scene of the 1924 *Thief* with the rose tree prominently in the centre.

Figure 6.6 The garden scene of the 1940 *Thief*.

While Korda certainly foreignised scenic elements of his film, he also created foreignised characters. The differences between the antagonists of the 1924 and 1940 films are very telling. In the 1924 American film the enemy is represented by a Mongol Prince, played by the Japanese actor Sojin, who comes to Bagdad as one of the suitors for the princess. When she refuses him, he decides to take over the city of Bagdad by force with his Mongol soldiers. This invasion of the 'bad guys' and the ensuing conflict of sword against sword is an interesting spin on the American Western struggle between cowboys and Indians. Hollywood Westerns of the early twentieth century often contained some variation of the conflict between whites and Native Americans, with the latter often ostensibly attacking the former. The Mongol invasion of this film looks and feels a lot like the conflict between cowboys and Indians. While the other is different (the enemy is Mongolian rather than Native American), the dichotomy is the same. Fairbanks even had racially determined stipulations of difference: his bad guy looked significantly different from the other actors.

The enemy of the 1940 British version, on the other hand, is not an exterior antagonist, but an interior one. And instead of a physical conflict, the main quarrel in Korda's film is a power struggle between a prince and his treacherous advisor. The adjustment of the plot here is significant, for it allows Korda to deal more heavily with themes of the royal right to power, complications of those rights, the idea of corruption in high places and the image of noble royalty betrayed by evil advisors. Jaffar, played by Conrad Veidt, makes the ultimate European bad guy because he is an abuser of his political power. By 1940 Veidt had become known for playing Nazi spies. He played a spy in *I Was a Spy* (1933) and again in *The Spy in Black* (1939), and was later to play the German Major Strasser in *Casablanca* (1942). He was, at least for European audiences, a recognisable bad guy, and more importantly, he had played the usurper of legitimate political power. His physical appearance makes his espionage and subterfuge all the more insidious because, unlike the Japanese actor Sojin of the American film, Veidt blends in with the rest of the white British actors. Korda's 1940 version offered a sophisticated alternative to the Hollywood black-and-white conflict.

One last significant element of difference is that of the representation of Arabic iconography. The 1924 version of the film established elements that came to be known as the iconic 'Arabian' style. This includes large domed structures, giant pots in the streets, flying magic carpet, turbans and snake charmers. Korda, in his remake, kept almost all of these elements. However, he also threw into the mix an interesting variation on these themes, some of which that relied heavily on Hindu influences. The most striking example of this is the deadly 'silver maiden', a mechanical object Jaffar uses to do his killing (see Figure 6.7). This six-armed, blue-skinned 'maiden' looks suspiciously like the Hindu goddess Kali, who is often portrayed with dark or blue skin and multiple arms. In Hindu mythology Kali is the

Figure 6.7 The silver maiden of the 1940 film, vaguely reminiscent of the Hindu deity Kali.

consort of Lord Shiva, and is commonly associated with both time and death. Popular renditions of her often portray her as dark or violent. And though she would not have been a household name in 1940s-era Britain, the image of a many-armed, blue-skinned female statue would undoubtedly be recognisably Indian. In 1940 India represented one of the last vestiges of British imperialism, the last crown jewel of the ailing British Empire. Bringing images from and allusions to India into the film highlighted the power of British Imperialism. Thus, though the portrayal of Middle Eastern theocracy and artwork is just as misrepresented as it was in the American film, accurate representation was not ever the point. Korda was simply wielding British imperialism.

CONCLUSION

Korda's *Thief* won Academy Awards for Cinematography, Art Direction and Special Effects. It was, as Korda had planned, a noteworthy representation of Britain's ability to rival anything Hollywood could produce. *Magill's Survey of Cinema* recognised it as "arguably the best Arabian Nights motion picture ever made, and a strong contender for the best fantasy film ever made as well. . . . Although [the 1924 version] was one of the most spectacular and imaginative of silent films, the 1940 remake surpasses it on all counts" (Magill 1980: 1703). The crowning moment for

Korda personally came in June of 1942 when Alexander Korda became Sir Alexander Korda, the first person ever to be knighted for his film contributions (Kulik 1975: 258).

The 1940 film adaptation *The Thief of Bagdad* represents a timeless classic as far as fantasy films go. Directors Martin Scorsese and Frank Coppola, in a commentary track on the 2008 DVD release of the film, both comment on their childhood impressions of Korda's film and its influence in their own film careers. In a 2008 movie review, *Cineaste* reviewer Rahul Hamid notes that the 1940 *The Thief of Bagdad*, "[t]hough merely the frothy entertainment of another time, leads the viewer to the history of both England and the Middle East and to ponder the stakes of their representation" (2008: 69). This vague comment about the "stakes of representation" of both England and the Middle East is perhaps more insightful than Hamid intended. Because of its crucial place in British film-making history, the 1940 *Thief* is actually very much about the stakes of representation, though much less about representation of the Middle East than it is about that of the historical and cultural context of mid-twentieth-century Britain and its nationalistic tensions. Such tensions provide a broader understanding of how Orientalist stereotypes were perpetuated and solidified. The exoticised, romanticised images of Arabia and Bagdad were vehicles for Korda's foreignising agenda, a background for his competition with Hollywood. Thus, though Korda may have contributed to the canon of domesticating adaptations of Middle Eastern culture, he was not doing so intentionally. Rather, his agenda with the 1940 *Thief* was targeted at the American cultural film environment. Understanding the film's significance means not only understanding Orientalism and western domination, but also recognising Alexander Korda's personal agenda, British nationalism of the 1930s and the relevance of Translation Studies. Using the vocabulary of Translation Studies allows us to explore this film in terms of its domesticating and foreignising elements, recognising a complex set of agendas more dynamic and complicated than they have been given credit for being.

Translation theory and the politicisation of translation are ideas that can—and should—increasingly be applied to Adaptation Studies. The transfer of one language to another has many nuanced similarities to film adaptation—which is, essentially, a translation from one language (literary) into another (film). Applying translation theory to *The Thief of Bagdad* (1940) showcases an exciting new approach to Adaptation Studies, helping us understand the nuanced work of the adaptor-as-translator in the process of film-making, as well as creating an understanding and awareness of the casualties occasionally inflicted during the transfer and packaging of culture as a film commodity.

Studies of this kind remain important since the issue of politicised translation has not gone away. As recently as May 2010, *The Economist* featured a news brief about the political legal battle involving a new translation of *The Thousand and One Nights* recently published in Egypt. The translation was "distinctly adult-oriented" (written in a similar vein as Richard Burton's nineteenth century translation), and caused quite a stir among an Islamist group called "Lawyers Without Shackles." This organization sued Egypt's ministry of culture on the grounds of Article 178 of Egypt's penal code, which punishes "'with imprisonment for a period of two years anyone who publishes literature or pictures offensive to public decency'" (54). Samia Mehrez, a professor at the American University of Cairo, claimed that such a lawsuit was completely political, and not about *The Nights* at all. "Cultural icons have been used as pawns in the political game between the state and the Islamists," she said. "It is the Islamists' way of getting back at the state, by embarrassing it, for the violence it inflicts on them" (54). The cultural and political struggle revolving around this new translation of the *Night* shows that an analysis of cultural appropriation through politicised, foreignised translation deserves continued attention.

WORKS CITED

Anonym. 2009. 'Michael Jackson, the Muppets and Early Cinema Tapped for Preservation in 2009 Library of Congress National Film Registry'. Library of Congress, 30 December. http://www.loc.gov/today/pr/2009/09–250.html (accessed 22 May 2010).

Anonym. 2010. 'The Puritans Won't Give Up'. *Economist* 15–21 May, p. 54.

Cooperson, Michael. 2006. 'The Monstrous Births of Aladdin'. In: Ulrich Marzolph (ed.), *The Arabian Nights Reader*. Detroit, MI: Wayne State University Press, pp. 265–282.

Cutchins, Dennis and Christa Albrecht-Crane. 2010. 'New Beginnings for Adaptation Studies'. In: Christa Albrecht-Crane and Dennis Cutchins (eds.), *Adaptation Studies: New Approaches*. Madison, NJ: Fairleigh Dickinson University Press, pp. 11–22.

Dalrymple, Ian. 1957. 'Alexander Korda'. *Quarterly of Film Radio and Television*, 11.3, pp. 294–309.

Eisele, John C. 2002. 'The Wild East: Deconstructing the Language of Genre in the Hollywood Eastern'. *Cinema Journal*, 41.4, pp. 68–94.

Felperin, Leslie. 1997. 'The Thief of Buena Vista: Disney's *Aladdin* and Orientalism'. In: Jayne Pilling (ed.), *A Reader in Animation Studies*. London: Libbey, pp. 137–142.

Hamid, Rahul. 2008. 'The Thief of Baghdad'. *Cineaste*, 33.4, pp. 69–70.

Handler, Richard. 1986. 'Authenticity'. *Anthropology Today*, 2, pp. 2–4.

Kennedy, Dane. 2000. '"Captain Burton's Oriental Muck Heap": The Book of the Thousand Nights and the Uses of Orientalism'. *Journal of British Studies*, 39.3, pp. 317–339.

Kulik, Karol. 1975. *Alexander Korda: The Man Who Could Work Miracles*. London: Allen.

Magill, Fank N. (ed.). 1980. *Magill's Survey of Cinema: English Language Films*. Vol. 4. Englewood Cliffs, NJ: Salem.

Makdisi, Saree and Felicity Nussbaum. 2008. 'Introduction'. In: Saree Makdisi and Felicity Nussbaum (eds.), *The Arabian Nights in Historical Context: Between East and West*. New York: Oxford University Press, pp. 1–23.

Nance, Susan. 2009. *How the Arabian Nights Inspired the American Dream*. Chapel Hill: University of North Carolina Press.

Niranjana, Tejaswini. 1992. *Siting Translation: History, Post-Structuralism, and the Colonial Context*. Berkeley: University of California Press.

Perry, George. 1985. *The Great British Picture Show*. Boston: Little, Brown.

Pronay, Nicholas. 1983. 'The "Moving Picture" and Historical Research'. *Journal of Contemporary History*, 18.3, pp. 365–395.

Robertson, Patrick. 1985. *Guinness Film: Facts and Feats*. London: Guinness.

Said, Edward W. 1978. *Orientalism*. New York: Pantheon.

Schacker-Mill, Jennifer. 2000. 'Otherness and Otherworldliness: Edward W. Lane's Ethnographic Treatment of *The Arabian Nights*'. *Journal of American Folklore*, 113.448, pp. 164–184.

Schickel, Richard. 1975. *The Men Who Made the Movies*. New York: Atheneum.

Shamma, Tarek. 2005. 'The Exotic Dimension of Foreignizing Strategies: Burton's Translation of the Arabian Nights'. *Translator*, 11.1, pp. 51–67.

Stockham, Martin. 1992. *The Korda Collection: Alexander Korda's Film Classics*. London: Boxtree.

Street, Sarah. 2009. *British National Cinema*. 2nd ed. London: Routledge.

Thief of Bagdad, The. 1924. Dir. Raoul Walsh. Perf. Douglas Fairbanks. United Artists, 2004. DVD.

Thief of Bagdad, The. 1940. Dir. Ludwig Berger, Michael Powell, and Tim Whelan. Prod. Alexander Korda. Criterion, 2008. DVD.

Venuti, Lawrence. 2008. *The Translator's Invisibility: A History of Translation*. 2nd ed. New York: Routledge.

Walsh, Raoul. 1974. *Each Man in His Time: The Life Story of a Director*. New York: Farrar, Straus and Giroux.

Yang, Wenfen. 2010. 'Brief Study on Domestication and Foreignization in Translation'. *Journal of Language Teaching and Research*, 1.1, pp. 77–80.

7 Molière Among the Penguins
John Wood's Translations for the Early Penguin Classics

Adrienne Mason

In a review of a recent translation of Rabelais in *Le Monde*, the historian Marc Fumaroli reminded his readers that translations of canonical literary texts play a key role in the diffusion of French culture and cross-cultural canon formation. People forget, he said, that writers such as Joyce, Cowper Powys, Bakhtin and Kundera all experienced Rabelais not through the original text but through modern translations, and the role of translation in relation to the European canon has consistently been overlooked. (2009: 2)

Fumaroli is right. Although the second half of the twentieth century saw Translation Studies emerge globally across higher education institutions, collective cultural amnesia can still obliterate translations of all kinds from the literary polysystem. More specifically the creative and interpretative status of those responsible for a translation is still not universally acknowledged or thought worthy of much critical attention. And yet, as Fumaroli went on to say, translated texts play an ambassadorial role representing their culture abroad with 'une autorité conquérante' (a conquering authority) which is every bit as valuable as elaborate policies of cultural diffusion (2009: 2). If that is the case, the way in which these texts are transformed and re-embodied by those involved in their production is crucial to that representation. And yet, as Lawrence Venuti has argued, attitudes towards that re-embodiment, particularly in the Anglophone world, are traditionally reductive.[1] Norms within the translation industry foster an illusion of transparency between the text and its translation so that the fact of the translation does not intervene to diminish the prestige and authority of the source text. Authority and authenticity are confused. When translations attract any critical scrutiny at all, reviews often focus narrowly on quiddities of interlingual transfer, as though translations happen in a vacuum, independently of the context in which they are produced and the end-users (readers or spectators) for whom a translation is the sole or primary means of access to the source text. Only if the translator has independent literary prestige is the creativity and value of a translation recognised in its own right, and even then, the wider collaborative, interpretative nature of text production seldom enters the equation.[2]

In this respect research into translation for the stage has blazed a trail productively across disciplinary boundaries, fusing textual and performance methodologies and setting translated texts in a much wider communicative context (see, e.g., Coelsch-Foisner and Klein 2003; Baines, Marinetti and Perteghella 2012). As regards translations for the page, however, the collaborative context of text production is rarely explored. It is often difficult to assess the impact of factors such as the publishing house, editorial policy, marketing strategy or commercial viability on the nature and diffusion of a translation because publishers' records are seldom available. And yet these interactions govern not only the choice of translator and titles for translation but the way the text is translated and, crucially, its market share. A translation which appears in a prestigious series has a profound and lasting impact on the way that texts are represented and received across the globe. Such was the case for translations which appeared in the early decades of the Penguin Classics series launched by Penguin Press. The series rapidly rose to a dominant market position, and, happily, the archives of Penguin Press are now in the public domain.[3] In this paper, therefore, I shall use unpublished material in the editorial files to examine the first theatre texts published as Penguin Classics, namely John Wood's two collected volumes of Molière translations, which were commissioned in the 1950s.[4] Like most other texts in the series, Wood's translations were commercially extremely successful and widely diffused across the world in the UK and the US. They have survived until the present day, albeit in a revised form, as part of Penguin's current Black Classics list.[5] I shall argue that the production and diffusion of these translations as well as their position within the contemporary literary and theatrical system resulted from a collaborative, negotiated and, in some ways, aleatory process, which was at least as much dependent on the status and commercial success of the publisher as on the translator and the translation strategy involved.

Let us look first, therefore, at the birth of the Penguin Classics series, which was by any standards a landmark in UK literary translation.[6] In just the first twenty years of this iconic series, between the launch of the series in 1944 and E. V. Rieu's retirement as its general editor, 150 genuinely new translations of European classical texts were commissioned, attractively produced and sold at an affordable price. This was an astonishing achievement. Commissioning a new translation is an expensive process, and most other contemporary series of budget World Classics, notably Penguin's direct competitor, Dent's Everyman's Library, relied on cheap reprints of translations already decades old. The creation of Penguin Classics was a high-risk venture, the result of collaboration between two remarkable and idiosyncratic publishers, E. V. Rieu, the first general editor of the series, and Allen Lane, the founder of Penguin Books.

Mentioned in a letter from E. V. Rieu to Allen Lane, 19 October 1944 (Hare 1995: 186), E. V. Rieu was the educational manager and managing director of Methuen when Allen Lane invited him to launch a new series

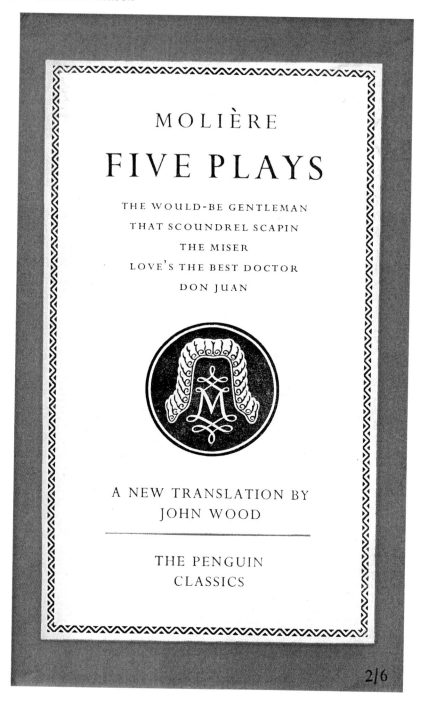

Figure 7.1   The Miser and Other Plays by Moliére, translated by John Wood (Penguin Books, 1953). Reproduced by permission of Penguin Books Ltd.

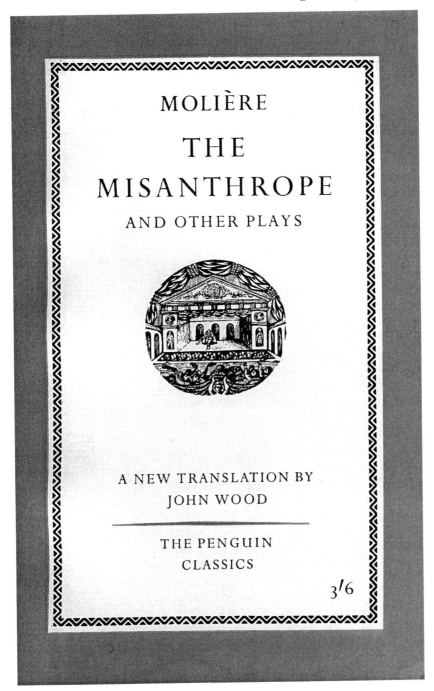

Figure 7.2   Le Misanthrope and Other Plays by Molière, translated by John Wood (Penguin Books, 1959). Reproduced by permission of Penguin Books Ltd.

devoted to translations of canonical European texts across different genres. Paradoxically, the whole enterprise seemed like a *folie à deux* to Lane's more conservative colleagues in Penguin. E. V. Rieu's own translation of Homer's *Odyssey* was to be the first volume to appear, and that venture alone seemed foolhardy. Translations did not conventionally sell well in UK and US markets. There were already many translations of the *Odyssey* to choose from, and only two had sold more than 3,000 copies (187). Who would want to buy or read another, let alone a whole series of new translations of other much-translated classics?

Allen Lane had a ready answer. Books were expensive and too often beyond the pockets of those with modest means. "People' want books . . . they want good books, and . . . they are willing even anxious to *buy* them, if they are presented to them in a straightforward intelligent manner at a cheap price" (in Lewis 2005: 88). This was a democratising vision which E. V. Rieu unequivocally shared and applied to the way in which translations were done. He claimed that the traditional, predominantly scholarly market for translations of Latin and Greek could be extended to a much wider reading public if a different, appropriative translation strategy was adopted. As he explained in a letter inviting the Greek scholar H. D. F. Kitto to translate three of Euripedes' plays, "I have tried to select works that have a perennial value (for all and not for scholars only), and that can be presented to the very wide and miscellaneous Penguin public . . . It is not erudition that we want to teach, it is appreciation".[7]

Nowadays, this may seem to be a statement of the obvious. A fluent, easily assimilated and enjoyable translation is recognised as the industry norm for commercially viable literary translation in the UK, however uneasy academics may feel about the hegemonic cultural and linguistic implications of that practice.[8] But Rieu's view was coloured by norms of academic translation prevalent at the time in the educational market, especially for Latin and Greek texts. The market for these was commonly assumed to be the 'semi-languaged'—in other words readers with a rudimentary knowledge of Latin or Greek who needed help to experience the text directly. For readers like these, a semantic translation with as little syntactical restructuring as possible and plentiful footnotes was functionally appropriate, but syntactically and stylistically cumbersome as a result. In addition, the language used was often archaic, particularly when, as was so often the case, the translation in question was an ageing reprint. Rieu was determined that Penguin Classics would be allow the reader to experience a translation in a completely different and much more exciting way.

An editorial blank cheque is a rare sight. But Allen Lane gave Rieu a free hand to propose the titles, choose his own translators, pay them well and, crucially, devise his own editorial strategy. Rieu's watchword was simple but significant: readability. Above all, the reader must enjoy a text unimpeded by translatorial or editorial intervention. Scholarly apparatus was to be kept to a bare minimum, and footnotes in particular were to be used sparingly or, preferably, not at all. Any explanatory material could perfectly well be supplied in a brief introduction. As Betty Radice put it in a 1972 obituary,

> He always held that translation should be into contemporary but not too topical prose, and be intelligible to all, not only to scholars of the original. He aimed at what he called the 'principle of equivalent effect', meaning that 'translation is the best which comes nearest to creating in its audience the same impression as was made by the original on its contemporaries'. To his translators, his advice was simply 'Write English', and 'Read it aloud' as a test of whether the English written was natural, durable, and free from translationese, literary archaism and current slang.[9]

The principle of equivalent effect is, of course, based on a fallacy: we can neither determine nor recreate the effect which the source text had on its first readers. But it is still commonly used to describe a communicative translation strategy which moves the text closer to the cultural and linguistic frameworks of the reader and minimises the effort needed for the reader to assimilate it.[10] Rieu's primary concern was to maximise the reader's enjoyment. For him a translator was predominantly a writer and he took a fairly cavalier attitude to the depth of a translator's first-hand knowledge of the source language or culture. Among the three principles of translation identified in a piece called *The Faith of the Translator*, knowledge of the source language and culture came a poor third (Rieu 1950: 17–19). First and foremost was the translator's knowledge of the target language and second a love for the original work itself. Transmitting that enthusiasm was more important than historical context or semantic or syntactic niceties and the public he described was, in theory at least, more interested in appreciation than self-improvement.

Most of Rieu's translators shared his views, and John Wood was no exception in many respects. He unequivocally shared Rieu's enthusiasm for a translation strategy designed to stimulate interest but, as we shall see, his priorities were somewhat different. He wanted to use the opportunity afforded by publication to foreground Molière as actor and director as well as author, and to produce a text which could be used in performance. He used his introduction to explain the dramatic contexts in which the plays were performed and to produce a text that was 'actable' as well as readable. He clearly assumed that these two ambitions were compatible. Before we explore that further, however, let us look first at Penguin's early French list and consider how the French titles and their translators, including Wood, came to be chosen for these early Penguin Classics in the first place.

Writing in 1960, Richard Hoggart commented on the "timeliness" of the Penguin venture, targeting a new young readership, "more mixed in its social origins" and including "sixth-formers, young clerks and teachers,

undergraduates, adult students, trade unionists and solitary single readers" (27–28). It is not hard to detect in this profile the importance of the
burgeoning education market both for Penguin as a whole and for Penguin
Classics in particular. Rieu's disavowal of scholarly translation techniques
was undoubtedly disingenuous, at least in terms of the target market even
if his preference for enthusing rather than instructing his readers was not.
The educational market was about to take off. Before the outbreak of war
in 1938, only a meagre 2% of the UK population were in full-time education at the age of nineteen, but this had expanded to 7% by 1962 (Committee on Higher Education 1963). The national policies underpinning the
plans for postwar reconstruction and expansion would have been familiar
territory for E. V. Rieu, fresh from his role as educational manager for
Methuen, and so would the shifting nature of the curricula.[11] An expanding market for sixth-formers and first-generation students of all kinds was
on the horizon and a series of new translations of modern European classics in a modern idiom could provide a ready source of cultural capital. The
implicit educational agenda is very obvious from the outset in relation to
the first French titles and to the choice of their translators.

There were strong commercial arguments in favour of adding French
titles to Penguin Classics. The cultural prestige of France had not at that
stage suffered the rapid decline it would experience in the later decades of
the twentieth century and beyond. *The Times* was still reporting daily on
cultural events in France. French cultural policy had traditionally recognised the importance of the diffusion of French culture abroad, and this was
reinforced by the postwar mini-boom in translation as a means to improve
international relations (see Venuti 1992: 5). French was the major modern
foreign language taught in UK schools and canonical literary works still
figured on school as well as university syllabuses. The US market was also
ripe for expansion. It was no accident that virtually all the titles published
in Penguin's lists, of French and other modern European classics were 'set
texts' for both school and university.

That said, there is a slightly random feel about these initial titles and a
certain eccentricity in the choice of translators. Although Rieu took a personal interest in all the early Penguin Classics, he was less directly involved
with the French titles as with the Greek and Latin classics, and as early as
1944, he told Allen Lane that he was consulting friends about the titles for
the French list (Hare 1995: 186). These included members of the academic
establishment, some of whom Rieu probably knew through his contacts at
Methuen. Not all of these, however, were necessarily experienced translators. John Butt, the translator of Voltaire's *Candide*, the second French title
to appear, was a case in point. Butt, who was at that time an academic at
Bedford College, London and general editor of the Twickenham Edition
of Pope's poetry, which had been commissioned by Methuen, had worked
closely with Rieu,[12] but he was not an obvious choice to translate from
French. He was an English specialist and by his admission did not feel

particularly well qualified for the job.[13] Personal contacts were equally clear in the choice of Leonard Tancock, who translated one of the earliest French texts in the list, *Manon Lescaut*,[14] and Tancock, a London academic in modern French literature at University College, referred to Rieu as "my old friend".[15] By 1966 Tancock himself had translated no fewer than six texts for Penguin and had also been acting as adviser and assessor for the series for some time.

Rieu's reliance on friends or acquaintances in academic circles may explain why Wood's Molière volumes were not commissioned as early as one might have expected. In the first twenty Penguin Classics to be published, two volumes of Maupassant's *contes* figured with *Candide* alongside *Mme Bovary*, *Manon Lescaut* and *Le Père Goriot*. All were translated by teachers or academics, and all were solid representatives of the French canon, but they are all prose works, which was odd in relation to the prominence of classical French theatre in school and university curricula. *Manon Lescaut*, the first text promoted by Tancock, must have seemed a very surprising choice when nothing from Molière, Racine or Corneille had appeared.[16] In fact, Wood's first volume of Molière translations, *Five Plays*, did not appear until 1953, well after the first translations of Chekhov and Ibsen, Euripides and Sophocles; and his second volume, containing *Le Misanthrope* and *Tartuffe*, two of the best known plays, did not follow until 1959. Even more surprisingly, Molière remained the sole representative of French theatre in Penguin's list until John Cairncross's translations of three Racine plays appeared in 1964 while Corneille did not figure at all until more than ten years after than that.

So how did Wood come to be chosen to translate Molière, and how were the plays for translation chosen? Again personal contact probably came into the equation. It is clear from the files that Wood knew Rieu personally and was well connected in London. However, he was based in Yorkshire, and there is no evidence that he was a close friend.[17] Like many of his fellow translators, Wood had solid academic connections through his role as a member of the North Riding Country Council Education Committee, but his primary interest seems to have been the link between drama and education. The publicity blurb for *Five Plays* indicates that his "particular field" was drama and, unlike his publishers, he was interested in the performability and in securing the performance rights from the outset.[18] His only comment on the contract in June 1952 was to reserve performing rights and ask for the insertion of a notice to the effect that these should be negotiated through the League of Dramatists. Moreover, the short time which elapsed between the finalising of the contract in June 1952 and the delivery of the manuscript in August of the same year suggests that he had already completed much of the work for that volume beforehand, so some of the translation may well already have been used in performance.[19] He had already started working on the verse plays for the next volume a few months after completing his first volume.[20] The fact that René Varin, the cultural attaché at the French Embassy in London, was interested in a performance of one of the plays for the annual Molière dinner in 1953 is further evidence that Wood combined practical experience of the theatre at least in an academic context together with his role as a translator.[21]

However that may be, Rieu clearly allowed Wood himself to play a significant role in the choice of the plays which make up both his Molière volumes. The advertising blurb for *Five Plays* is explicit in that respect, and Rieu habitually asked his translators to draft their own blurbs.[22] According to Wood's draft for the blurb, any selection of plays "must be arbitrary and personal" since such a small sample can "offer no more than a taste, a first sample, of the power and range of Molière's genius".[23] Fair comment, no doubt, given that there are over thirty to choose from, but the blurb goes on to say that while three of the plays (The *Would-Be Gentleman*, *The Miser* and *Don Juan*) are major works, the other two (*Scapin* and *Love's the Best Doctor*) are "happy examples of Molière's delight in pure entertainment".[24] In Wood's second volume too, there is a comparable awareness of Molière's stagecraft with a similar choice of less well-known but theatrically interesting plays. Wood's introductions to his two volumes document the different contexts in which the plays were performed and his inclusion of less well-known plays reflected a desire to showcase the full range of Molière's dramatic output by including, notably, comedy-ballets and farce, of which he claimed Molière showed "complete mastery" (Wood 1962: 9). In that sense, Wood was ahead of his time. The Penguin team was clearly indifferent to issues such as performing rights or to non-textual elements of the plays, whereas Wood was very keen to include the Lully's music alongside the relevant translations. His efforts to persuade Penguin to do so fell on resolutely deaf ears,[25] but it is to Wood's credit that he was keen to introduce Anglophone readership to some of Molière's less well-known plays and to convey something of their wider interest as theatre texts.

Prima facie Wood's strategy in producing a performable text could have conflicted with Rieu's clear reader-oriented editorial policy. But 'performability' is a catch-all term. It can only be defined within a given context and, arguably, on a case-by-case basis. Fortunately, thanks to Rieu's enlightened practice of inviting his translators to write their own introductions and blurbs, we have more evidence about the Wood's strategy for the translation than is often the case. Wood took full advantage of this opportunity to explain the challenges he faced and his overall approach. The paratextual material for *Five Plays* makes clear that he saw no contradiction between what he hoped to achieve in his translations and the series in which they would appear.

The advertising blurb, which initially was used as a wrapper on the front cover, predictably begins with the claim that a new translation was overdue. According to Wood, "[T]he version most familiar to English readers dates from the eighteenth century" and "its idiom is far removed from contemporary English". Moreover, it goes on, "Lack of effective translation may account, in part, for the neglect of Molière, which has long been a reproach and a loss to English theatre". This is a lacuna which Wood clearly hoped to fill since he goes on to make an explicit connection between the translation strategy and his desire for his version to be performed. "The translation", he says, "keeps close to the original and seeks to retain something of the vigour and felicity of Molière's language in an English which is at once readable—and actable".[26]

A blurb is, of course, advertising copy and not to be taken at face value, but Noel Peacock's excellent synoptic analysis of Molière's plays in translation confirms many of the claims made by Wood in the blurb and in the introduction to his first volume (see Classe 2000: 956–996). Wood was right to draw attention to the flurry of translations and adaptations of Molière in Restoration London and to the subsequent loss of interest during the Romantic period and beyond. This relegated Molière to "the school and the study" as he puts it, until stirrings of interest in the early decades of the twentieth century, hinted at a revival (Wood 1962: xxv).[27] Wood was probably also right to argue that until his own first collection of plays, the translations most easily accessible to English readers dated back to 1739, since it was the translations in the ten-volume Baker and Miller collected works which were the reprinted by Everyman (Baker and Miller 1739). There was no collected volume of George Graveley's flamboyant translations until 1956, and other potential rivals did not emerge until after Wood's translations had been commissioned. Wood was therefore early in the field, and the real postwar acceleration of interest charted by Peacock did not emerge till later.

Interestingly, however, Wood's rationale for new translations contains a distinction which helps to position his work in relation to performance. Wood refers favourably to Miles Malleson's adaptations for the stage, which presumably supported his claim that Molière's fortunes on the English stage had begun to take a turn for the better.[28] But while Wood clearly had no purist objections to versions which rework the source text, it was not what he sought to do in either of his two volumes.[29]

This is stated explicitly in the introduction to *Five Plays*. Possibly in deference to Rieu, for whom equivalent effect and readability were watchwords,[30] Wood also invokes the notion of equivalence as a strategic objective but expands it to include a reference to performance: "In general the translation seeks to keep close to the original wherever the equivalent word or phrase can be found. Where it cannot, the aim has been to create the equivalent effect and to keep within the bounds of dramatic effectiveness" (Wood 1962: xxvi). As indicated earlier, we can only conjecture the true communicative impact of a source text so the term 'equivalence' establishes only the need to decide on a specific relationship between source and target—in other words it states the problem rather than the solution. But Wood did have the space to enlarge on the kind of relationship between source and target texts which he hoped to establish (xvi–xxviii). The challenges posed by Molière's texts are predictable enough, but Wood's honest analysis of instances of unavoidable translation loss highlights the tension between his desire to produce a text which is both semantically reliable and performable, calling into question the distinction he himself perceived between translation and adaptation.

Let us take just a few examples of the linguistic conundrums which taxed or defeated Wood. In relation to Molière's prose plays, Wood finds subtle shifts in register, so important for the communication of character and social position, a particular bugbear. Molière's language, Wood claims, could "outrage the purists" without straying too far from classical French. A shift between standard English and modern slang and Americanisms would, he says, sharpen the contrast too far (1962: xxvi), so he has taken refuge in milder solutions, such as 'wallop', 'smack across the face', 'bawling'. Even so, he is still left with a version that is more direct (by which he presumably means less subtle) than the distinctions in the archaic registers of seventeenth-century French. Equally vexing for Wood was the archly stilted "jargon amoureux" of Molière's ill-starred young lovers. It "simply will not pass as it stands", he wrote, while the "inroads of the tushery school" have made the terms of derogation and abuse, which occur throughout the plays, almost impossible to reproduce: "[A]ll the debasing ingenuity of centuries of euphemism . . . have . . . made 'odds bodikins', ' 'sdeath', ' 'slife', and many another expression unusable now though they are what is required" (xxvii). Again, Wood' solutions leave him dissatisfied: "[O]ne is driven to ring the changes on scoundrel, knave, villain, rascal, fool, idiot, dog, traitor, slut, hussy, and creature" (xxvii).

Regional dialects are another brain-teaser. The patois of the peasants in *Dom Juan* has been handled by "a synthetic west country alternative [which] is offered with suitable diffidence", and Wood consoles himself by the sceptical reflection that Moliere's original was probably equally inauthentic (1962: xxvii). Similarly, comedy based on mispronunciation, such as occurs in *The Would-Be Gentleman*, or heavily accented French, such as the use of Gascon and Swiss in *Scapin*, are equally intractable. Faced with the polyglot interlarding of different languages in the Turkish interlude in *The Would-Be Gentleman*, Wood goes even further and admits defeat. It is "quite untranslatable", and he does not hesitate to say that a producer may "alter it if he thinks fit for the stage" (xxvii). In the end "much depends on the actor and one may perhaps leave it at that" (xxviii). In other words Wood's search for equivalence in terms of finding close modern parallels collapses. In practice, Wood is obliged to allow that in performance, the boundary he has identified between translation and adaptation is unsustainable and it will be up to the director and performer to manipulate and adapt the translation for the receiving audience.

In his second volume, Wood faced an even more perplexing problem since he was confronted with the translation of the verse comedies. Wood had rightly admitted in his introduction to *Five Plays* that his selection of plays was unrepresentative of Molière since some of the greatest work was in verse (1962: xxvi), and this was to be remedied in his second volume, *Le Misanthrope*. However, a verse translation would have forced Wood to abandon his desire to stay as close to the source text as possible. Instead, he opted for a straightforward prose translation:

> Molière uses metre and rhyme . . . to give the effect of brilliance appropriate to the scene and to provide a witty, ironic, or comic counterpoint to the scene . . . the effect of translation, in *Le Misanthrope* in particular, is to make the speech more direct than the original, the more so since much of the preciosity has no tolerable modern equivalent. What one has sought to do is the preserve the rhetorical line of the speeches, the sense of mounting rhythms, of successions of phrase upon phrase, sentence on sentence. (Molière 1959: 20)

Such a strategy, Wood argues, can be justified since Molière's use of verse is not lyrical or intensely emotional. It is essentially part of linguistically complex comic writing, so arguably a prose translation can be functionally adequate for an English audience, albeit with a degree of unavoidable translation loss (Molière 1959: 20).

The discourse of loss and deficiency is, of course, commonplace among translators, but Wood's analysis of his translation seems to indicate that his text was a constant negotiation between the desire to produce a stage-oriented version of his text which would attract performers, while resisting the kind of radical manipulation which would have taken his audience even further from seventeenth-century drama. As E.-A. Gutt has pointed out, a translation designed to read like a piece originally written in the contemporary target language is an invitation to the reader to process and interpret the text in the context and time-frame of the receiving rather than the source culture.[31] Such appropriative strategies minimise the interpretive effort needed from the receiver, and Wood, following his editor's policy, needed to produce a text which kept Penguin readers well within their comfort zone. That said, as his desire to publish Lully's music confirms, he wanted to retain and preserve the source text as far as he could in a text which could credibly be staged. In other words he stopped short of radical or creative rewriting when confronted with the intractable linguistic and social impasses he encountered in Molière's texts and was, as a result, left with an uneasy compromise. Only the ingenuity of the producer and the actors could square the circle.

In many respects, it is hard not to conclude that Woods, despite his best efforts, remained a translator for the page rather than the stage. Moreover, by publishing with Penguin in a series with the explicit aim of introducing world classics in a *readable* form across all genres, Wood's translations were bound to be considered as texts intended to be read rather than performed. The editorial team, as we have seen, was supremely uninterested in whether they were used as performance texts or not. The reviews, though they are few and far between, confirm this and are clearly oriented to the book market. *Five Plays* appeared when Penguin Classics were still establishing a reputation so the files record only one favourable review in *The Scarborough News*.[32] However, *The Misanthrope* fared slightly better, probably because by 1959, Penguin had established a clear market lead and new titles for Penguin Classics were by then attracting rather more critical attention. The *Manchester Guardian* noted that in the batch of new titles in which *The Misanthrope* appeared "a casual observer might almost be forgiven for not noticing that some others are in the same race. The latest additions [to the Penguin list] are well up to standard".[33] *Tribune* commented that "[t]he dramatist's work is given a plain English dress, which reveals, among other things, his family relationship with John Osborne" while the *Press and Journal* headed an enthusiastic review as "Molièrein racy prose", applauding a "first-class translation" with a colloquial style which was "highly readable" and "ideal for Molière, enemy of preciosity".[34]

Clare Finburgh has argued persuasively in a recent article, that it is the

> theatre and performing industries [which] determine what is 'performable' in response to what they believe audiences wish to see' and in practice, even for subsidised theatre, 'performability' ultimately means 'marketability' since productions have to be financially viable even in nationally subsidised companies. (Finburgh 2012: 233)

National companies certainly did not rush to use Wood's translations although the RSC apparently did consider his text for a production of *Scapin*,[35] and Wood produced *The Imaginary Invalid* for the York Festival in 1959.[36] By contrast, Miles Malleson's adaptations, staged at roughly the same time both in London and the provinces, were being well received. They were adapted to suit the conventions of the UK stage and so, commercially, were much less risky than the work of a relative unknown with limited theatrical experience (Classe 2000: 959). Should we therefore simply assume that Wood's translations were unsuitable for performance because despite his best efforts, his work appeared in a successful but reader-oriented context and that translations which attempted to modernise but not to transform the English stage were simply too "stiff" and "workmanlike" to work as performable texts (Classe 2000: 959)?

Tempting though that conclusion may be, Wood's translations undoubtedly *were* performed, though it is not possible to ascertain where or how often these performances took place. Moreover, Wood had been financially shrewd when he insisted on protecting the performance rights. As he confirms in a letter to E. V. Rieu: "[H]aving reckoned up what I have received from [royalties] and in performing royalties over the 10 years since the first volume of Molière appeared—I feel that I should send you a word of thanks".[37] In all probability, the widespread dissemination of Wood's translations across the Anglophone world owed a good deal less to the ingenuity of his translation than to the Penguin Classics' target market, Penguin's pricing strategy and the cumulative publicity value of their very successful distribution of "branded goods".[38] All Penguin series had consistent and recognisable cover designs, and a good trademark. They were clean, smart, modern and, above all, cheap. They were in other words both attractive and accessible. Penguin Classics were targeting the educational market in practice if not in theory and that may help to explain why educational institutions almost certainly accounted for many, if not most, of the performances to which Wood refers. Despite the direction to apply to the League of Dramatists inside the front cover, Penguin rerouted a significant number of requests for performing rights and these came exclusively from staff connected with colleges or schools.[39] So, too, did numerous requests for the right to reproduce the translations in anthologies or collected volumes of plays particularly from US organisations, where Wood was invited to tour and speak on Molière.[40] Whatever else, Wood's translations were widely known and readily available at low cost to the groups likely to be interested in them.

We cannot know how these ephemeral productions were staged or received by their audiences, but equally we should not ignore or underestimate the importance of a performance market which was educationally oriented. The performance of a semantically oriented but accessible translation may not ever have had wide appeal in the commercial theatre, but it was able to provide a useful complement to the academic study of a theatre text. This was particularly the case in a period where, as we have seen, live performances of Molière in commercial or subsidised theatres were relatively rare and other visual media were generally unavailable. Grappling with Molière's linguistic complexity and the theatrical conventions of seventeenth-century France in the source language was—and still is—a challenge for students of French or European theatre. An appropriative, domesticating translation, which at the same time sought to parallel some of the characteristics of a different and alien theatrical system, could offer a point of entry into the dramatic conventions of another time and culture and act as a valid transitional mechanism for the semi-languaged or those interested in acquiring cultural capital by experiencing a difficult classical text on the stage.

If spectators (or readers) are to be open to cultural otherness, they have to be willing to engage actively with a 'resistant' translation or *mise en scène*. Such willingness is an act of trust, which can be nurtured and acquired over time. Although a domesticating strategy of this kind is in so many respects reductive and limiting, to deny an inexperienced audience the possibility of receiving a translation within a familiar context is ultimately elitist. It can, in the right circumstances, be a rite of passage. As general editor of Penguin Classics, Rieu had spotted the importance of this initiatory function in developing his editorial policy for 'readability', and Wood's aspiration to produce an 'actable' translation was cast in the same mould for a similar educationally oriented public. Whether or not Wood's translations were ever 'actable' must surely depend on the criteria applied at the time and the context in which they were performed. The history of their genesis and diffusion illustrates the fact that the appearance of any translation, whether for page or stage, is firmly anchored within the economic, cultural and political imperatives of the literary or theatrical systems within which it is produced.

NOTES

1. Lawrence Venuti explored this long-established phenomenon in his seminal work, *The Translator's Invisibility: A History of Translation* (1995).
2. This is evident across different genres but especially so in translation for the stage. One might use Seamus Heaney's *Beowulf* as an example of a poetry text, or Timberlake Wertenbaker's translations of Marivaux and Michael Frayn's of Chekov in relation to theatre texts. As regards performances of Molière reviewed or advertised in *The Times* between 1950 and 1960, only the actor, Miles Malleson, is regularly mentioned by name as the translator.
3. The archives are housed in the University of Bristol. I am indebted to Penguin Press and to staff in the Special Collections team of the University for their permission and help in accessing them. The files used are referred to by their code number in the Archive.
4. Wood's first volume was entitled *Five Plays* and contained Wood's translations of *Le Bourgeois Gentilhomme*, *Les Fourberies de Scapin*, *l'Avare*, *L'Amour médecin*, and *Don Juan* with the English titles of all five on the front cover (Molière 1953). The second, published six years later also contained five plays but foregrounded *Le Misanthrope* in the title. It also contained *The Sicilian or Love the Painter* (*Le Sicilien ou L'Amour peintre*), *Tartuffe or The Imposter* (*Tartuffe ou l'Imposteur*), *The Doctor in Spite of Himself* (*Le Médecin malgré lui*) and *The Imaginary Invalid* (*Le Malade imaginaire*) (Molière 1959).
5. Clear records of sales figures are not readily available in the archives, but print runs for Penguin were generally fairly small (around 25,000–30,000) with reprints as necessary. This was certainly the case for Wood's Molière and in a letter to Alan Glover, dated 18 March 1958, in which Wood complains about the delay in reprinting saying, "My solvency may depend on it". DM1107/L13.
6. Penguin's twenty-fifth anniversary in 1961 attracted a great deal of attention in the quality press. Penguin Classics were singled out for praise in every significant press tribute. These can be consulted in Penguin's Scrapbook for that anniversary which is held in the archive.
7. Letter à H.D.F. Kitto, 21 octobre, 1944, D1938/1.
8. Codes of practice such as those outlined by the Chartered Institute of Linguists (CIoL) confirm this. See for example their criteria for their professional translation diploma which includes a paper on literary translation. For a distinction a translation must "read like a piece originally written in the target language" (CIoL n.d.: 9).
9. *Proceedings of the Royal Society of Literature.*

10. The current criteria specified by the CIoL specify a choice of language and register "appropriate to the subject matter and the spirit and intention of the original" (n.d.: 8).
11. It was no accident that after Rieu's retirement in 1964, his editorial heirs, Betty Radice and Robert Baldick, quietly but quickly restored the paratextual scholarly apparatus proscribed by the editorial policy of their predecessor.
12. The Butt papers relating to the Twickenham edition are housed at the Bodleian library and contain an extensive correspondence between Butt and Rieu.
13. "[I]n spite of what I suppose I may regard as the success of *Candide* I still feel a good deal of temerity at stepping out of my normal role". Letter from John Butt to E.V Rieu, 13 August 1963, DM 1107/L126.
14. The date of the contract does not survive in the files, but Tancock records a "long delay" in receiving the galleys in a letter of 14 June 1949, so it was probably one of the earliest commissions. DM1107/L13.
15. This reference, dated 8 June 1966, appears in a letter to Miss Willey, a staff member at Penguin. Tancock also makes clear that he and Rieu had regularly discussed the nature and objectives of the series. DM1107/L13.
16. A letter from Tancock to Allen Lane, dated 7 July 1954, makes clear that Tancock, at least, had never expected *Manon* to be a best-seller and sales of 70,000 which he mentions as the total by December 1953 were modest by Penguin's standard. DM1107/L13
17. Copies of Rieu's direct contacts with translators are not regularly preserved into the editorial files but Wood alludes to a number of direct exchanges with Rieu in letters to others. In one surviving letter to the latter, dated 30 March 1963, Wood uses the surname as a form of address, beginning his letter "Dear Rieu" and ending it "All good wishes". The use of surnames or 'dropping handles', as it was sometimes called, was an indication of friendship between men but tone of the letter is courteously formal rather than easy or personal. *Le Misanthrope*, Wood's second volume of translations was dedicated to René Varin from the French Embassy. DM 1107/L89.
18. DM 1107/L36.
19. DM 1107/L36.
20. Letter to Alan Glover, 31 December 1952. DM 1107/L36.
21. Letter to Alan Glover, 30 June 1953. DM 1107/L36.
22. See an exchange of correspondence between Rieu and members of the production team at Penguin in DM/1107/L89.
23. The blurb for *Five Plays* has survived in DM 1107/L36.
24. Interestingly this even-handed recognition of the value of Molière's less well-known plays is maintained on the front cover of the first edition of *Five Plays*. None of the plays is foregrounded as the leading title; all five are listed on the front cover in identical format. Wood could not unilaterally have decided on the titles and Penguin's policy seems to have varied. Paradoxically, although *The Misanthrope* was foregrounded in the early editions of Wood's second volume, a memo of 1967 suggests that it would be changed to *Five Plays* the next reprint. The opposite happened with the initial *Five Plays* which became *The Miser and other plays* in 1962. DM 1107/L36.
25. A series of letters to that effect can be consulted in DM 1107/L36.
26. The blurb is preserved on an undated typewritten A4 sheet in DM 1107/L36.
27. The French government made available a relatively generous post-war budget for cultural diffusion and this enabled national theatre companies, such as the

Comédie Française and the Théâtre National Populaire to bring productions to
the London stage. This may also have stimulated interest in translated versions.

28. "Mr Malleson has shown recently that the old spell still holds" (Wood 1962: xxvi).
29. In his second volume of translations, *Le Misanthrope*, Wood refers the reader back to the introduction to *Five Plays* so we may infer that he used the same translation strategy in both. He spends some time, however, in the preface to his second volume explaining to the reader how he sought to compensate for translating verse into prove by seeking to 'preserve the rhetorical line of the speeches, the sense of mounting rhythms, of successions of phrase upon phrase, sentence on sentence" (Molière 1959: 20).
30. Wood acknowledges the debt to Rieu's "example and precept" at the end of his introduction (Wood 1962: xxviii).
31. See E.-A. Gutt's discussion of this point (1998: 50).
32. Letter from Wood to Glover in 1959, DM/1107/L89.
33. 24 July 1959. Available in DM/1107/L89.
34. 14 August 1959.
35. Letter to J. Croall, 17 January 1966. Wood must have been disappointed when this exploration did not go further. DM/1107/L89
36. Letter from Wood dated 8 September 1957. DM 1107/L36
37. Letter to E. V. Rieu, 30 March 1963.
38. See an interview with Ben Travers recorded in 1970 and documented in Hare (1995: 4–5).
39. Records of these can be found in the relevant editorial files, DM 1107/L36 and DM/1107/L89.
40. See the relevant editorial files, DM 1107/L36 and D.M/1107/L89.

WORKS CITED

Baines, Roger, Cristina Marinetti and Manuela Perteghella (eds.). 2012. *Staging and Performing Translation: Text and Theatre Practice*. Basingstoke, England: Palgrave Macmillan.
Baker, Henry and James Miller. 1739. *The Works of Molière: French and English*. London: Watts.
Chartered Institute of Linguists. n.d. *Diploma in Translation: Handbook for Candidates*. London: IoL Educational Trust. http://www.iol.org.uk/qualifications/DipTrans/DipTransHandbook.pdf (accessed 26 February 2013).
Coelsch-Foesner, Sabine and Holger Klein (eds.). 2003. *Drama Translation and Theatre Practice*. Frankfurt am Main: Peter Lang.
Committee on Higher Education. 1963. 'The Future Demand for Higher Education and the Places Needed'. In: *Higher Education: Report of the Committee Appointed by the Prime Minister Under the Chairmanship of Lord Robins 1961–63*. London: HMSO, pp. 48–74. http://www.educationengland.org.uk/documents/robbins/robbins06.html (accessed 20 June 2012).
Finburgh, Claire. 2012. 'The Politics of Contemporary French Theatre: How "Linguistic Translation" Becomes "Stage Translation"'. In: Roger Baines, Cristina Marinetti and Manuela Perteghella (eds.), *Staging and Performing Translation: Text and Theatre Practice*. Basingstoke, England: Palgrave Macmillan.
Fumaroli, Marc. 2009. 'Rabelais, la langue du roi'. *Le Monde*, 10 July, p. 2.
Gutt, E.-A. 1998. 'Pragmatic Aspects of Translation: Some Relevance-Theory Observations'. In: Leo Hicks (ed.), *The Pragmatics of Translation* (Topics in Translation 12). Clevedon, England: Multilingual Matters, pp. 41–53.

Hare, Steven. 1995. *Penguin Portrait: Allen Lane and the Penguin Editors, 1935–1970*. London: Penguin Books.

Hoggart, Richard. 1960. 'The Reader'. In: *Penguins Progress 1935–1960*. Harmondsworth, England: Penguin Books, pp. 27–28.

Lewis, Jeremy. 2005. *The Life and Times of Allen Lane*. London: Penguin Books.

Molière. 1953. *Five Plays*: The Would-Be Gentleman, That Scoundrel Scapin, The Miser, Love's the Best Doctor, Don Juan: *A New Translation by John Wood*. Baltimore: Penguin Books.

Molière. 1959. The Misanthrope *and Other Plays: A New Translation by John Wood*. Baltimore: Penguin Books.

Molière. 1962. *Five Plays*. Harmondsworth: Penguin Books.

Peacock, Noel. 2000. 'Molière 1622–1673: French comic dramatist'. In: Olive Classe (ed.). *Encyclopaedia of Literary Translation*. Vol. 2. London: Fitzroy Dearborn, pp. 956–996.

Rieu, E. V.1950. 'The Faith of a Translator'. In: *Penguins Progress 10*. Harmondsworth, England: Penguin Press, pp. 17–19.

Venuti, Lawrence. 1992. *Rethinking Translation: Discourse, Subjectivity, Ideology*. London: Routledge.

Venuti, Lawrence. 1995. *The Translator's Invisibility: A History of Translation*. London: Routledge.

Wood, John. 1962. 'Introduction'. In: Molière, *Five Plays*. Harmondsworth, England: Penguin Books.

Part III
Emerging Practices

8 Half-Masks and Stage Blood
Translating, Adapting and Performing French Historical Theatre Forms

Richard J. Hand

INTRODUCTION

In the history of world theatre, most plays were *not* written or performed in English. Over the decades, key achievements in international drama have found their way into English through translations, adaptations and appropriations. Some playwrights have done well: Anglophone readers and audiences have a choice of English Ibsens, Strindbergs and Chekhovs to consume. However, other achievements are less generously represented. Interestingly, this is particularly the case with French dramatists. There have, of course, been numerous Molières in English over the years, but later figures of French theatre are less prominently translated. The French stage offers a rich mine of material and my own research in translation and theatrical practice has explored and unearthed notable works of French theatre for the English eye and ear. In particular, in this chapter I will investigate three manifestations of French theatre from a personal, practical perspective: Victor Hugo, the Grand-Guignol and Octave Mirbeau.

A translation theorist such as Aaltonen distinguishes "between *theatre translation*, to refer to those pieces intended for performance, and *drama translation*, or translations of plays that are not meant for stage, that is, text oriented" (Riera 2010: 107n). This differentiation is not without its contentions, but in my own case I have been encouraged or compelled to opt for the principle of 'theatre translation': translating and publishing plays with an aspiration to the drama studio and stage rather than a 'literary' or 'critical edition' approach. Concomitant with this is the inference of 'performability' which is outlined (as 'speakability') by Louis Nowra:

> The translated play, unlike the novel or poem, must be 'speakable.' If anything destroys an audience's interest in a play it is dialogue that sounds translated. Ironically one often does a disservice to the playwright by translating him as closely as possible and yet, by making the play attractive to an audience and speakable, one has, on occasions, had to move far from the original. But what is the 'original?' (1984: 15)

Although Nowra's assertion seems plausible, his final question is all-important and reflects a debate that will be taken up by many others, including Clare Finburgh who takes issue with the notion of 'playability' (2011: 231) and its recurrence in theoretical approaches and the theatre industry.

The qualities of performability/speakability/playability may well be as subjective and ephemeral as notions of linguistic 'equivalence', but other aspects of the translating process are especially important. As Jorge Braga Riera writes, "(Not) only must translators be aware of the languages involved in the translating process, but also of the cultures where languages operate; that is, they must be familiarized with both source and target languages and cultures" (2010: 107). An acknowledgement of the necessity of a 'cultural' awareness certainly underpinned my own work in Hugo, the Grand-Guignol and Octave Mirbeau. The theatre scene and cultural scene of Paris beneficially enlightened the translation process, not least in seeing these theatrical manifestations in relation to *flânerie* (the Parisian art of urban wandering), Walter Benjamin's *Das Passagen-Werk/The Arcades Project* and cultures of eroticism and the macabre (see Hand 2010b). For some critics, this extends beyond garnering a degree of cultural familiarisation. Jenny Wong, for instance, seems to indicate the profound implications of the translation process when she contends that to "translate from one language to another inevitably means to exchange one worldview for another" (2012: 108).

The 'meshing' of linguistic translation with cultural contextualisation and an exchanged 'worldview' takes on additional significance when it comes to translating works of theatre. Sándor G. J. Hervey, Ian Higgins and Michael Loughridge argue,

> The translations of stage drama that are most successful from the performing point of view are usually based on compromises between reflecting some of the features that confer merit on the ST [source text] and adopting or adapting features of an existing TL [target language] dramatic genre. (1995: 139)

As will become evident in this chapter, the process of locating existing dramatic genres and individual works in English was a prudent option if not a necessity, above all when it comes to the continuing adaptive processes of actual or ideal stage interpretation. However, it would be a mistake to think that this is simply a process of compliance, making examples of French theatre 'fit' the English-language audience. Clare Finburgh, for example, is passionate about the explosive potential of translations when she insists that "[f]oreign languages, styles and genres must be allowed to interrogate, even to radically disrupt the target culture" (2011: 244). In the following case studies, it could be argued that the introduction of these quintessentially French works and forms strives to disrupt a perception of theatre history but also, above all with the Grand-Guignol, introduce a radical and disruptive genre onto the Anglophone stage.

VICTOR HUGO: HISTORICAL MELODRAMA

Although Victor Hugo (1802–1885) is the preeminent figure of French Romanticism if not French Literature as a whole, there is an enigma to his legacy. Hugo was a prolific writer, but his international repute abides with his fiction. Furthermore, his novels *Notre-Dame de Paris* (*The Hunchback of Notre Dame*, 1831) and *Les Misérables* (1862) have remained as classics not least because of their appeal as sources for adaptation into works of stage and screen. *Notre-Dame de Paris* was first filmed in 1905 before being interpreted by, among others, Universal (1923), RKO (1939) and Disney (1996). *Les Misérables* is likewise popular with countless adaptations across the performance media including the most successful stage musical in history: Claude-Michel Schönberg and Alain Boublil's 1980 version. The long historical accounts of Paris and Notre-Dame itself in the 1831 novel and Hugo's passionate argument on the necessity of sewers in *Les Misérables* would be surprising to find in an adaptation, but around and through those major components there are arresting and grippingly dramatic 'stories'. Given the inherent 'drama' to Hugo's prose works and the adaptation of them, it is somewhat ironic that an important and successful dimension to Hugo's oeuvre—namely his own stage plays—has been eclipsed. Moreover, when Hugo's plays have had a lifespan into our own times it has been in adaptive form: for example Hugo's *Le roi s'amuse* (1832) is certainly much more famous in the guise of Giuseppe Verdi's 1851 operatic adaptation: *Rigoletto*.

Claude Schumacher developed *Hugo: Four Plays* (Methuen, 2004) with a view to redressing the neglect of Hugo's drama. I was commissioned to translate *Lucrèce Borgia* (*Lucretia Borgia*, 1833) and *Ruy Blas* (1838) for this edition. Schumacher made it clear—partly in the spirit of Louis Nowra quoted at the start of this chapter—that something between the *performable* and the *literal* was desired. In the case of the Methuen translations,

> This is one reason (Schumacher) requested a prose translation of *Ruy Blas* not the rhyming Alexandrine couplets of the original: adhering to the original lyrical patterning of the original would have maintained, as it were, the *rhythm and pulse* of the original but not the closeness of semantic *meaning*. Although the scripts would not be cut or radically restructured, the editor wanted plays that could be efficaciously spoken and enacted by English-language performers and presented to a twenty-first century audience. (Hand 2010a: 19)

As an example, let us look at the opening of *Ruy Blas*. In Hugo's original it reads,

> Don Salluste: Ruy Blas, fermez la porte, — ouvrez cette fenêtre.
> *Ruy Blas obéit, ouis, sur unb signe de don Salluste, il sort par la porte du fond. Don Salluste va à la fenêtre.*
> Ils dorment encore tous ici, — le jour va naître. (Hugo 1985b: 11)

In the 2004 translation this becomes,

> Don Salluste: Ruy Blas, close the door. Open the window.
> *Ruy Blas obeys and then, after a sign from Don Salluste, exits by the tour upstage door upstage. Don Salluste walks over to the window.*
> Everyone is still asleep. Dawn will be breaking soon. (Hugo 2004: 289)

The twelve beats of Hugo's Alexandrine lines and the close rhyme of the couplets (*fenêtre/naître*) will continue throughout the play. In English this was loosened up: the meaning and action is adhered to, but the dialogue has become more realistic, colloquial and conversational. Furthermore, it is worth adding that although Hugo's original play could have been translated with an eye/ear to rhyme and rhythm (e.g., "Ruy Blas, close the door at once — open the window/They are still asleep, daybreak will soon start to glow"), this would probably have become oppressive. The adherence to a strict rhyming system would be unusual for the audience of the present day, and yet it is worth noting how controversial Hugo's *Lucretia Borgia* was in the 1830s for being written in prose.

After the publication of the Methuen plays, I was commissioned to direct one of the scripts at the Gatehouse Theatre in London for the 2007 International Victor Hugo Festival. I opted for *Lucretia Borgia*, Hugo's "highly dramatic, audaciously violent and erotic re-imagining of one of the most (in)famous figures of the Italian Renaissance: the ultimate *femme fatale*" (Hand 2010a: 20). Hugo's play has an historical setting, bringing to life personages and incidents that are documented and/or legendary. However, the *dramatic* is more important to Hugo than accuracy or historical 'truth': the play is a vivid and sweeping melodrama that exploits themes of revenge with heightened set pieces, consistent dramatic irony and enormous poetic license. For contemporary production, Hugo's play presents a mixture of the irresistible and the challenging. Working with a large ensemble to develop an historical epic full of heightened passion and irony was a delightful prospect but one was immediately struck by the difficulties of wrenching this play out of its historical context. The codes and conventions of early nineteenth-century French melodrama might be difficult material with which to captivate a contemporary, English-language audience. In the rehearsal process this was most tellingly revealed when it came to developing sequences in which characters in half-masks are unable to recognise each other—a situation contemporary actors found, initially, somewhat absurd until they were able to locate a convincing zone of interpretation. Similarly, some of the long speeches threaten to be awkwardly declamatory to the modern actor and spectator and inventive dramatic strategies were required to make these sequences 'work' (see Hand 2010a: 26–27).

As well as the challenges presented by generic conventions, there were other challenges presented by Hugo himself. As will be familiar to readers of his novels, Hugo had a fascination for history. In the stage directions of *Lucretia Borgia* (and some of his other plays) there are long descriptions of the stage décor and furnishings. For example, Hugo evidently savours the details of Don Alfonso d'Este's palace:

> *A hall in the ducal palace of Ferrara. Tapestries of Hungarian leather decorated with golden arabesques adorn the walls. Magnificent furniture in the style of late-fifteenth-century Italy, including a ducal throne covered in red velvet with the Este coat of arms embroidered on it.* (2004: 243)

Realising the precise details of Hugo's scenic demands threatens to be as oppressive as utilising the rigid lyrical structure of the spoken words in *Ruy Blas*. Moreover, the precision of Hugo's 'authentic' scenographic vision here is ironic given the poetic license with which he interprets history in the rest of the play: the furnishings may be realised with something of a restorer's eye, but Hugo extrapolates the myth of the Borgia family, above all Lucretia, taking it far beyond historical fact.

In the 2007 stage production of *Lucretia Borgia*, we opted against setting the play in the sixteenth century and selected a very different temporal setting:

> In the production we would set the play in the Italian states of the 1920s: the era of the rise of Fascism combined with an exciting Modernism; the shift from pre-First World War certainties into a cataclysmic mood of uncertainty; the shift in the performance aesthetics of film from screen melodrama to Expressionism. The production was governed by a 'Ritz' style of black tie and ball gowns, with recurrent elemental colors of blood red, rich gold and cold blue. The final, nightmarish scenes of the play transformed into an Expressionistic aesthetic (the 'other' 1920s). The overall effect was an adaptive 'time tunnel:' the reanimation of sixteenth-century Venice and Ferrara through 1830s French Romanticism set in the 1920s for a twenty-first century audience. (Hand 2010a: 23)

To this end, setting the production in the 1920s necessitated the rewriting of sentences that were highly specific in Hugo's own 'historical' vision. For example, at the beginning of the play, an anecdote surrounding the Borgias is recounted,

JEPPO: Very well. It was in the year of Our Lord, fourteen hundred and
ninety . . .
GUBETTA: (*in the corner*) Fourteen ninety-seven.
JEPPO: Quite so! Fourteen ninety-seven. In the early hours of a Thursday
morning . . .
GUBETTA: No. *Wednesday.* (Hugo 2004: 214)

In the production this became,

JEPPO: Very well. It was twenty-two years ago . . .
GUBETTA: (*in the corner*) Twenty-three.
JEPPO: Quite so! Twenty-three years ago. In the early hours of a Thurs-
day morning . . .
GUBETTA: No. *Wednesday.*

This type of textual adaptation was necessary to avoid the awkward
spectacle of characters in 1920s costume locating themselves in the sixteenth century.

Lucretia Borgia is a masterpiece of French theatre which—despite its
radical abandonment of an Alexandrine structure—is still an essential
example of 1830s Parisian melodrama. However, in creating a viable stage
interpretation of the play, a concerted negotiation of codes and conventions was required. The play also features sequences of extraordinary violence: the denouement to the play features an orgy that turns into slaughter
thanks to the infamous Borgia poison and Hugo's troubling fantasy ending,
in which Lucretia is stabbed to death and dies with *un cri de joi/a cry of joy*
(Hugo 1985a: 1426) at the hands of her own son who, only at the last, rea-
lises he has committed matricide. Heightened and histrionic, the sequence
might be the stock-in-trade of melodrama but might risk being risible in
the present day. However, the audience was presented with a nightmarish
vision drawn from the aesthetics of Expressionism and a gruesomely realistic stage effect as Lucretia's throat was cut: there were more audible gasps
and shudders than sniggers, perhaps making the 2007 London audience
react like their 1833 Parisian counterparts: despite the difference, equivalence is found. Arguably, the thunderous finale of melodrama will make
Lucretia Borgia an influence on a French dramatic genre at the other end
of the century: namely, the Théâtre du Grand-Guignol.

GRAND-GUIGNOL: HISTORY

In the history of popular theatre, one of the most unusual examples is the
Grand-Guignol. The Théâtre du Grand-Guignol (1897–1962) was a Pari-
sian phenomenon, the 'theatre of horror' which has put the phrase 'Grand-
Guignol' into the dictionary of many languages to mean heightened,

over-the-top horror performance. The Grand-Guignol itself opened in 1897 in a reclaimed space, a deconsecrated chapel in Montmartre, with the intention of being a showcase for stage naturalism in the mould of the Théâtre Libre, the intimate, avant-garde theatre established by André Antoine in 1887. The Grand-Guignol was founded by Oscar Méténier, a theatre enthusiast whose main profession was working as a senior secretary for the Commissioner of the Parisian police force. Even if the Grand-Guignol desired to build on the success and genre of Théâtre Libre, its destiny was written large in those first evenings. On the opening night of 3 April 1897, the Grand-Guignol presented a collection of short, naturalistic plays, including Oscar Méténier's own play *Mademoiselle Fifi* in which a French prostitute murders a Prussian soldier during the Franco-Prussian war of 1870. This play was the sensation of the first night and went on to be performed at the theatre hundreds of times. The grim setting and bloody theme of this play set the tone of the Grand-Guignol's success. In addition, although the chapel had been deconsecrated prior to being turned into a theatre, this was done minimally: throughout its lifespan, the Grand-Guignol would retain its ecclesiastical panelling, tall angels carved into its rafters and the smell of decades of altar candles and incense, aspects which would underline the taboo nature of the theatre and its repertoire. Yet another ingredient was Oscar Méténier himself: it is recorded that he would, dressed all in black, regale the audience queuing outside with lurid details of crime cases on the files of the Parisian police. Méténier was merely talking about his day job to entertain the audience while they waited to fill the tiny auditorium, but he had inadvertently invented the 'horror host' preshow of popular culture.

Méténier was custodian of the Grand-Guignol for scarcely a year before Max Maurey took over. Over the next sixteen years Maurey used his entrepreneurial and marketing skills to full-bloodedly develop the Grand-Guignol into the 'theatre of horror'. Maurey would evolve Méténier's inadvertent preshow into the gimmick of the house doctor who would assist any overwhelmed spectator, a device that will have a legacy in William Castle's showmanship that will place life insurance salesmen and safety zones in selected cinemas which screened his horror films. As for the Grand-Guignol repertoire, Maurey's thinking was that if the audiences loved *Mademoiselle Fifi*, they should have more. It is here that the influence of the 'blood and thunder' melodrama within *Lucretia Borgia* and other plays will become detectable: plays which culminate in sensational, violent endings. While Hugo used historical sources, the Grand-Guignol writers used more contemporaneous 'facts' including those found in *faits divers*, the short news stories that filled the popular press, sometimes with graphic illustrations: tales of true crimes; tragic cases of vengeance or abuse; or atrocities and outrages committed in the streets of Paris or far-flung corners of the globe. In addition, the writer André de Lorde (the 'Prince of Terror') would join the Grand-Guignol in 1901 and his prolific output would include plays that were researched in close collaboration with experts from the worlds of science, psychology or anthropology: experts who could help de Lorde create realistic details in his formulaic stage plays. The horrors synonymous with the Grand-Guignol will never stray far from the feasible terrors of the world we live in: the Grand-Guignol stage will never present the supernatural or fantastical; its horrors will be brutally sadistic, sometimes extraordinary, sometimes mundane, but always possible. Maurey also introduced comedies (often sex farces) into the evenings of short plays thus inventing *la douche écossaise*, the formula of interspersing horror with comedies.

However, even if the Grand-Guignol emerged out of Antoine's Théâtre Libre and its chief writer de Lorde strove for verisimilitude, the Grand-Guignol developed its own style of acting. The Grand-Guignol, in effect, conjoined the traditions of naturalism and melodrama. It was a very small theatre and the settings of the plays could be as intimate as they were 'real'. At the same time as being naturalistic in the feasibility of its settings and characters, the Grand-Guignol play needed to make a rapid journey from the everyday into the heights of horror. The plays were typically one-act works and the theatre became famous for set-pieces of special effects: stage blood that congealed in front of the audience; the dismemberment of heads, hands, fingers or eyeballs; functioning guillotines and sizzling pokers; acid attacks that melt the face or torture techniques that strip victims of their skin. The challenge for the actor was to take the spectator from the banal utterances of the commonplace to the screams of the victim and the spiteful laughter of the avenged. In other words, in an ideal performance the Grand-Guignol audience was taken on a seamless journey from naturalism into melodrama. The most celebrated actor of the Parisian Grand-Guignol was Paula Maxa who emphasised the performer's need to develop skills of focus and control in a Grand-Guignol performance (Pierron 1995: 1393) otherwise risk the audience's destructive laughter. Mel Gordon reinforces this when he states that a "false note in the acting could thoroughly ruin a twenty-minute scenario" (1997: 25–26).

The idiosyncratic nature of the form and its unique domicile in a grim and atmospheric cul-de-sac a few minutes' walk from the sex industry hub of Place Pigalle, meant that there were difficulties when attempts were made to export it. It may have been *à la mode* in Paris, but it would reveal the difficulties of cultural transposition. In 1908 the Parisian Grand-Guignol went on tour, performing its repertoire in French in London, Berlin and Rome. The expedition was a financial and critical disaster as, according to Gordon, the theatre reviewers and foreign audiences took to neither the horror plays nor the sex comedies (1988: 35). Certainly in London, the influential critic Max Beerbohm was unimpressed by the Parisian ensemble and reacted to the sensationalism of the repertoire by saying, "I am rightly ashamed of yielding to it" (in Trewin 1958: 20). Despite this inauspicious start, the success of the Grand-Guignol would lead to other attempts to export it. Between 1920 and 1922 Jose Levy (with the invaluable support of Sybil Thorndike and Lewis Casson) led an ambitious experiment to create a

Grand-Guignol theatre in London. Using the Little Theatre, a suitably small venue with a reputation for avant-garde works on a backstreet near Charing Cross station, Levy used translations of the original French repertoire as well as endeavouring to nurture home grown talent by securing new and well-established writers to produce short horror plays and comedies. At the time, short plays were a fairly radical idea for Britain let alone the intense, sometimes explicit, plotlines of the genre's terror plays and comedies. This conscious attempt to import a distinctly French genre in translation had the potential to disrupt, radically, the target culture and the process would not be easy. While the pre–First World War London audiences watched the French actors of the 1908 tour with a degree of disdain (if at all), the 1920s translated form which created London's Grand-Guignol garnered critical attention and a popular following.

The English plays written for London's Grand-Guignol presented very 'British' drama adhering to the conventions of Paris. For example, Reginald Berkeley's *Eight O'clock* (1920) presented a prisoner awaiting his execution and is an example of British liberal drama with an emotional effect as we learn of the deprived circumstances of the condemned man's upbringing and the desperation of his social situation. Similarly, H. F. Maltby's *The Person Unknown* (1921) is distinctly anglicised vision. Maltby's play concerns a maimed war veteran who returns to confront the woman who encouraged him to enlist and to claim the 'kiss' she pledged him. The play is an anti-war play which presents a provocative picture of the fault-lines of the British class system: the arrogant woman is a successful music-hall star who stirred up the passions of her audiences to join the military, including the naïve working class man with the disfigured face who breaks into her apartment to take his kiss and her life. At the same time, *The Person Unknown* is also a radical adaptation of Maurice Level's *Le Baiser dans la nuit* (1912), a classic of the Parisian repertoire, in which the male victim of a crime of passion which left him hideously disfigured by vitriol lures the woman who did it to him for a 'final kiss' of forgiveness only to exact an equivalent act of revenge on her. Both of the plays are 'grotesquely erotic in their gendered conflict' (Hand and Wilson 2007: 148) with the key difference that in the British play there is a social and ideological message to the drama while in the French origination, passion is all.

Another example from the British Grand-Guignol also reveals the complexities of cultural transposition. The well-established writer Joseph Conrad visited the Little Theatre and was inspired to transform his 1915 short story 'Because of the Dollars' into *Laughing Anne*, a play for the British Grand-Guignol. The play was rejected by Levy for, in Conrad's words, "[t]oo much darkness; too much shooting" (in Partington 2000: 180). However, the flaws of the play extend beyond the scenographic demands and props. The central, villainous character in the play is the Man Without Hands, a ruthless gangster who leads a pack of criminals. For John Galsworthy, despite the fact the same character features in the short story, the decision to think of placing the maimed figure on the British stage doomed the play to rejection and failure: "Conrad probably never realised that a "man without hands" would be an almost unbearable spectacle; that what you can write about freely cannot always be endured by the living eye" (Galsworthy 1924: vii). However, it is interesting to note that the Parisian Grand-Guignol abounded with maimed characters who have lost—or will spectacularly lose—a variety of limbs. Conrad has merely adapted his short story (where the Man Without Hands was perfectly acceptable) onto the stage: but while the maimed man would have been fair game in Paris, in London this would have been a cultural import too far. Shakespeare may have presented us with the blinding of Gloucester in *King Lear* but this British play following the conventions of a peculiar French genre was too much, for John Galsworthy at least (indeed, *Laughing Anne* would not be performed until 2000).

The British Grand-Guignol would be of particular concern for the theatre censor (the Lord Chamberlain's Office) and it was a relationship that would ultimately lead to the British Grand-Guignol's demise. The notorious 'blue pencil' excised problematic words and scenes but a large number of plays were completely banned. In particular, plays that were originally French were most problematic in the censor's eyes and a number were banned outright including Wilfred Harris's *Save the Mark*, a comedy about an adulterous love-bite adapted from Marcel Nancey and Jean Manoussy's *La Ventouse* (1916); the horror play *Blind Man's Buff*, a translation of Charles Hellem and Pol d'Estoc's *Aveugle!* (1907); and 'the lunatics have taken over the asylum' scenario *Dr Goudron's System*, a translation of André de Lorde's popular Edgar Allan Poe adaptation *Le Système du Docteur Goudron et du Professeur Plume* (1903). Eventually, it was the furore surrounding the staging of Christopher Holland's *The Old Women*, a translation and premiere staging of André de Lorde and Alfred Binet's *Un crime dans une maison de fous ou Les Infernales* (1925), that leads to the British Grand-Guignol's demise. As we can see, Levy's experiment in Grand-Guignol reveals an attempt to 'radically disrupt' the British theatre scene. Or rather, this was how the attempt was construed by the institutionalised system of censorship (Levy, after all, was simply a devout Francophile who adored the Grand-Guignol genre, rather than a firebrand). The story of the British Grand-Guignol reveals the complexity when an attempt is made to introduce the narratives, conventions and set-pieces of a distinctive homegrown genre into a target culture.

GRAND-GUIGNOL: IN PERFORMANCE

The Grand-Guignol may have been too racy for some in the 1920s, but in the twenty-first century, who cares? In performing Grand-Guignol in our own time, one is confronted with the simple fact that the name and legend of the genre itself excels the reality of the form. If anything, stage blood (so famously used by the theatre) has become ubiquitous. The theatre itself closed down in 1962, in an era when Henri-Georges Clouzot's *Les Diaboliques* (1954) and Alfred Hitchcock's *Psycho* (1960) had already begun to redefine horror for the popular audience and would pave the way for future horror culture. Indeed, despite the many examples of horrors executed in the Grand-Guignol repertoire that can be singled out or highlighted and the extant examples of sensational posters, production stills and other publicity material that have survived, the repertoire itself is often characterised by surprising subtlety. There may be a furious climax but the journey to that point is carefully and steadily managed, primarily through the script and its dialogue. The modern spectator could be forgiven for expecting buckets of blood and on-stage annihilation. The reality, however, is that the legendary stage horrors of the Grand-Guignol are usually created by inference and suggestion or sleight of hand, the careful manipulation of small syringes filled with stage blood and trick knives which can be safely operated.

These issues became a particular challenge when commissioned to direct a reconstruction of 'a night at the Grand-Guignol' for the 2009 Abertoir horror festival. The Abertoir festival is an annual event that has run in Aberystwyth since 2005. The festival features screenings of classic films and world premieres as well as special events such as talks and question and answer sessions with actors and directors associated with horror movies. Although there would occasionally be live performances by rock groups which may have a particularly gothic image or association, the presentation of live theatre was unusual. The audience would comprise horror movie fans who would regularly sup on screen terrors but were not accustomed to theatre. Working with the Grand-Guignol form, one is aware how the phrase casts a long shadow: everyone in the audience would have heard— and possibly occasionally used—the phrase 'Grand-Guignol'. Yet wouldn't the reconstruction of a night at the Grand-Guignol seem quaint if not anodyne for the hardened horror film fanatic? The trick mechanism of props is easy to detect if a spectator resists the performer's attempt to misdirect his/her gaze; 5 milliliters of stage blood (sticky and made from a corn syrup base) squirted from a concealed syringe cannot cut the terror that CGI and liters of screen blood can, effects that took hours or even weeks to build and prepare. However, theatre has a distinctive advantage: its *liveness*. The stage action could not be paused or stopped and with the heightened enacted horrors and squirts of stage blood that leap out towards the auditorium, an audience used to film can suddenly find itself in the ultimate 3D cinema.

The two horror plays produced in the Grand-Guignol triple bill for Abertoir were Maurice Level's *Le Baiser dans la nuit* (1912) and Jean Aragny and Francis Neilson's *Le Baiser de sang* (1929), two representative and popular works from the Parisian repertoire presented in the published translations by

Hand and Wilson (2002): *The Final Kiss* and *The Kiss of Blood*. In Level's *Le Baiser dans la nuit/The Final Kiss*, the first act presents Henri together with his brother, doctor and lawyer as he refuses to appear in court to testify against Jeanne, the woman who assaulted him with sulphuric acid. In discussing the translation/adaptation published in 2002 Hand and Wilson write, "This is the freest adaptation in the present collection. In producing the adaptation, the decision was made to shorten the work into one act, reduce the number of onstage characters, streamline the exposition, and abridge some of the longer monologues" (2002: 182). The 2002 version opens with a doctor and nurse examining the hideous wounds of Henry who sits with his back to the audience. This radically streamlined version was used for the Abertoir festival. Another advantage in using this script as the opening piece in an evening of theatre is that it facilitated an effective piece of pre-show with the doctor and nurse conducting an impromptu medical examination of selected spectators as they enter the auditorium. After this, the doctor and nurse could step onto the stage to examine Henry and the first play begins.

Jean Aragny and Francis Neilson's *Le Baiser de sang/The Kiss of Blood* (1929) opens in an operating theatre in which we witness a trepanation. The script describes the sequence in great detail and is full of dialogue which reinforces what we *are* seeing and what we *think* we see. The patient dies under the knife of the eminent surgeon Leduc which establishes the mood and trajectory of the play. After the operation, a gentleman called Joubert bursts into the surgery complaining of agony in his finger. After a long sequence in which Leduc can find nothing wrong with Joubert's digit and humours and dismisses him, in a rapid, ferocious sequence Joubert cuts off his own finger with a scalpel. Joubert's irrational behaviour is, we discover, due to his guilt for murdering his wife, Hélène. In fact, she survived the murder attempt and 'haunts' Joubert, demanding revenge. Hélène's kiss on the finger which pulled the trigger of the gun caused him to slice it off. At the end of the play, Hélène returns to kiss Joubert's hand which he cleaves off with an axe before collapsing dead:

Joubert: I'm in agony! Agony! The axe! Where's the axe?!
              (He rushes forward, takes the axe from the fireplace and hacks his hand off at the wrist.)
Leduc: Stop him! Stop him, I say!
Dr Volguine: My God!
Joubert: No more pain! No more pain! *(He falls.)*
Prof Leduc (bending over Joubert): Dead! He's dead!
Hélène: Revenge! *(Manic laughter.)* Ha! Ha! Ha! (Hand and Wilson 2002: 264)

As is evident above, the stage directions at the final moments of the script are minimal: Joubert *"s'élance et à coups de hache se coupe le poignet"*

(Pierron, 1995: 1132), he "hacks his hand off at the wrist". For the Abertoir production and its horror fan audience, this was a moment too critical to squander, not least as it was the closing sequence of the triple bill. This account reveals the decisions taken:

> (The) rehearsal process developed the scene into an example of the grotesquely erotic: an example of extreme violence being in parallel with, and allusive to, an erotic, perhaps even pornographic, narrative. The climax of the play in performance compelled the actor playing Joubert—kneeling down and sweating—to brandish his hand to Helene and press himself against her body while blood continued to drip from the stump at the end of his arm. Similarly, in rehearsal the actor playing Helene located an ecstatic response to her husband's self-inflicted amputation and demise: this gradually evolved into the actor triumphantly licking the oozing blood and inserting the stump into her mouth. (Hand 2010b: 78–79n)

This interpretation would probably have been unthinkable in the original production at the Parisian Grand-Guignol, but this moment in the production was unabashedly heightened to satisfy an audience used to seeing films such as *Saw* (James Wan, 2004), *Hostel* (Eli Roth, 2005) and *Antichrist* (Lars Von Trier, 2009) or, in terms of classic gore, the 1960s exploitation films of Herschell Gordon Lewis through to horror milestones like *The Texas Chainsaw Massacre* (Tobe Hooper, 1974). The translation of the French original was transmogrified into being a sequence befitting the context of its commission and production. It is an example of translation shifting into intertextuality to fulfil the generic expectations of a crucial moment of horror performance. However, the scripted dialogue and action—and the speeches themselves—were adhered to. In other words, the structure of the sequence was used as a lynchpin to the performance. To this end, it is necessary to discuss Hélène's triple utterance: "Ha! Ha! Ha!"

As in other places in the Grand-Guignol, when Hélène bursts into manic laughter we are witnessing a character become a (stage) lunatic. However, in production this was expanded so that *all* the characters' descended into individual insanities. Although Antonin Artaud never mentions the Grand-Guignol in his writing, his concepts of cruelty and plague in the theatre were contemporaneous with it. Using Artaud-based workshops in rehearsal was a welcome shift away from exploring naturalism and melodrama. We were able to locate individual 'madnesses': Hélène finds the delirium of her ecstatic triumph; Joubert collapses into suppliant degeneration; the super-rational and egotistical Leduc is rendered into traumatic shock; and Volguine is frozen in introverted and appalled horror. The world has gone mad: all reason has unraveled.

It is worth stressing that as well as negotiating between a 'lost' historic form of popular horror performance and contemporaneous 'equivalents', the production located an overarching principle influenced by a specific horror film. *The Kiss of Blood* is a script which is, as it were, in two halves. The first half is set in Leduc's surgery with all the wipe-clean paraphernalia and hierarchy of the medical world. The second half takes us to Joubert's home and it is within this domain that we are led to the dénouement of horror, retribution and madness. In our design principal, we kept the first half as white as possible: the lighting, the uniforms worn by the medical staff, the equipment they used and the section of skull the surgeon removed from the doomed patient's head. By the same token, when we get to Joubert's house, the theme was oppressively gothic: dark coloured clothes and props, and subdued, brooding lighting which left the corners of the stage in oblivion. The inspiration for this was taken from Alfred Hitchcock's *Psycho*, essentially the juxtaposition between the mundane, brightly lit world of the modern office, freeway and shower room tiles and the gothic world of the Bates mansion where we witness the profound horror and madness of its occupant. There is also an equivalent construction of abject females in *Psycho* and *The Kiss of Blood*: Norman Bates lives with the oppressive fantasy figure of his mother and believes her to be 'real', Joubert beholds his corporeal wife as a fantasy figure.

OCTAVE MIRBEAU: SATIRICAL DRAMA

One of the most interesting writers associated with the Grand-Guignol is Octave Mirbeau (1848–1917). Although obviously not as celebrated as Victor Hugo, Mirbeau was a giant of French letters in his own right, acclaimed—and sometimes denounced—by his contemporaries. He was a 'living' voice in the France of his time, who made his presence in French culture felt through his acerbic journalism, his experimental and sometimes scabrous fiction and, comparatively late in his career, his extraordinary plays. Mirbeau was a prominent figure, defending contemporary artists and commenting on political controversy. Interestingly, Mirbeau was drawn to the Grand-Guignol and wrote some plays for the theatre. The four Mirbeau plays staged at the Grand-Guignol were all character-driven comedies which playfully satirised aspects of contemporary French society such as sexual relationships: for example *Vieux ménages* (first staged in 1894 and revived for the Grand-Guignol in 1900) presents an embittered elderly couple, whose mutual and irreconcilable resentment can amuse us with its *Schadenfreude*; in *Les Amants* (1901) we behold the complicated courtship ritual between two young lovers whose frustrations and distrust fuel their passions as much as any superficial, physical attraction. These plays are perhaps a surprisingly 'light touch' when we consider Mirbeau's reputation as a writer.

In the present day, Mirbeau is most famous for his Decadent novels *Le Jardin des supplices* (*Torture Garden*, 1899) and *Le Journal d'une femme de chambre* (*The Diary of a Chambermaid*, 1900), provocative works of erotica that can still shock the reader with their sadomasochistic excesses and have lost none of their power as brutal satires of the bourgeoisie and imperialism. *Le Journal d'une femme de chambre* shows bourgeois France from the point of view of the servant Célestine and we witness the sadistic abuse and exploitation that the self-assured middle classes mete out upon the workers in their service. *Le Jardin des supplices* takes the reader into the Far East where we see the pleasure seeking of affluent western tourists who can indulge their every whim (including cannibalism) and gain sexual pleasure from the suffering and torture of victims in the colonies. Although Mirbeau may not have written horror plays for the Grand-Guignol himself, the theatre adapted *Le Jardin des supplices* with its production of Pierre Chaine and Andre de Lorde's *Le Jardin des supplices* (1922). In tackling this work, the Grand-Guignol could only ameliorate the plot: the relentless catalogue of horrors perpetrated in the novel becomes embodied in two principle sequences of violence (stripping the skin off the back of a prostitute; and the blinding of a woman with a hot needle). Chaine and de Lorde's adaptation makes the story more blatantly 'political' with a plot of espionage and subterfuge which enables the sadistic horrors in the work to receive just retribution and 'cause'. Although this is more in keeping with the British reworking of the Grand-Guignol genre when it is imported across the English Channel, a staging of *Le Jardin des supplices* in1920s London would have been unthinkable.

As we have seen, Mirbeau was less shocking in his short plays than in his fictional prose. Mirbeau also wrote some full-length plays which were presented—to great popular, critical and financial success—on the stage in France and across Europe (but less conspicuously in Britain). Mirbeau's two most successful plays *Les Affaires sont les affaires* (1903) and *Le Foyer* (1908)—recently translated as *Business Is Business* and *Charity* (Hand 2012)—are, at first glance, conventional comedies of manners: perfectly structured plays with delicious wit and highly developed characters. But beneath the surface lurks the same, mischievous Mirbeau who eviscerated society in his Decadent fiction. Both plays are uncompromising and damning satires on the hypocrisies and injustices of contemporary France. *Les Affaires sont les affaires* was produced in Britain, although Sydney Grundy's 1905 adaptation of it—to judge by the copy held in the Lord Chamberlain's Office archives at the British Library—was a very much tempered and substantially shortened version, almost certainly because a more accurate translation would have been deemed far too risqué for the British theatre censors of the time. At the heart of *Les Affaires sont les affaires* is the demonic Isidore Lechat, a self-made millionaire and wannabe politician who tyrannises anything and anyone who crosses his path. Callous, adulterous, unscrupulous, Lechat is many things. But one thing is constant: he is always democratic in his wickedness, persecuting without any qualms the birds in his garden as much as his servants, his rivals or his own family. This demagogue has only one soft spot, his devotion to his son and heir, the reckless Xavier. Mirbeau develops this relationship with ruthless intent.

Mirbeau's final play *Charity* (1908) is "another three-act comedy of manners in the Molière tradition . . . in the same mould as *Business Is Business* but takes as its theme *charity* rather than *business*" (Hand 2012: 5). The plot is centred on a charity home run by Baron Courtin, a prominent and respected liberal politician. Courtin is a richly constructed figure whose personality and psychology is developed for us not least through his day-to-day dealings with characters from all walks of life. Courtin is a character as Gargantuan as Isidore Lechat but infinitely more empathetic and charismatic. However, despite his insight and his habit of taking the moral high ground, Courtin ultimately teeters on the precipice of doom because of his own self-interest and corruption. This is encapsulated in Courtin's high-profile pet project of the charity home. Despite its noble intentions and principles, the audience gradually comes to realise that "far from offering salvation to the destitute adolescent girls it houses it creates greater problems: financial corruption, physical and sexual abuse, and death" (6). Through the construction of Courtin, Mirbeau posits an ideological condemnation of the deep-seated corruption that lies behind the rhetoric and sanctimony of the self-appointed guardians of the dispossessed. In watching *Charity*, we see the self-proclaimed integrity and superiority of those with moral authority inexorably unravel before our eyes. The fact that Courtin manages to 'get away it' is a theatrical decision that can only make us angrier and, Mirbeau hopes, more politicised.

Given Mirbeau's acute gaze on his nation's political scene and his profession as a journalist, it is no surprise that these plays are highly developed satires on contemporary France with allusions to personalities and cases, both famous and forgotten. They are as concerned with the contemporary political scene as Hugo's plays draw on the accurate historical details of the past. Can Mirbeau's theatre, this well-crafted and passionate drama which gives such a vivid picture of *la belle époque*, have any relevance to our own time? Certainly a lot of the subplots and characters in the plays and the themes of corruption and sleaze that permeate the 'democratic' society he presents can be easily detected in the contemporary world if one wants to look for it. However, a lot depends on how we choose to interpret the works, how we 'translate' the texts for ourselves before even translating them onto the page. In the 2012 Octave Mirbeau plays collection, although countless annotations and footnotes could have 'explained' Mirbeau's frame of reference, this was neither desirable nor permissible. The result is plays that are adaptations as much as translations, not least as "certain historical details and rhetoric (especially in *Charity*) have been edited or streamlined|" (Hand 2012: 7–8). Furthermore, these pre-Brecht political plays are reminiscent of George Bernard Shaw and John Galsworthy when rendered into English, a relationship between French and British genre that is consciously nurtured and negotiated in the process.

At the time of writing, the 2012 Mirbeau stage translations have not been performed. If they do eventually reach the stage, some essential decisions will be required. Although a performance set in *la belle époque* would be completely viable, both scripts could be effectively updated. The themes of injustice, corruption and exploitation seem, sadly, perennial or, rather, as pervasive as they were in Mirbeau's era. Although much has been done to the scripts already in order to 'loosen up' aspects of historical detail and register, further work would be required to make Mirbeau's acerbic satires fully mesh into a vision of the twenty-first century: disruptive comedies that make us look at the faults of our own society while simultaneously making us laugh. This is an endeavour that could be rewarding: to appropriate Hervey, Higgins and Loughridge, the merit of Mirbeau's plays can be optimised by the further adoption and adaption of contemporary, probably English-leaning, features.

CONCLUSION

Working on historical theatre forms neglected in English (i.e., the historical melodramas of Victor Hugo, the French popular theatre form Grand-Guignol and the satires of Octave Mirbeau), one is faced with numerous challenges in terms of translation, rehearsal and performance. To create viable works of theatre, one embarks on a process of compromise and negotiation at each stage of a three-level symbiotic journey (translating plays from French into English; the development through adaptation of a performance script; and eventual stage production). Just as source language words are translated into a target tongue, aspects of the unique nexus of traditions, codes and idiosyncrasies of a source culture are also imported. The historical and linguistic conventions inherent in Hugo's 1830s plays can be relaxed and reworked for a present-day audience. Historically, bringing the Grand-Guignol to Britain has been problematic and controversial, while in the twenty-first century the genre risks being all too tame on a post-Lord Chamberlain stage. To this end, popular culture and genres of the past and the present are negotiated: indeed, horror movie culture does not only help a horror performance come to life (and death), it is probably impossible to ignore. The outspoken journalist Octave Mirbeau may have had specific *cause célèbres* and legislation—and recognisable politicians and businessmen—of *la belle époque* in his sights when he wrote his full-length plays, but they can strike a chord for the contemporary viewer when we identify the themes and archetypes he has created. However, all is not compromise or a procrustean process whereby over-specified details are stripped away and the slightest 'risk' to comprehension is mollified. English translations of plays which are neglected literary dramas or risqué popular genres can help to refresh, perhaps even disrupt, an Anglophonic perspective on theatre and performance history. Bringing these works to light on the English language page and, ideally, stage can permit a reinterpretation of theatre and performance history by increasing the available repertoire of plays and genres. In this respect, the introduction of new translations and productions of neglected non-English classics and popular genres into a culture can benefit us. It can compel us to look at and question our own theatrical traditions and worldviews not least in that it affords our eyes and ears the opportunity to take in something *very old* yet *very new.*

WORKS CITED

Finburgh, Clare. 2010. 'The Politics of Translating Contemporary French Theatre: How "Linguistic Translation" Becomes "Stage Translation"'. In: Roger Baines, Cristina Marinetti and Manuela Perteghella (eds.), *Staging and Performing Translation: Text and Theatre Practice.* Houndmills, England: Palgrave Macmillan, pp. 230–248.
Galsworthy, John. 1924. 'Introduction'. In: Joseph Conrad, *Laughing Anne and One Day More.* London: Castle.
Gordon, Mel. 1997. *The Grand Guignol: Theatre of Fear and Terror.* New York: De Capo Press.
Hand, Richard J. 2010a. '"It must all change now!": Victor Hugo's *Lucretia Borgia* and Adaptation Practices in Theatre'. In: Dennis Cutchins, Laurence Raw and James Welsh (eds.), *Redefining Adaptation Studies.* Lanham MD: Scarecrow Press, pp. 17–30.
Hand, Richard J. 2010b. 'Labyrinths of the Taboo: Theatrical Journeys of Eroticism and Death in Parisian Culture'. In: Karoline Gritzner (ed.), *Eroticism and Death in Theatre and Performance.* Hatfield, England: University of Hertfordshire Press, pp. 64–79.
Hand, Richard J. 2012. *Octave Mirbeau: Two Plays.* Bristol, England: Intellect.
Hand, Richard J. and Michael Wilson. 2002. *Grand-Guignol: The French Theatre of Horror.* Exeter, England: University of Exeter Press.
Hand, Richard J. and Michael Wilson. 2007. *London's Grand-Guignol and the Theatre of Horror.* Exeter, England: University of Exeter Press.
Hervey, Sándor G. J., Ian Higgins and Michael Loughridge. 1995. *Thinking German Translation: A Course in Translation Method, German to English,* London: Routledge.
Hugo, Victor. 1985a. *Oeuvres Complètes: Théâtre I.* Paris Robert Laffont.
Hugo, Victor. 1985b. *Oeuvres Complètes: Théâtre II.* Paris Robert Laffont.
Hugo, Victor. 2004. *Plays.* Ed. Claude Schumacher. London: Methuen.
Nowra, Louis. 1984. 'Translating for the Australian Stage (a Personal Viewpoint)'. In: Ortrun Zuber-Skerritt (ed.), *Page to Stage: Theatre as Translation.* Vol. 48. Amsterdam: Rodopi, pp. 13–28.
Partington, Wilfred. 2000. 'Joseph Conrad Behind the Scenes'. *The Conradian,* 25:2, pp. 177–184.
Pierron, Agnès. 1995. *Le Grand Guignol: Le théâtre des peurs de la belle époque.* Paris: Robert Laffont.

Riera, Jorge Braga. 2010. 'The Adaptation of Seventeenth-Century Spanish Drama to the English Stage During the Restoration: The Case of Calderón'. In: Catie Gill (ed.), *Theatre and Culture in Early Modern England, 1650–1737: From Leviathan to Licensing Act.* London: Ashgate, pp. 107–130.

Trewin, J. C. 1958. *The Gay Twenties: A Decade of the Theatre.* London: MacDonald.

Wong, Jenny. 2012. 'The Transadaptation of Shakespeare's Christian Dimension in China's Theatre—to translate, or Not to Translate?' In: Laurence Raw (ed.), *Translation, Adaptation and Transformation.* London: Continuum, pp. 99–111.

9 Bridging the Translation/Adaptation Divide
A Pedagogical View

Laurence Raw and Tony Gurr

The relationship between translation and adaptation has been of considerable significance during our teaching careers. In 1991 Laurence described his experiences teaching British and comparative Cultural Studies in Turkish universities in a paper originally delivered at the University of Warwick, in which he tried to show how the study of a text such as Terence Rattigan's *Separate Tables* (1954), coupled with a video version of the play (John Schlesinger's 1983 adaptation starring Alan Bates), could be used as a basis for comparative intercultural studies.[1] In another paper he suggested that this kind of approach could be enhanced by invoking what Alan Sinfield called those "stories" (1989: 23) by which we make sense both of ourselves and the foreign cultures. By investigating the foreign culture through the medium of their own cultures, learners could not only come to terms with differences between the two, but also change their own view of the world by exposing their own cultural identity to the contrasting influences that the foreign culture and language might exert. A course created in this way might reveal the different stories upon which individual British and Turkish cultures were based, and thereby promote an understanding of how intercultural knowledge derives as much from the resources of the group as from references to specific texts.

What seemed workable in theory did not always work in practice. While learners admired Bates' performance on its own terms as a study in emotional repression, they found it difficult to relate Rattigan's depiction of human behaviour to their own experience. The context of *Separate Tables*—a seedy private hotel in Bournemouth in the early 1950s—was just too remote from them, both culturally and historically. A year or so later, Laurence re-encountered some of the learners; by now most of them had either moved on to graduate studies or entered the world of work. They explained that the Rattigan text had proved problematic for them, as they first had to translate his rather precise use of English into an idiom they could understand, and subsequently try to adapt themselves to his thematic preoccupations. For them translation and adaptation constituted two distinct processes of adjustment: one of them linguistic, the other cultural. This experience proved beyond doubt that inter- or cross-cultural learning can only take place if learners and educators alike can appreciate the ways in which they make sense of the world. As a British-educated academic, Laurence's conception of 'translation' and 'adaptation' was very different from that embraced by his learners, the majority of whom came from the Republic of Turkey's two principal cities, Ankara and İstanbul.

Inspired by this recollection, we will begin this chapter by showing how 'translation' and 'adaptation' have developed models of textual transformation that have proved highly effective in promoting western interests in different contexts. This helps to explain why Laurence's learners thought as they did: much of their language education in high school (as well as university) education was inspired by this model. We subsequently show how 'translation' and 'adaptation' have acquired specific cultural meanings in the Turkish context to denote different types of writing: the distinction between the two plays an important part in shaping learners' views. Inspired by the theories of narrative put forward by psychologist Jerome Bruner, we propose an alternative framework for looking at translation and adaptation that identifies both processes as different yet fundamentally interrelated; they are transformative processes by which individuals can come to terms with the world around them. We offer case studies of our own work with different groups of learners and educators to support our case. Following Maria Tymoczko's recommendation, we seek to expand the intellectual field that will "expand the conception of translation [and adaptation], moving it beyond dominant, parochial and [culturally] stereotypical thinking about . . . processes and products" (2007: 132). By focusing on processes such as transfer and re-presentation, we believe that translation and adaptation should be looked at from a more inclusive perspective that acknowledges the presence of "a globalizing world demanding flexibility and respect for differences in cultural traditions" (132). This is an important move: we should acknowledge the post-positivist view that problematises notions of what constitutes a "fact" and emphasises the significance of perspective. In Brunerian terms, we need to understand the ways in which individuals construct their own narratives (or "stories", to invoke Sinfield's term), and how such stories shape the ways in which they think. This post-positivist view should inspire new approaches to teaching adaptation (or translation), with the emphasis placed on negotiation and collaboration between educators and learners.

As indicated above, translation proved an effective means of disseminating values from the west into other territories, chiefly by promoting particular models of textual transformation.[2] One such model was the notion of translation as transfer, in which "transfer is figured in terms of transporting material objects or leading sentient beings (such as captives or slaves in one direction or soldiers and missionaries in the other) across a cultural or linguistic boundary" (Tymoczko 2007: 6). An early instance of this process at work can be seen in the writings of St. Jerome, where he observes that "like some conqueror [Hilary the Confessor] marched the original text, a captive, into his native language" (in Robinson 1997: 26). Note the metaphor here that represents Hilary as a generalissimo-like figure embarking on a linguistic conquest. This same military-like precision influenced government policy in the Republic of Turkey in the early years after its creation in 1923, when Mustafa Kemal Atatürk created a western-style foundation for his new national culture. He established a Translation Bureau with the stated purpose of commissioning translation of a series of 'western classics', to be distributed to all schools and higher education institutions, as well as drawing on the expertise of European refugees from Nazi Germany such as Erich Auerbach. Atatürk's policy used the idea of translation as transfer to further national interests, as translators made use of the newly emergent Turkish language (forcibly purged of Ottoman, Persian and other neologisms), incorporating a series of words borrowed from western languages, chiefly French. Atatürk was determined to suppress his country's Ottoman past and reinvent it as a forward-looking, dynamic state that would ultimately compete both culturally and artistically with its western allies.

The translation as transfer model has exerted considerable influence over generations of learners in the Republic of Turkey. According to one contemporary programme in Translation Studies, for instance, learners are expected to "develop translation skills to the highest possible level in terms of text analysis and terminological studies", as well as "develop knowledge and understanding of Turkey-EU relations, and concepts in political science and cultural studies". Developing 'translation skills' in this model requires learners to understand the ways in which the source texts works, and use that knowledge to find the closest possible equivalents in the target text: in other words, to remain 'faithful' to the source text (Anonym. 2012) In the foreign language–learning classroom, the main pedagogical emphasis is placed on grammar—rather than listening or speaking—in the belief that learners will achieve success in their future careers if they can speak the most 'correct' form of the language. Neither of these approaches is exclusive to Turkish academia (notions of fidelity continue to occupy the Translation Studies agenda in different contexts),[3] but the ideological purpose behind them remains significant, nearly ninety years after the Republic was first established. Bülent Bozkurt suggested in 1998 that the construction of departmental curricula in language, literature and Translation Studies played a large part in sustaining "Turkey's socio-political and cultural standing in relation to [B]ritain and the world" (1998: 8). Western ideas should be rendered as faithfully as possible into Turkish, so as to create future generations of culturally sophisticated learners. Learning 'proper' (i.e., grammatically correct) English is important as a means of communicating with the outside world. Given the pervasiveness of these beliefs in university departments of humanities, it is not surprising that Laurence's learners wanted to make sure they translated *Separate Tables* as faithfully as possible into Turkish before trying to comment on it.

However, this is not the only process of transformation that has penetrated the Republic of Turkey since the 1920s. The Translation Studies scholar Şehnaz Tahir Gürçağlar has analysed the translations of Selâmi Munir Yurdatap and Kemal Tahir, two writers who worked on the publishing margins in the mid-twentieth century (Gürçağlar 2008). Unlike their colleagues in the Translation Bureau, they were not preoccupied with introducing western-inspired material into the national culture; rather they produced popular texts that appropriated well-known fictional figures—Sherlock Holmes or Mike Hammer—and set them in local situations, while showing a marked indifference towards the authorial provenance of the source texts. Tahir created new versions of Mike Hammer's work set in İstanbul, all of which appeared under a range of pseudonyms ("F. M. İkinci" or "the second" being one of them). Neither he nor Yurdatap valued fidelity; they were much more concerned to take advantage of the rapidly expanding market for locally published texts, often issued in serial formats. Yurdatap's version of Bram Stoker's *Dracula* was reshaped according to the narrative structure of a Turkish folk tale, with the emphasis on action and the fantastic over dramatic or lyric features (Gürçağlar 2008: 211). Using the term coined by Julie Sanders, we might describe them as "appropriations" in which the desire to meet the popular audience's demand took precedence over artistic motives (2006: 27). At the time when they appeared, however, they were described neither as translations nor adaptations but *romanlar* (novels)—a genre assigned by the publishers to short stories and novellas as well as larger works (Gürçağlar 2008: 248). In fact there is no equivalent word in Turkish for 'appropriations' or 'adaptations': depending on the context, the words *çevirmek* (to translate) or *hazırlamak* (to prepare verbally, either for spoken or written delivery) are generally employed. To 'adapt' translates either as *alışmak* (to get used to), *alıştırmak* (to get accustomed to) or *uyum sağlamak* (to suit a new purpose, as in the phrase, 'Adapting our native cuisine to suit the available food resource of our country'). André Lefevere remarked a long time ago that this untranslatability is due less to the lack of syntactic or morphologic equivalents, and more to do with the absence of poetological equivalents: "Language is not the problem. Ideology and poetics are, as are cultural elements that are not immediately clear, or seen as 'misplaced' in what would be the target culture versions of the text to be translated" (1990: 26). The Turkish word *uyum sağlamak* (to suit a new purpose) is the important term here: Tahir and Yurdatap did not write 'appropriations' or 'adaptations', but set out to create new texts of their own that consciously repudiated the notions of fidelity associated with the Translation Bureau's versions of the same texts. They wrote "indigenous books" (Gürçağlar 2008: 187), containing new terms and new characterisations in the target language that had little or nothing to do with the source texts. Gürçağlar invokes Gideon Toury's concept of "pseudo-translations" to describe them (2008: 244–246), based on the assumption that they were written for two culture-specific purposes; to meet the popular audience's demand for simple, well-told stories, and to prove the effectiveness of Kemal Atatürk's language reforms. Yurdatap and Tahir were but two examples of a popular movement for rewriting texts according to local conventions that dominated the cinema as well as book publishing. *Dracula* was remade as *Dracula in İstanbul* (*Drakula İstanbul'da*) in 1953, with the Christian iconography—for example the cross that kills the vampire—silently removed. This form of textual transformation continues to this day in various media outlets—especially television. Jonathan Lynn and Anthony Jay's award-winning comedy *Yes Minister/Yes Prime Minister* (BBC, 1980–1987) was recently remade for Turkish television, with the addition of new characters such as a comic tea-person, who regularly made unannounced entrances, delivered one or two wisecracks and left. The comedy *Ugly Betty* was transferred to İstanbul and ran for two seasons: while preserving the basic framework of the sitcom, it incorporated elements of melodrama (the struggle between good and evil, easily recognisable characters such as the innocent woman vs. the devious man) derived from *Yeşilçam*, the popular form of cinema that dominated the Republic of Turkey's cinema screens for four decades between 1950 and 1990.[4]

For Laurence's learners in the early 1990s, the concept of 'adaptation' meant two things: first, it was seen as a popular form of textual transformation that lacked the academic credibility associated with translation. To become a good translator, an individual needed to pursue a course of under- and postgraduate study to develop their capacity in both source and target languages, as well as learn translation theory. Only then would they have acquired sufficient experience to translate the source text 'properly'— keeping as close as possible to the author's perceived intentions. An adapter, on the other hand, had the freedom to manipulate the source text so as to accommodate the demands of the target audience—for example local readers or filmgoers. Perhaps more interestingly, the concept of 'adaptation' was perceived as a secondary interpretive process; something that took place once the translation had been accomplished. When Laurence's learners had finished translating *Separate Tables*, they tried—and mostly failed—to adapt it to their respective contexts.[5] Their understanding of 'adaptation' was somewhat paradoxical: on the one hand, it connoted freedom, giving writers (and readers) the power to construct their own texts with little concern for fidelity; on the other, it was seen as something inferior to translation, the kind of thing reserved for pulp fiction and mass-market media rather than the academy.

While this viewpoint is culture-specific, it has been trenchantly taken up by western Translation Studies scholars writing about adaptation: in 2007 Lawrence Venuti criticised Robert Stam's *Literature Through Film* (2005) on the grounds that Stam invoked "a dominant critical orthodoxy based on

a political position (broadly democratic, although capable of further specu-
lation . . . that the [adaptation] critic applies as a standard on the assumption that the film should somehow inscribe that and only that ideology"
(2007: 28).[6] Venuti proposes that Adaptation Studies should learn from
Translation Studies' example: rather than drawing on an author-determined
methodology, Translation Studies concerns itself with the "recontextualiz-
ing process . . . the creation of another network of intertwining relations
by and within the translation, a receiving intertext . . . [as well as] another
context of reception whereby the translation is mediated by promotion and
marketing strategies" (30).

However, Venuti's argument does not acknowledge the possibility that
the term 'adaptation' can be interpreted in different ways. The Turkish
educational theorist and head of primary education, İsmail Hakkı Tön-
guç, played an instrumental part in creating the Village Institutes, a bold
experiment designed to introduce mass education to the rural areas of the
Republic of Turkey between 1940 and 1954. The curriculum included
both practical (arts and crafts, agriculture) and academic (mathematics,
literature, science) courses, and included regular weekly meetings where
educators and learners collaborated on future plans. In his manifesto for
the project, published in 1944, Tonguç emphasised the importance of the
Institutes as a way of encouraging people to rely

> on their own assiduity. They do not strive to enter anything they can-
> not undertake or accomplish without the help of others. They believe
> in their creative work. They consider reading and educating themselves
> one of their primary missions . . . They *adapt* . . . as [one of their] main
> principles. They urge individuals comprising the nation to act in the
> same way. They strive to protect the positive values they possess under
> any given condition. (in Altunya 2012: 100, italics ours)[7]

Tonguç views adaptation as a process whereby individuals learn to come to
terms with the world and thereby acquire self-reliance, while at the same
time understanding the significance of community as a means of sustaining
the "positive values" of a nation. Tonguç continues, "[C]ooperation . . . is
an indispensable principle [of adaptation]. Apart from using common sense
and power, this principle provides interaction between individuals, groups,
and regions" (102). At the weekly meetings, everyone in the Institute discussed the extent to which "the goal [either academic or practical] had been
achieved, what the profits and losses are, what the reasons for failure (if
any) are, and how they can be overcome" (102). Feedback is an important
aspect of adaptation, so long as it is offered constructively in a mutually
supportive environment.

Yet it is also true that the act of translation can be viewed through a
similar psychological prism. The only way that translators can understand
the significance of their work is to rely on their 'somatic feel' for the source

text—for the sense of words, phrases and their meaning. They should question the way things look on a page and not worry about keeping close to what the source text's author wants to say; instead they should concentrate on what the author implies, even if that means going against what he or she holds most sacred. They should look beneath the source text's surface to discover what they believe is its basic meaning. By such means the translator can create an "imaginative construction" of the source text that the translator—and no one else—believes truly represents the whole (Robinson 1991: 156). They articulate their dreams, and at the same time intervene, subvert, divert and even entertain. They are transformed from "neutral, impersonal, transferring devices" into creative individuals in their own right, drawing on their personal experiences—emotions, motivations, attitudes, associations—and showing how such experiences "can contribute to the worlds they inhabit" (260). Both translators and adapters draw on the kind of transformative processes that are fundamental to human growth and development.

The link between translation, adaptation and psychological development can perhaps be better understood by looking at the work of the psychologist and educational theorist Jerome Bruner. In *Making Stories* he argues that all our transformative acts can be approached as narratives designed to render the strange familiar, transform uncertainty into certainty and normalise the unexpected. By such means individuals transmute experiences into "collective coin which "can be circulated . . . Being able to read another's mind need depend no longer on sharing some narrow or interpersonal niche but rather on a common fund" (2002: 16). Group interactions thrive on the interplay of narratives, on the sharing of common ideas that "come to terms with the breach [i.e., the unexpected or the uncertain] and its consequences", producing an outcome or resolution (17). Bruner expounds his theory by suggesting that narrative gives us the power to make sense of things, even when they don't appear to make much sense, citing the psychologists George A. Miller, Karl H. Pribram and Eugene Galanter to support his point. They believe that narratives are an expression of the desire to plan, "the elementary neuro-psychic unit of human consciousness and action" (28). Planning requires a working knowledge of how our world works and, more importantly, how others will react: "[T]hanks to the regularizing power of culture, our plans usually work out quite quietly and well" (28). This is why group interactions are vital, for it is only by regular association with others that we can (largely) guarantee the success of a plan or narrative. Telling others about ourselves and our feelings transforms our ideas of who we are, what happens, and explanations about what we are doing at any given moment into story form.

However, narratives do not always comprise the familiar; individuals often construct them in such a way as to "create a conviction of autonomy, that one has a will of one's own, a certain freedom of choice, a degree of possibility" (Bruner 2002: 78). This is what might be termed the desire for originality. In Bruner's view our concept of narrative creation is dominated by contradictory forces: autonomy (i.e., the desire to be original) and our commitment to group values (that frequently depend on sacrificing autonomy in favour of familiarity). How individuals resolve that conflict is very much down to choice: some create original narratives by freeing themselves from "precedent obligations" to the familiar and opting for "a self-generated peripeteia" instead (83). This may engender "new trends and new ways of looking at ourselves in the world" (84).

Bruner suggests that these competing narratives (original vs. familiar) help us make sense of our lives; they are the basis for communal life yet can simultaneously threaten those who try to sustain that community. Hence strategies have to be developed for dealing with such conflicts—for example legal systems that restrict "incompatible interests and aspirations" (2002: 93). As individuals, we can either accept such structures—that reinforce community values—or create "self-defining" stories of our own. Bruner invokes a term coined by Claude Lévi-Strauss to describe all human beings: they are "*bricoleurs*" (90)—improvisers, creators of narratives designed to "tell about ourselves to ourselves", while remaining loyal to the group networks surrounding them. Sometimes our narratives invoke "old stories" as a means of dealing with the unfamiliar; occasionally they incorporate entirely new stories of our own creation. More often than not they combine both elements.

In terms of learning issues, Bruner believes that good pedagogy consists of helping learners to discover their "good self" by constructing their own narratives (and thereby develop their abilities as *bricoleurs*)—as well as forging a lasting commitment to others. Selfhood without commitment "constitutes a form of sociopathy—the absence of a sense of responsibility to the requirements of a social being" (2002: 69). Group interactions refine our abilities to create original narratives—through feedback, for example.

Bruner's theory of narrative formation applies equally to the acts of translation or adaptation. Narratives are constructed from different source-texts and transformed into "collective coin" (Bruner's term) by means of a set of familiar conventions. These conventions vary according to context—Selâmi Munir Yurdatap and Kemal Tahir rewrote popular western classics to incorporate Turkish folk narratives. Through feedback from others involved in the process of disseminating and reprinting translations—particularly publishers—those narratives (whether adaptations or translations) are subsequently reshaped according to a "common fund" of beliefs that challenge the translator's status as a primary creative force, as well as affecting their ability to retain control of their own work. However, these constraints do not affect the potential for constructing new narratives. It is this mix of constraint and reward, exploitation and autonomy that renders translation and adaptation so fascinating.

However, this framework might prove difficult to implement in contexts where translation and adaptation are viewed as completely different.

This was certainly the case with another group of learners whom Laurence worked with in the 2010–2011 academic year, on a course titled 'Drama: Analysis and Teaching'.[8] For the most part the learners were accustomed to courses such as 'Translation', in which they were expected to translate texts from English to Turkish and vice versa, looking for the closest possible linguistic equivalents in creating their target texts. Their assessment was very much dependent on the educator's understanding of how 'faithful' their translations were to the source texts. Bearing this constraint in mind, Laurence dispensed with the notion of a content-based pedagogy (that required learners to read the text closely, translate it and subsequently comment on its themes) and asked them instead to think of a Shakespeare play as a basis for their personal development. What mattered was the ways in which individual learners consumed or adapted to the text. As long ago as 1934 John Dewey emphasised that a learner-centred approach is one in which "elements that issue from prior experience are stirred into action in fresh desires, impulsions and images" (65). Yet this stirring can only be achieved if learners understand the significance of the Shakespearean text to their development as individuals. Hence they should be encouraged to engage collaboratively with a variety of issues—textual, thematic, sociological, cultural—posed either by themselves or the educator.

Bearing this in mind, Laurence created a syllabus based on the learners' own experience: what they understood from a Shakespeare play depended very much on what they knew, believed and valued. It also involved interacting the learners' prior learning with his learning as an educator: for example by acknowledging their belief—reinforced throughout their educational careers—that translation was identified as a more 'academic' form of textual transformation than adaptation. The choice of plays was determined through negotiation: Laurence and his learners read through whatever Shakespeare plays they wished (either in English or in translation), and subsequently tried to convince other members of the class that their choice of play was the best. This was an interesting task, as the learners set aside their notions that a text had to be translated first before it could be understood, and looked at the plots instead. Some of them liked the rough-and-tumble of *The Comedy of Errors*, others the brutality of *Hamlet*. *The Comedy of Errors* was particularly popular; its setting in Ephesus was recognisable to learners brought up in the west of the Republic (Ephesus is about one hour's drive from İzmir). However it was decided collaboratively that the principal objective should be to select texts that could best fulfil the learning outcomes—in other words develop learner abilities and encourage self-reliance, as Tonguç recommends. Eventually the group settled on *Romeo and Juliet* and *Hamlet*, the subject matter of which seemed especially applicable to most learners' experiences. Familial rivalry forms the subject of innumerable popular filmed melodramas (with their roots in Yeşilçam) in the cinema and on television.

In determining how the plays would be approached, the group once again kept the learning outcomes in mind. The need to translate a text seemed less attractive when compared to the idea of creating new narratives inspired by the Shakespearean text. Different groups of learners chose one of the two plays—*Romeo and Juliet* or *Hamlet*—and devised a variety of approaches to adapting it. Some opted to subdivide into groups of two or three, each charged with the responsibility of rewriting one act at a time; others worked in larger groups to adapt the play as a whole. The emphasis throughout was on negotiation: learners made their own decisions as to which characters to retain and which to omit, and whether the plots needed simplifying or not. Laurence's role as educator was confined to that of a collaborator, offering feedback on the learners' various drafts and their subsequent rehearsals. The language of communication was left open: learners used either Turkish or English.

All the learners shifted the plays' locations from Verona and Denmark to the Republic of Turkey. This decision was not only inspired by their cultural backgrounds but also by their knowledge of the conventions of *Yeşilçam* melodramas; they wanted to show that they could have something to say both to themselves—as performers—as well as the audiences witnessing their performances. One example will serve to illustrate the kind of creative work the learners produced: one group of four girls (Seçil, Hande, Begüm, Hazal) rewrote the balcony scene in *Romeo and Juliet* ("You are more beautiful than the morning sun. You are more beautiful than the stars at night" (II.i.43 ff.). Juliet (Hazal) simpered, but her enjoyment was abruptly curtailed by the Nurse's (Begüm's) entrance, asking whether she wanted a cup of Turkish coffee to drink before going to bed. According to the nurse this was essential, as Juliet needed to have her fortune told before she could marry Paris. Juliet tried her utmost to put the Nurse off, while Romeo (Seçil) waited patiently below for her to return to the balcony. Eventually Romeo and Juliet parted, and Juliet returned to the Nurse, breathlessly urging her to "forget the coffee". In Juliet's view her destiny had already been determined; she did not need anyone to read her coffee dregs. In spite of her family's objections, she would marry Romeo.

Each group created a series of supporting materials designed to accompany their narratives—for example a series of questions that might be asked to audiences (or other groups in the class) that would prompt reflection on the themes of the plays—family, conflict, love and revenge. This scheme of work was inspired by the learners' desire for professional development; if they became educators in the future, and took their learners to a theatrical performance, how could they sustain interest on what was happening on stage?

This process of transforming the Shakespearean text resembled what the French-Canadian playwright Michel Garneau describes as "tradaptation", in which canonical texts are invested with new meanings designed to force the target culture to confront itself through exposure to the rewritten source text. Tradaptation involves processes of translation and adaptation that resist distinctions between the two (in Brisset 1988: 206). According to locally constructed definitions, the learners created an adaptation, not a translation, in which textual concerns mattered less than having the freedom to create new versions of the Shakespearean text. In truth, however, such value judgments hardly mattered: learners used their narratives to embark on a process of personal adaptation as Tonguç might have defined it. They used their experience of Shakespeare to develop abilities such as self-reliance, collaborative organisational thinking, negotiation and decision making.[9]

Tony's view of pedagogy has been greatly influenced by the model developed at Alverno College, Milwaukee that cultivates learner abilities throughout all its disciplines—communication, analysis, problem solving, valuing in decision making, social interaction, developing a global perspective, effective citizenship and aesthetic engagement (Anonym. 2011). The distinctive feature of this ability-based approach is that educators make explicit the expectation that learners should be able to do something with what they know. Alverno have also developed a multidimensional process of judging the individual in action. Their innovative assessment of both course-based and integrative assignments uses educators and trained assessors, often volunteers from the wider business community, to observe and judge a learner's performance based on explicit criteria. This kind of approach enables learners to respond to and shape the world in which they live.

As a freelance instructional abilities and institutional effectiveness consultant, working mostly with administrators and educators of English Language, Tony works to establish what might be described as cultures of "learnacy" based on the construction of new narratives. This approach is designed to develop what the psychologist Jean Piaget once defined as the ability of "knowing what to do when you don't know what to do" (1986: 45). Notions of teaching 'correct' English through grammar have been set aside; instead educators are encouraged to become involved in a process of co-creating learning objectives, lesson plans and modes of assessment, while at the same time being open to revising individual points of view. Creating such narratives should not only prevail amongst educators; it should encompass learners as well. As part of the group-focussed programme of study at Anadolu University's School of Foreign Languages (AU-SFL) in Eskişehir in the centre of the Republic of Turkey, Tony ran video-based classroom observation and feedback sessions on classes run by Çağdaş Gündoğdu, a teacher and head of one of the school's Learning Units. Gündoğdu recorded his impressions in a series of blog posts: in one class, for instance, Tony suggested that different types of interactions between learners might be introduced, moving away from the educator-centred method of teaching. The difference was pronounced: Gündoğdu wrote, "The students were real contributors. The lesson was smooth and there occurred no problems" (2012a). Gündoğdu also describes "a new path" of learning, in which learners were given the opportunity to make decisions for themselves. Another blog post explained what a difference this made to the classroom dynamics:

> [In the past] I helped them too much with the tasks [so] that they felt too comfortable, so that they did not feel the need to reveal their full potential to achieve what was expected of them . . . [now] I understand better at this very moment that a talented teacher is the one who leads learners to discovering their talents and using them to attain goals. (2012b)

In a third post Gündoğdu describes some activities designed to teach possessive adjectives; these were recorded on video, and learners were invited to comment on their own performances. One of them commented that "she was not really aware of what she was speaking; another pointed out that he really had no idea why [he was making mistakes], still another said . . . [he] thought it was the right thing to do because you [Gündoğdu] were not correcting". However another learner commented that perhaps they "would have stopped speaking" if the mistake had been corrected. This reflection session proved revelatory for educator and learners alike: Gündoğdu found out exactly how much time was spent explaining the purpose of the lesson, giving little or no time for collaborative learning. The experience was cathartic: "I figured out the real value of sharing, and I knew that could be done only with my colleagues but also with my students . . . Then I promise myself in this very post that I will always do more than my best to . . . help my students of any level discover their true potential" (2012c). In another blog-post, Aysun Güneş, Head of a Learning Unit at the same institution, describes her experience of working with Tony to create a team of educators over a nine-month period. The first few weeks were difficult: "we [the team] generally fight with the problems that arose. In this step people generally try to adapt themselves or accept the role entitled to them" (2012). The only way individuals could deal with any problem was to "ask some questions . . . and . . . criticize". The influx of new educators into the team raised further issues concerning "relationships and . . . [how] the community (within the organization) support how things are working or not working effectively".

Tony's work with educators emphasises collaboration as the source of change. Through continual negotiation and reflection, educators learn how to create new narratives based on alternative teaching and/or organisational styles, as well as acquiring a newfound sense of self-belief. This discovery spurs them on to further collaboration with fellow educators and learners alike. Tony's role as an educator is not to be judgmental, but to ask questions and make suggestions designed to prompt further reflection; this is what prompted such a change in Gündoğdu's pedagogical practice. For Tony's educators, as for Laurence's learners of Shakespeare, adaptation was not viewed as a textual practice, but rather a psychological process to help them come to terms with the world around them, as well as developing their abilities.

By treating one's disciplinary specialism as a springboard for creating new narratives, both textual and psychological, we believe that these case studies start to answer some important questions—such as justifying the importance of our respective subjects for educators and learners alike. We have also emphasised the importance of adapting or translating our experience as educators into something that proves significant for our learners, both intellectually and professionally. Finally, we have tried to show how learner responses form a significant component of the ways in which the courses are constructed, based on the belief that collaboration is a fundamental basis of change in the way educators and learners think about the purpose of their courses, both intellectually and professionally.

In a recent piece the Translation Studies scholar Dirk Delabastita proposes a threefold distinction between different levels of reality: the *status* of discursive phenomena (including translations and adaptations), which he defines as "what they are claimed to be or believed to be in a given cultural community"; their *origin* ("the real history of their genesis, as revealed by a diachronically oriented reconstruction"); and their *features* ("as revealed by a synchronic analysis, possibly involving comparisons") (2008: 235). This model allows for alternative conceptions of adaptation and translation, such as those discussed earlier on in our piece. Delabastita quotes his fellow scholar Theo Hermans, who emphasises the futility of "fixing stable units for comparison . . . of excluding interpretation, of studying translation in a vacuum" (in Delabastita 2008: 245). Delabastita offers instead "a conceptual tool to make such a discussion [of how translations and adaptations work in different contexts] more effective", by envisaging "all kinds of possible relationships between various kinds of 'translation' and various kinds of 'non-translation'" (245). The "radically open and atavistic view of translation" proposed in his model "ends up questioning the existence of Translation Studies as an autonomous discipline" (245). Although we do not believe that Translation Studies' future is in any danger, we share Delabastita's concern that both Translation and Adaptation studies need to negotiate difference, to understand how they are understood in various contexts. However, we also think that this process of negotiation is a complex one—involving textual, cross-cultural and psychological issues. Translation and adaptation are fundamental to the process of constructing knowledge for learners and educators alike. Hence pedagogy becomes extremely significant as a means of stimulating learning, developing abilities and promoting further research into the futures of both disciplines. By involving learners in every classroom exchange, we can work towards a better understanding of the essential concepts, issues and objectives of translation and adaptation, as well as acquiring a greater awareness of how they relate to one another.

NOTES

1. For more on the idea of intercultural practice, see Laurence Raw, "Intercultural Competence: Does it Exist?" in *Exploring Turkish Cultures* (Newcastle-upon-Tyne: Cambridge Scholars Publishing, 2011): 12–21.
2. Much of the following discussion about the translation-as-transfer model is based on Laurence Raw's essay "Identifying Common Ground," in Raw (ed.), *Adaptation, Translation and Transformation* (New York and London: Continuum, 2012): 5–8.
3. For an example, see Richard Philcox's essay "Fidelity, Infidelity, and the Adulterous Translator." *Australian Journal of French Studies* (2009). *Readperiodicals.com*. Web. Jul. 25, 2012.
4. For more on the Turkish *Ugly Betty*, see Laurence Raw, "Updating Popular Cinema: *Ugly Betty* on Turkish Television," in Janet McCabe and Kim Akass (eds.), *TV's Betty Goes Global: From Telenovela to International Brand* (London and New York: I. B. Tauris, forthcoming.
5. This model could also be used to describe Christopher Hampton's versions of Ibsen's *A Doll's House* (1975), and *An Enemy of the People* (1998), both of which are based on Michael Meyer's translations from the Norwegian.
6. In Stam's defence, he does point out in the introduction to the book that, by adopting "a broad intertextual as opposed to a narrow judgmental approach," his analysis will be "less moralistic, less implicated in unacknowledged hierarchies [. . .] oriented not by inchoate notions of 'fidelity' but rather by attention to specific dialogical responses, to 'readings,' 'critiques' and 'interpretations' and 'rewritings' of source novels" (Stam 5).
7. Despite their benefits, the Institutes were violently attacked by various pressure-groups. Conservatives opposed the idea of co-education, while landlords objected to the fact that many of their tenants were beginning to question the landlords' authority. In political terms, the Institutes were accused by right wing politicians of fostering a subversive, unruly, anti-traditional generation dedicated to Marxist values. Eventually the government bowed to pressure from the opposition and closed the Institutes down in 1954.
8. This account is based on Laurence's article "Shakespeare in Education: Creating Learning that Lasts." *Literature, Media and Cultural Studies Newsletter* 37 (July 2010): 19–23.
9. According to Derek Bok, this is what today's learners are looking for from any course: "[They] are more inclined to value education chiefly for its utility in achieving the material [and professional] success they regard so highly. For such students, useful skills matter more than ever" (Bok 2006: 36).

WORKS CITED

Anonym. 2011. 'The Eight Core Abilities: Abilities for Today and Tomorrow'. Alverno College, Milwaukee, WI. http://www.alverno.edu/academics/ouruniquecurriculum/the8coreabilities (accessed 12 April 2012).

Anonym. 2012. 'Faculty of Arts and Sciences: Department of Translation and Interpretation'. Atılım University Graduate Program 2012. http://mtb.atilim.edu.tr/grad_programs.php (accessed 25 July 2012).

Altunya, Niyazi. 2012. 'A General Overview of the Village Institute System'. In: Ekrem Işin (ed.), *Mindful Seed, Speaking Soil: Village Institutes of the Republic 1949–1954*. 2 vols. İstanbul: İstanbul Research Institute Publications.

Bok, Derek. 2006. *Our Underachieving Colleges: A Candid Look at How Much Students Learn and Why They Should Be Learning More.* Princeton, NJ: Princeton University Press.

Bozkurt, Bülent. 1998. 'The Future of English Departments in Private and State Universities'. *Hacettepe University Journal of English Literature,* 7, pp. 3–6.

Brisset, Annie. 1988. *A Sociocritique of Translation: Theater and Alterity in Quebec, 1969–1988.* Trans. Rosalind Gill and Roger Gannon. Toronto: University of Toronto Press.

Bruner, Jerome. 2002. *Making Stories: Law, Literature, Life.* Cambridge, MA: Harvard University Press.

Delabastita, Dirk. 2008. 'Status, Origin, Features: Translation and Beyond'. In: Anthony Pym, Miriam Shlesinger, Daniel Simeoni (eds.), *Beyond Descriptive Translation Studies: Investigations in Homage to Gideon Toury.* Amsterdam: John Benjamins, pp. 233–246.

Dewey, John. 1934. *Art as Experience.* New York: Minton, Balch and Company.

Drakula İstanbul'da [Dracula in İstanbul]. 1953 [2002]. Dir. Mehmet Muhtar. Perf. Ümit Deniz, Cahit İrgat, Ayfer Feray. And Film. DVD.

Gündoğdu, Güven Çağdaş. 2012a. 'Blessed With a Revelation!' *Teachers Reflect,* 29 May. http://teachersreflect.wordpress.com/2012/05/29/blessed-with-a-revelation (accessed 11 June 2012).

Gündoğdu, Güven Çağdaş. 2012b. 'Resurrection'. *Teachers Reflect,* 31 May. http://teachersreflect.wordpress.com/2012/05/31/resurrection (accessed 10 June 2012).

Gündoğdu, Güven Çağdaş. 2012c. 'What Makes You Happy?' *Teachers Reflect,* 2 June. http://teachersreflect.wordpress.com/2012/06/02/what-makes-you-happy-2/ (accessed 10 June 2012).

Güneş, Aysun. 2012. 'Building a Team Spirit at a State University in Turkey—2 (a Kind of Reflection)'. *Language Teaching Tips,* 6 June. http://languageteaching-tips.wordpress.com/2012/05/04/64 (accessed 17 Jun. 2012).

Gürçağlar, Şehnaz Tahir. 2008. *The Politics and Poetics of Translation in Turkey.* Amsterdam: Rodopi.

Lefevere, André. 1990. 'Translation: Its Genealogy in the West'. In: André Lefevere and Susan Bassnett (eds.), *Translation, History, and Culture.* London: Pinter Publishers, pp. 14–29.

Philcox, Richard. 2009. 'Fidelity, Infidelity, and the Adulterous Translator'. *Australian Journal of French Studies,* 47:1. http://www.readperiodicals.com/200901/2122679401.html#b. (accessed 25 Jul. 2012).

Piaget, Jean. 1986. *The Origin of Intelligence in the Child.* Trans. Margaret Cook. London: Routledge.

Raw, Laurence. 2010. 'Shakespeare in Education: Creating Learning That Lasts'. *Literature, Media and Cultural Studies Newsletter,* 37, pp. 19–23.

Raw, Laurence. 2011. 'Intercultural Competence: Does It Exist?' In: *Exploring Turkish Cultures.* Newcastle-upon-Tyne, England: Cambridge Scholars Publishing, pp. 12–21.

Raw, Laurence. 2012. 'Identifying Common Ground'. In: Laurence Raw (ed.), *Adaptation, Translation, and Transformation.* London: Continuum, pp. 1–20.

Raw, Laurence. Forthcoming. 'Updating Popular Cinema: Ugly Betty on Turkish Television'. In: Janet McCabe and Kim Akass (eds.), *TV's Betty Goes Global: From Telenovela to International Brand.* London: I. B. Tauris.

Robinson, Douglas. 1991. *The Translator's Turn.* Baltimore: Johns Hopkins University Press.

Robinson, Douglas. 1997. *Western Translation Theory From Herodotus to Nietzsche.* Manchester, England: St. Jerome Publishing.

Separate Tables. Dir. John Schlesinger. Perf. Alan Bates, Julie Christie, Irene Worth, Claire Bloom. HBO/ HTV Wales, 1983. DVD.

Shakespeare, William. 2005. 'Romeo and Juliet'. In: John Jowett, William Montgomery, Gary Taylor, and Stanley Wells (eds.), *The Oxford Shakespeare: The Complete Works*. 2nd ed. Oxford: Clarendon Press, pp. 369–401.

Sinfield, Alan. 1989. *Literature, Politics, and Culture in Post-War Britain*. Oxford: Basil Blackwell.

Stam, Robert. 2005. *Literature Through Film: Realism, Magic, and the Art of Adaptation*. Malden, MA: Blackwell Publishing.

Tymoczko, Maria. 2007. *Enlarging Translation, Empowering Translations*. Manchester, England: St. Jerome Publishing.

Venuti, Lawrence. 2007. 'Adaptation, Translation, Culture'. *Journal of Visual Culture*, 6.1, pp. 25–44.

Yes Minister/Yes Prime Minister.1980–1987. Dirs. Peter Whitmore, Sidney Lotterby. Perf. Paul Eddington, Nigel Hawthorne, Derek Fowlds. BBC. DVD.

10 Scenic Narration
Between Film and Theatre
Ildikó Ungvári Zrínyi

INTRODUCTION

Scenic narration is one of the most exciting problems of visual drama-turgy. Which are the elements that bear the burden of telling a story, and which are the fragments that replace the explicit form of the whole story? Postdramatic or contemporary theatre widens the possibilities of interpret-ing the signs: the possibility of story(telling) does not die, only that in its fragmented status it is more suitable to the pluralism of a contemporary worldview. Hans-Thies Lehmann states that "within the de-hierarchized use of signs post-dramatic theatre establishes the possibility of dissolving the logocentric hierarchy and assigning elements other than logos and lan-guage" (2006: 93), and this applies more to the visual dimension in the sce-nic narration. It is obvious from these statements that the pictorial and the performative turn are responses for the crisis or even the end of logocentric thinking, giving way to the flow of images, on the one hand, and to actions happening in a performative space between the bodily presence of specta-tor and the actor, on the other. It is from this double point of view that we examine narration in an intermedial performance, in a specific theatrical language situated between film and theatre. The forms of visual narration in this case function through recycling, which is in close relation to adapta-tion and translation, and as the analysis will refer to, with other forms that work with the appropriation of texts, be they verbal or scenic ones.

The process of image production is investigated in the following train of thought from a communicational-anthropological point of view. Today's audiencing uses more and more complex devices to decrease or even elimi-nate the distance between actors and spectators, involving the senses to a greater extent. Audiencing appears to be an objectifying and objectified position at the same time, and these dynamics are widely explored by con-temporary theatre. As a matter of fact, this kind of reciprocity is grasped in the definition of theatre by Luke van den Dries, who states, "Theatre is the production of human (inter)action in a common operation executed by both actors and spectators, in the course of which both partners could be considered as producer and product of the other" (in Vanhaesebrouck

2004). Thus this relation gives room to a complex, mutually creating process, which unmakes/annuls the spectator's passive gaze, and the process of receiving images becomes a specific one.

Hans Belting, the author of *An Anthropology of the Image* (2011), says that all that we see is interpreted on the basis of our image-experiences. From this point of view, bodily motion and the flow of the image-movement continue a dialogue with the spectator, who is willing to receive the still images, while being guided by mental images. In the process of reception, the images are continuously melting and slipping over one another, their multiple relation creating a wide field of perception and interpretation, which gives birth to unusual relations, intertextual references and synaesthetic[1] experiences. Those images which are finally emphasised are recorded by the receiver, not on the spot, but in their past forms, for, as Belting says, "in the enigma of the image presence and absence are inseparably interwoven" (33).

The images created this way always have a *punctum*, which, according to Barthes, is that part of the image which attracts or wounds and touches the observer, while the *studium* is the conventional description of the things represented on the surface of a photograph (1981). In the case of theatre, finding the punctum is an event, and the images of the movement being melted together, after a rhizomatic stage the punctums of the images form the knots of visual narratives.[2] In ritual theatre the relation of the punctums happens according to the well-defined order of liturgical language. On the contrary, in postmodern theatre according to Helga Finter, the affects belonging to the punctum lead to inner experience, perceptive passion (1985).

Images can be filmic images, and Finter speaks about an overall characteristic of the filmic eye and montage in postmodern theatre (1985). Such images like in Wilson's or Purcarete's oeuvre create the terrain of intermediality, that is the land between different media, or at least two: film and theatre. However, postmodern theatre uses not only the combination of these two, but also different types of historical media in the midst of contemporary theatre (e.g., the mousetrap scene in Mugur's *Hamlet*, where the Renaissance dumb show is placed in the medium of a contemporary performance language). This example of a historical theatre genre and its medium is identified by a distinct place, with characteristic poses and gestures, body usage, costumes as opposed to the postmodern language of the whole performance. Such remediation[3] appears in a puppet show scene and some market place theatre forms in Serban's *Cries and Whispers*, the analysis of which performance follows on the next pages.

What we call 'theatre media' in the examples used above is not identical with a genre or style, but it is a way of communicating in the frame of a specific theatrical genre, and according to the culturally canonised and technically determined forms of communication. Because of this last characteristic, it is difficult to grasp the functioning of the medium: Dieter

Mersch says a medium is characterised by a certain materiality that never shows itself; the medium does not draw attention to its own materiality (2004). In the same sense Samuel Weber speaks about the scenic medium: he considers it a means which "effaces itself and thus be defined by the quality of being diaphanous, or transparent" (2004: 100). In the following train of thoughts we will use the term *theatre medium* as a means or a channel, the functioning of which is hidden by the fact that it mediates theatrical events by culturally (and theatrically) canonised forms, between which there are very close relationships in a given period of time, and this is due to the specific (technical) possibilities of communication characteristic to the given era. For example, cultural practices in ancient Greek culture show certain connections among them, which become obvious for us if we examine the way of using spaces, the characteristic perception (some senses being more active than others) and so on. McLuhan states the first period of communication was an oral one and was dominated by the ear and hearing (this is the tribal period in McLuhan's theory).[4] This is true in a way to ancient Greek rituals and theatre as well, where spoken word was very important, but we must admit that the image (of the dancing chorus in the orchestra and the heroes on the *proskenion*) became more and more important as the presentation took place in huge theatres (the Greek *theatron* meaning 'place of seeing'). Very important from the point of view of the medium was that the scenic structure and its image were ordered by the convention of dancing rituals before the temples of the Greek gods, the crowd dancing in front of the building. To turn back to the question of the senses and the size of the place, in the ideological event when the tetralogies were presented, the hearing component of the ritual structure was modified by the huge auditorium, and by transforming the participants into an audience sitting in their assigned seats. Although the spatial structure remained the same, the proportions changed and influenced not only audience's perception, but also the transmission of energy between the spectators and actors/chorus. A considerable part of information was transmitted via images and the mediation of energy happened similarly through images.

What is important, as the example above illustrates, is that it is not only the relations given by seeing, hearing, smelling and touching, in other words the kinetic, proxemic structures in a theatre medium (the distance between the performers, whether they can touch each other, what can they see from a specific angle—the whole or just a fragment; the relation and possibility of interaction of the actors and spectators etc.) which are important, but also the conventions which produce theatricality and which determine the usage of the living body and its gesture scenarios,[5] the production of images and the circulation of energies between the actors and the audience.[6] The conventions are a result of how, from the use of the theatrical signs, within which the most important and complex is the actor's living body, specific media arise. The body functions as an analogue code, therefore it is difficult to examine the signs it engenders;

but it offers multiple possibilities to analyse its functioning in terms of the performance, of the ceremonial play and of the anthropological entities, which differ from epoch to epoch. For instance, the scene from *Cries and Whispers* where Maria, one of the three sisters, examines her face and body in the mirror of the folding screen, would not function in a proscenium arch theatre but only in a small studio hall, where the spectators sit so close to the scene that they can see their own faces behind Anna's face in the mirror. The situation is similar to a marketplace scene, where the masquerader shows various amazing things (the folding screen is pushed from behind by Anna, the servant)—and the doctor is explaining what one should see in the picture. This way, the medium of the performance is shaped by the conventions of the marketplace theatre: one can discover the situation of the film audience, and, to some extent, that of the museum visitor's, who is looking at a moving installation. Ways of viewing are always decisive in the identification of a theatre medium. We must mention here, that the whole scene happens in the semi-dark and the object of viewing is composed by a living body and a folding screen (an object) and the moving images, which makes the whole scene function in a kind of aestheticised marketplace medium.

It is instructive/edifying to follow how these media are created in the scenic language of a performance. What is interesting about this attempt of adaptation—*Cries and Whispers* directed by Serban in 2010—is that it does not simply use a film excerpt but that it recycles the filmic material into both a filmic performance language with its own medium and a theatrical performance language with its medium. These two media appear within the same performance, curiously in the same place at a given period of time and still very distinct. As we shall see, recycling is a form of adaptation which makes the coexistence of these two media possible.

RECYCLING FILM IN THE MEDIUM OF THEATRE

The performance *Cries and Whispers* at the Hungarian Theatre of Cluj[7] gives the actors the possibility to play multiple identities: the story is a rehearsal and a *making of* preparation for shooting the film *Cries and Whispers*. Andrei Şerban, the Romanian-born American stage director, works with a Hungarian company from Transylvania. In an interview, Şerban tells us that he often looks at theatre with a film-director's eye, hiding behind a fictitious camera.[8] The idea of presenting the filmmaking process widens the frame of the play and creates a prologue to the play (in the foyer) which thematises the process of creation. Storytelling thus allows the interruption of the main narrative and the building into the performance of some texts from the memories of Bergman, *Laterna Magica*, and a specific stage language is formed, giving room both to the filmic elements and to real theatrical situations and events.

Thus the play begins in the foyer, where a catwalk stage is placed, all along the foyer with Bergman's chair on it. The actors step into the play with their own (Hungarian) actor identity: the main actor, Zsolt Bogdán, is having personal discussions with his acquaintances from the audience around the catwalk, then as he climbs onto the catwalk, he enters the role of Bergman and distributes the roles of the film to the actresses—some of them saying that they have played similar roles at the Theatre from Cluj. Then Bogdán, now in the role of Bergman, invites the audience to participate in the creation of a film inside the red room. From that moment on the actors are playing Swedish actors and a Swedish stage director, who are in the middle of rehearsing the film *Cries and Whispers*. And they step into the roles of Bergman's film heroes—Anna, Karin, Maria, Agnes—while Bogdán plays not only the role of Bergman, but also that of the doctor, Karin's and Maria's husband, sometimes at the same time, using two chairs and two suit jackets. Beyond these three levels of the play there is a fourth one: the ideal level of the film, which is shown only for a few minutes at the end.[9]

Inside the red room—which reminds us of a theatrical space for there are rows of chairs on one side of the room—there are props to create the illusion of filmmaking: a camera, a clapperboard, an assistant in a red kimono continuously producing a voiceover. But the play often makes the impression of a theatre rehearsal as well, and the performance uses both languages. Thus, besides the fact that they play many roles, the actors' identities and skills are burdened by being go-betweens, mediating between the pictorial language of film and the performative language of theatre. Şerban recycles the story and the film in many ways: the order of the scenes is overthrown and he includes texts and stories from Bergman's autobiography. We follow here Carlson's classification of postmodern theatrical recycling (which speaks as a first case of well-known situations, plot, well-known heroes and experiences, which is used at full length in *Cries and Whispers* (2003).

The second way of recycling things is with ironic purposes. Şerban uses this in those moments where he treats Joachim's death scene ironically—here the bodkin is revealed to be a false one, and the tragic pathos is suddenly transformed into civil laughter and badinage of the actors. Another example is the puppet-theatre-like scene after the burial, where Bergman plays the role of the two brothers-in-law simultaneously, with the help of two suit jackets, chairs and extra mimes. The story as a whole is not treated with irony, for as Şerban states, the performance is meant to be an homage to Bergman. Both examples show that, on the one hand, recycling in most of the cases goes hand in hand with intertextuality, and on the other, that the scenic text allows a playfulness, which in most cases, due to the ironic detachment, results in a change of media.

Carlson's third type of postmodern recycling is based on those experiences of the spectator which are used by the theatre from a commercial point of view: advertising a certain type of story (a romantic one, or, on the contrary, one full of horror scenes), certain famous actors, playwrights, stage directors, and so on using their fame to appeal to the nontraditional theatregoing public. Andrei Şerban's fame is used to advertise the performance of *Cries and Whispers* and references are made to both his status as cult director as well as theatre director. Carlson's recycling theory is useful because it allows the questioning of elements, situations, stories and artistic interpretation to be recycled from the viewpoint of the here-and-now of the theatrical performance. Recycling always implies appropriation as well as intertextuality, and, of course, both recycling and intertextuality are in relation with other postmodern techniques, such as bricolage, remake, adaptation, pastiche, palimpsest and so on.

The performance thus offers the actors the possibility to use different theatrical languages: recycling and intertextuality offer changing the various fictitious and real identities. The use of the text is another component, for verbal text is completed and very often overwhelmed by nonverbal sounds, cries, whispers, ticking of clocks and other nonverbal elements, such as gestures and images. A curious convention is introduced by the voiceover, which continuously tells the audience what the actors are doing, while they often do not do what the voice says they do. Translation somehow becomes one of the main themes of the performance: translating theatre into film, Hungarian actor to Swedish actor, text to gesture and so on. The whole text of the performance is continuously translated into Romanian, and the final film excerpt from the original film directed by Bergman has no translation, and is projected in the place where the former Romanian translation appeared.

SITUATIONS, FRAGMENTS OF EXPERIENCE

Şerban challenges some conventions of audiencing, thus starting a recycling process from the beginning. The performance place itself is a proposal for using a new theatre language, for it is a new studio hall with seventy-five seats and no stage, where spectators and actors are close to each other and the space is not governed by the logocentric inheritance of classical perspectivalist theatres. This is due to the fact that the playing area is wide and not too deep, and thus offers different angles for the spectators instead of one privileged perspective. It does not offer those logocentric, text-based models of identification as in the case of classical text-theatre but it offers more immediate forms such as market play theatre, Brechtian theatre, cinematic theatre and so on.

In the performance there are recycled experiences connected to theatrical genres and media which are created on the borderline of theatre and everyday theatricality—for at the beginning the spectators get museum slippers which remind them of their museum experiences; there is a catwalk that reminds them of their fashion show experiences, but also the marketplace experiences, where stars and exceptional people and magic appear on a platform. The platform always creates a multiple theatrical medium, where actors, ventriloquists, contortionists and magicians appear very close to the spectators. In accordance with the medium, various states of the actors are exposed as well as various positions for the spectators. This is exactly what Şerban wanted: to break the classical pattern of audiencing, by making the spectators stand, lean on the wall, sit on the edge of the catwalk. In this way he deconstructs the medium of the classical performance in favour of the marketplace scenario. The barker, played by Bogdan/Bergman, moves freely in the space, he climbs the red wall and appears on top of it, speaking from there to the actors who stand on the podium, and to the audience, who stand beneath him: this reminds us of the gods standing on the *theologeion* in the ancient Greek model—Bergman's status would be that of God.

When going into the theatre hall, the spectator may identify personal experiences connected with Japanese culture and Noh Theatre: in the red room there are folding screens, little black table and two assistants in red kimonos. The first assistant moves in the space according to the representation of non-being of characters in the Noh theatre, she is the person who produces a continuous voiceover.

RECYCLING OF IMAGES

The play in the foyer thus offers to the audience various ways of identification through its different experiences belonging to different media. It offers various statuses and identities to the actors, too—from civilian to the Cluj actress whose roles in the past are similar to the one she is performing now, to the Swedish actor's status, and in the end they become spectators of the Bergman's Swedish film which is projected onto the wall.

Şerban's images are characterised by hauntedness and past-like appearance: with the help of a the fog machine, images become signs of remembrance and the Bergman film quotation appears in the end as an afterimage, for it is past-like compared to the events on the stage. The image bears the pattern of the wall, thus the theatrical room appears through the filmic image.[10] Filmic images come into being due to the work of lights: the gestural space of the red room is a sensuous space, where the light brings close detail to what otherwise would not be seen by the theatre audience—the space is made utterly perceptible by the continuous play and alteration of closeness and distance, of the ticking of clocks and whispers. The character of Bergman mixes the theatrical reality by means of theatre before our eyes. A good example of this process is when he, by the power of conviction and fantasy, transforms the directorial chair into the Chinese emperor's throne and back again.

Bogdan/Bergman uses the same theatrical methods to initiate Agnes into death with the symbolic use of a thin scarf: he covers her with the scarf soaked with clay, as if he was going to make a death-mask, then he brushes the paint on Agnes's face, using painfully practical gestures. Although he initiates her into death by these gestures, the declaration of death does not mean the end. Though her eyes are being closed and candles lit, her life does not end, and as her body has been injected with death, this throws doubt and ambiguity over the living bodies—they need to prove they are alive. Agnes's body hangs on Maria's body, and Maria tries to get rid of this indefinably elusive burden, then calls Anna with despair, who takes her into her arms and draws her to her naked breasts, as if she suckled her. Bogdan/Bergman only blows out the lights when Agnes calms down in Anna's love. This complex symbolism alters spatial perception, subverts the order of life and death, just like the scene where Agnes as Agnes from the film (and not as an actress at the rehearsal) steps to the spectators and takes hold of their hands. Light is the means of this radical subversion, the scandal of missing from life and still being there: yellow light is cast upon her face when she is dying (see Figure 10.1). This yellow light is cast on the faces of her sisters as well, when they surround the dead body, and due to the power of the symbol, we feel they are also dead. When the priest says his prayer over the dead body, and is imploring the soul to intercede with God, yellow light falls on his face, then turns into green and disappears in the centre of the face. A few moments later Karin is cast in the dead-yellow light, when she looks at the glass shard, this is the shard she later uses to stab her pubis, and this suggests the painful secret of her dying marriage.

Figure 10.1 Agnes and the yellow light (photo: Daniela Dima; reproduced with kind permission of the Hungarian Theatre of Cluj).

Perception is directed in this strange context by the continuous change of viewpoints: Bogdan also achieves this change with his specific gesture with which he tries to capture the sight, to identify images, to compress into image what is so rich in human life situations. The function of the gesture would be to identify things (this is characteristic of the theatrical context), and the gesture results in images that are outlined and frozen or simply created by light: Karin rubs her temple, the mother appears in the fog; Karin is looking at the shard, the doctor gives an injection, Maria's face in red, Agnes's face in pain—images that have their own *punctums*, as a photo or film image does, and they are separating from the body and creating a virtual space, which is characteristic of cinema, and which opens up the space of the red room in all directions (similarly to the hypertext, hyperrealities, but also to the life mediated by new media). The technique of the performance language is to show the real place in a live manner, then sublimate it into images, and then to re-open it into countless new images and realities, thus creating the multitude of viewpoints. To this technique belongs the projecting of faces and their shadows on the wall, doubling in this way the perception of the same person. Bergman sometimes deliberately creates illusion with the help of the fog machine— Bergman carefully enfolds with fog the image of the mother, the figure of Anna leaning over the cradle of the baby (these images do not lack irony: Şerban mocks that functioning of remembrance which beautifies everything). And similar to a reflexive floor, there appear images that stress the self-reflexivity of the space: the folding screen that is often moved in the room reflects the image of various fragments of the audience. In these cases the folding screen is a mirror, but when it is illuminated, it becomes transparent and spectators lose their image in the mirror. The same thing happens when Maria examines the wrinkles on her own face in the mirror, and the audience sees her face getting older and their own faces in the same mirror which is moving. These continuous changes of the viewpoints draw our attention (just like Bergman's framing gesture) upon the fact that one always sees sights seen by others or visible to others, in the process of vanishing and transforming.

Thus light creates and delimits places, cuts images—lots of images: their separation from the place and the body means deterritorialisation. The human face deterritorialises from the body anyway, say Deleuze and Guattari, just like the map from the earth's body (1987: 170–172). The territoriality is the staying, the dwelling[11]—but these images become estranged by the crisp light. The dead masque put on the face also has deterritorialising power. The refrain or *ritornel* is that formation (in the sense of rhythm, nursery rhyme, musical repetition)[12] that would introduce rhythm into the faces—but Maria's face cannot be saved from the masques of getting older and becoming unprincipled, characterless, which makes its reflection in the mirror ambiguous.

The light, the use of close-ups, has the effect of filmic solutions; nevertheless they result in a complex sight, for in this medium of theatre the spectator can see not only the face in the image cut out by light, but the rest of the body, too, in a different light, as part of a different reality. The images emphasised by the light create a language that tells the initial story in another medium, calling for the filmic remembrance of the spectator, and the filmic images are created in Bergman's style, holding out the close-ups. Here we can find the characteristics of pastiche and the recycling of images which are created in Bergman's style but in different timing (a timing which functions according to the principles of the stage, therefore they are shorter than Bergman's silences). In the process of recycling images arise that are supposed, invented images, nonexistent memories. They are a result of the reconstruction of film shooting, and here we realise that these are variants which are part of the process of recycling; variants of the same situation do not help the story to emerge, because of their coordinating nature, and because they exclude the possibility of the linear storyline.

VIEWPOINT AND NARRATION

Şerban's handling of space and lights in relation to Brojboiu's set creates many simultaneous points of view which are characteristic of twentieth- and twenty-first century-theatre as spatial art (it also may be a characteristic of ritual theatre, as we described it in the first part of the chapter), and this is the result of a plurality of visual narratives—most of these images and viewpoints are not allowed by the Proscenium Arch model, and many of them are not characteristic to alternative or studio theatre forms either. From this context the landscapes of faces and details are outlined, nevertheless they cannot form an autonomous film narrative—although during the so-called 'shooting of the film' there is a voiceover (the assistant is reading the instructions) which follows the images created in the film style. This hypnotic sound doesn't really strengthen the film-like character; as a matter of fact, it undermines the status of the text, for performers often act in contrast (or do not act at all, or give variants of the action) as compared to the content of the text. Dominance of the text is in this way undermined and produces moments of exceptional theatrical delight. This way the distance of film image and theatre is thematised, and the deterritorialised images live their ongoing life in a patchwork-like context, in a medial polyphony, where the process of recycling and pastiche de-centres and re-creates the original film situations.

A good example of this functioning is Agnes's agony: it is presented with many viewpoints, creating many kinds of realities—for example when Bogdan/Bergman looks at the girls from behind—we see the work of the observer, too, but it is impossible to identify with it (see Figure 10.2). Or

Figure 10.2   The sisters, Bergman and Anna (photo: István Biró; reproduced with kind permission of the Hungarian Theatre of Cluj).

when Anna, the maid, is the observer, she is emphasised as a picture, and her face is deterritorialised, while Bergman, the eternal observer, falls back into dimness—and we cannot assume any of these viewpoints. Inasmuch as this room is like a *camera obscura*, in which the body of the observer is situated in its space, then it obviously means the fall of perspectivism—but at the same time it gives room to another kind of perception. Thus space becomes an intensely perceptive space: the ticking of clocks is amplified, the reflexive red surface auto-reflects until the furniture is covered by white sheets. The mirror-like red coating preserves its reflexivity only in the moments when there is light—dim scenes are ruled by a different order. The *camera obscura* model is contested by the fact that the audience's seats in the space form few but wide rows: the image cannot be in proper perspective, therefore the spectators see the details close to them from one angle, and those far from them from a different angle.

Knots of the narratives are formed not only by the clear and frozen images that have their distinguished *punctums* (such as the shard in Karin's hand, Agnes crying, with her mouth wide open). Dim moments also have their narrative value: sometimes they are well-worked-out images like the image of the naked Agnes after having been washed, or the sleeping Agnes and Anna; at other times a short sequence has the value of a narrative knot, for example when Maria looks at her face in the folding screen which is moving and serves as a mirror. The moving of the folding screen is an important, performance-like element of the scene, and it produces the rhizomatic multiplying of the images.

BETWEEN IMAGES AND SOUNDS: THE MEDIAL TERRITORY

The medium remains outside the images—outside the well-defined world of faces, postures—yet it is connected with the language of gestures and movements characterised by the original inconstancy and discursivity of the khora (see below). The formation of the medium occurs with the help of a strong, sense-provoking context; thus we may speak about different realities created by the continuous delimitation of a territory within the specific medium—we may call it medial territorialisation. Details outlined by the light (face, movement, poses) leave behind them a medium that is getting close to the language of gestures and movements. Theatre appears as a complex state which is prelingual and pre-expressive. The mediating character of the performance can be grasped when we see the images and hear the instructions in parallel, and perceive the gestures materialising between them which detach themselves from the image and try to recycle them. To grasp this phenomenon, we must turn to the *ritornel* (refrain) again.

The refrain in Deleuze and Guattari's conception is a territorialising assemblage that is transformed into variation by the rhythm: the refrain constructs rhythmic faces and sound landscapes, thus delimiting a territory, which at the same time makes the transition to deterritorialisation.[13] The refrain is a territorial assemblage in which "forces of chaos, terrestrial forces and cosmic forces" confront each other and converge in it (1987: 312). The refrain turns into variation owing to rhythm—rhythm and chaos are born in the in-between (313).

According to Hannes Böhringer, Nietzsche's teaching about Dionysian-Apollonian music and the eternal recurrence unite in the refrain (2009: 31). Böhringer, interpreting Nietzsche, states that the Apollonian music is what Deleuze and Guattari call the construction of a wall of sound, the building of the abode and the marking of a territory (1987: 311). Nietzsche connects the beautiful illusion of the world of dreams, inner fantasies and light to this. The Dionysian music is a labirynth, the privilege of the ear: "[S]ound invades us, impels us, drags us, transpierces us"—according to Nietzsche's ideas, it causes "ecstasy and hypnosis" (348). In Nietzsche's ideas the characteristics of Dionysian art are movement, dance, song and the release of nature's forces.

In *Cries and Whispers*, the above detailed medial context may be able to create both the Dionysian world of gestural language, action, movement, cries and whispers, and the Apollonian order of the gaze, denoted by strong lights, sight and illusion, the pictorial articulation, the aristocratic ticking of clocks. ("the refrain is a prism, a crystal of space-time" that "acts upon that which surrounds it"; Deleuze and Guattari 1987: 348). Such distinction of the theatrical and filmic language according to the classical dichotomy does not hold true to the world outside the performance—but it seems functional regarding this scenic language. The hurting of each other, Karin's hurting of herself, occurs in the individual world, in the life of lonely figures, in the light which accordingly seems to be negative; where

Figure 10.3   Bergman (photo: István Biró; reproduced with kind permision of the Hungarian Theatre of Cluj).

against the ritual washing of the dying woman, nakedness in a liminal space, Agnes and the nurse's last scenes take place in the dimness, in the world of bodily touch and closeness.

Bergman, the artist and director, gets closer to the events with his peculiar gesture embracing both worlds. He forms a frame with his fingers, a frame which is gestural and pictorial at the same time (see Figure 10.3). He works with the telephoto lens, but he also uses the fog machine to create illusion. The artist Bergman creates, actuates, watches or even deconstructs this world.

THE PLAYING FIELD AND ITS SURFACE

The khora[14] in Julia Kristeva's interpretation is a constantly changing articulation—an understanding and maternal, nourishing space, prelingual—and characterised by co-ordination (1984). The khora is the guidance of drives, says Kristeva; it may be compared only with vocal and kinetic rhythm. It shows the medial world of life and death which may contain both life and death—the harsh life may also be part of it with its terrifying face and smell of blood (e.g., Anna, after finishing her prayer, blows out the candle and starts eating an apple with rough and instinctive gestures).

Khora here appears not only as a place which is at the same time mirror and reflexive surface, it is also a place that needs to be protected, a place that is as red as blood (just like in the film), and it refers to life, to creation, but also to death. Plato's *Timaeus* discusses khora in relation to the foster mother, the nurse. Indeed, the place in *Cries and Whispers* is a feminine place for four women: it is a maternal, nourishing space where in the dim light Anna draws Agnes to her naked bosom and after her death she breast-feeds the girl who cannot die. This place loses its mirror-surface, generating tension when it is drawn into semi-darkness—there are shadows everywhere, and when light falls on things, they reflect it brilliantly. Agnes's deathbed is shown as a floating ship in the bright light which makes objects and shadows visible, interpretable forms. In the process of Şerban's recycling, the place and its medium, which in Bergman's film is "all-receptive" (to use Kristeva's term), gets quotation marks and is enclosed by the sharply articulated world of images and mirrors where the surfaces of the objects are estranged and hostile: the mirror that shows aging, Karin's knife and her V-shaped sleeves, the shard in her hand and so on. These objects are the props of the three sisters' life full of lies, compromises, lack of love: the dwelling and its furniture cannot abolish this strange and dangerous reflection; khora appears here as a masked bearer of imprints. It is not a receptive surface anymore: the rigid and inhuman or misinterpreted systems of culture estrange it and cover the khora with their images and reflections. A cruelly beautiful picture expresses this complex state of affairs: the mother-like Anna embraces Agnes who is weary of dying, while we know Anna's motherhood is mere self-delusion for her child lives only in her memories (see Figure 10.4).

The khora's resistance and mask break off in moments of human direct-ness, in the scenes with Anna and Agnes, for example when the no-longer-living Anna grabs the hands of the spectators; or during the darkness of

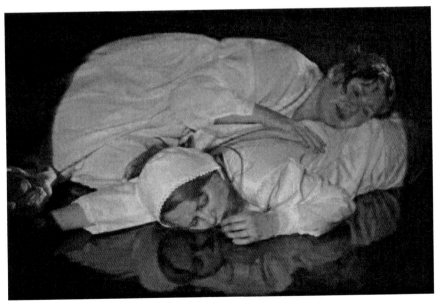

Figure 10.4 Agnes and Anna (photo: István Biró; reproduced with kind permission of the Hungarian Theatre of Cluj).

the film shooting, which refers to the process of creation (of both theatrical and cinematographic oeuvres), sometimes quite obviously in the case of the artistic confessions of the stage director, Bergman. The khora becomes synonymous with the life-giving, creative ground, which in Kristeva's opinion precedes the evident, the verisimilar, and is the continuous recommencement (1984).

THE RITORNEL AND THE MEDIUM

The rhythm of the performance is determined by the rapidly adopted convention, that during the 'rehearsals', the rhythmic light of the two reflectors outlines the scenes, images and characters from the process of the play; this rhythm creates time as well: when Bergman stops the rehearsal, the limelight disappears, the scene is illuminated (and very often the audience's seats, as well), and the director speaks to the audience and interprets some moments and situations. The interpretations and instructions often break moments of high tension—such as when the director finds Agnes' howling is false; he postpones Joachim's death, offering two variants, and the bloody scene transforms into some convivial joking around. The Deleuizian refrain is a striving for the (ideal) form (which is a characteristically European story), and this is obtained by the recycling of Bergmanesque film images, using pastiche. This filmic narrative thread is submitted to variations and to comments, thus from the intermezzos highlighting the artist's human problems, and from the observer's continuous presence a parallel language is created—and this strengthens a minor discourse[15] represented by the refrain: in its field man lives not point by point, but moves without beginning and end (Deleuze and Guattari 1987: 498). As the song is connected to the intermezzo (Böhringer 2009: 31), the intermezzo and ritornel are also connected to the terrain appropriated by light, but it is not subordinated to anything. Forms and conventions are born in this refrain—on the one hand, the images, on the other, the movement and gesture, as the equivalents of Apollonian and Dionysian art. The refrain, which is a continuous pre-articulation movement, to use Böhringer's expression, is characterised by the dimension of becoming; it crosses the pastiche-line, determining the way of recycling, up to the presentation of the 'ideal' image, the film excerpt with the idyll of three girls on the swing. These images appear on the screen; Agnes's memory about the joint swinging may be conceived as a picture the reverse of which is dominated by the chaos of screams, whispers and cries.

The functioning of the refrain can be grasped in the dynamics which are given by the alteration of the two media: film and performance or rather theatre, as it refers to the relationship with the audience. The distance of the viewer in the cinema scenes alternates with the feeling of taking part in events and space.

The distance is a peculiar one, because the spectators always know that they are in a room which they cross at the beginning of the performance, on one side of which there are backless seats for the audience. Therefore they see patchwork sights, for example film-like faces with theatrical bodies that are very near theirs (and this generates a different kind of circulation of energy). The change of medium does not refer to classical theatre media[16] any more—these are those media that use our patchwork experience of the mediatised life.

Theatre appears here as complex, prelingual and pre-expressive, the mediality of which materialises in variants of expression. According to this, two different languages appear: Karin's self-harming happens in light while the ritual washing of the naked dying girl happens in the semi-darkness, in the world of touching and closeness.

CONCLUSIONS

The continuous use of different media in a theatrical performance often raises the question of the autonomy of different components of the performance, which should be the bearers of narratives. In cases when the viewpoints multiply and the different media in performances preserve their autonomous status, the spectator is more active than in classical forms of theatre (as we could see in Şerban's *Cries and Whispers* and in Purcărete's *Faust*). Thus narration is subject to a medial polyphony, parts of which cannot be heard one by one, and the assembling of a dominant narrative out of the fragments and variants is almost impossible. However, out of the meeting of the different fragments new sensorial worlds are created; and, as we have seen, moving between different media opens up the initial genre and medium of film or performance. Recycling, as a form of adaptation and translation, creates this medial polyphony, which serves as an excellent ground for the playful coexistence of different narrative techniques.

NOTES

1. Lehmann uses the term with the meaning of 'communication across the senses' (2006: 85).
2. We borrow here the term *knot* from Eugenio Barba's writings, who says that words on the stage create knots which appear indissoluble and revelatory, and do not present solutions to the spectators (1995: 95, 153); the knots help the spectators to pose questions to themselves (1997). Here we extend the meaning of the term to visual events, too (as Barba probably also used it to denote not only verbal units, but nonverbal ones, too—he speaks about the knots of the story).
3. This term is used by Bolter-Grusin (1999).
4. The next periods in McLuhan's theory are: the literate age (hand-writing), the print age (printing press), and the electronic age.

5. A gesture scenario is a scenic event told by gestures, objects and a place, which often works on the stage even if some objects are missing, or even if objects are transformed by the actor's gestures (e.g., the mad Ophelia is carried out by a wheelbarrow instead of a coach in Vlad Mugur's Hamlet, 2002). The scenario's simplest form is the gesture program, which is an automatic gesture connected to one element (object or place), like lighting a cigarette, or making the sign of the cross at a given place. The scenarios and programs form gesture narratives (see Ungvári Zrínyi 2011)

6. Stephen Greenblatt speaks of the circulation of social energies in a given epoch in the form of different collective cultural practices (like exorcism in Shakespeare's time and during the Middle Ages). But we also mean here the energy produced by the actors, the way of transmitting it is often elaborated for a specific performance (Greenblatt 1989). Erika Fischer-Lichte thoroughly deals with the circulation of energy between audience and actors in her book *The Transformative Power of Performance: A New Aesthetics* (2008).

7. Ingmar Bergman, *Cries and Whispers*. Adaptation by Andrei Şerban and Daniela Dima. Hungarian State Theatre from Cluj-Kolozsvár, Romania, 2010, R: Andrei Şerban. Costumes and stage design: Carmencita Brojboiu, dramaturg: Kinga Kovács, light design: Sándor Maier Andrei Şerban.

8. Interview with Andrei Şerban. Playbill of the performance *Cries and Whispers*, 2010.

9. There is one more piece of information which was relevant only for a few days: during the three final rehearsals, which were open for a specialist audience, Şerban interrupted the rehearsal several times to give instructions to the actors.

10. This phenomenon will be examined with the help of the *ritornel* later on.

11. Here we use Hannes Böhringer's interpretation of deterritorialisation by Deleuze-Guattari (2009: 36.)

12. Deleuze and Guattari state that "the refrain is essentially territorial, territorializing or reterritorializing" (1987: 300); the song of a child "jumps from chaos to the beginnings of order" (311). (The English translator used the word *refrain* for the French *ritournelle*—while in Böhringer's essay the Hungarian translator J. A. Tillmann uses the word *ritornel*; see Deleuze and Guattari 1980.)

13. The three forms of refrain are (1) turning back to the beginnings of order through a child's song; (2) a forming a home like a circle by constructing a "wall of sound"; (3) one opens the circle a crack, to join the cosmic forces of the future (Deleuze and Guattari 1987: 311.)

14. The term occurs in Platon's *Timaeus* (n.d.)

15. Major discourse is characterised by the power of constants, while minor discourse presents the possibility of variants (Deleuze and Guattari 1987: 101–110)

16. We consider there are two types of classical historical theatre media: the medium of ritual theatre and the medium of perspectivalist theatre. From communicational-anthropological point of view, there are two other types: the avant-garde and the postmodern theatre media, of which the avant-garde is partly classicised (see Ungvári Zrínyi 2011).

WORKS CITED

Barba, Eugenio. 1995. *The Paper Canoe: A Guide to Theatre Anthropology.* London: Routledge.

Barba, Eugenio. 1997. 'Four Spectators'. *The Drama Review*, 41, pp. 96–100.

Barthes, Roland. 1981. *Camera Lucida*. New York: Hill and Wang.

Belting, Hans. 2011. *An Anthropology of the Image: Picture, Medium, Body.* Princeton, NJ: Princeton University Press.

Bolter, Jay David and Richard Grusin. 1999. *Remediation: Understanding New Media*. Cambridge, MA: MIT Press.

Böhringer, Hannes. 2009. *Daidalosz vagy Diogenész* [Daidalos or Diogenes]. Budapest, Terc.

Carlson, Marvin. 2003. *The Haunted Stage: The Theatre as Memory Machine.* Ann Arbor: Michigan, University of Michigan Press.

Crary, Jonathan. 1990. *Techniques of the Observer*. Cambridge, MA: MIT Press.

Deleuze, Gilles. 1986. *Cinema I: The Movement-Image*. London: The Athlone Press.

Deleuze, Gilles and Felix Guattari. 1987. *A Thousand Plateaus: Capitalism and Schizophrenia*. Minneapolis: University of Minnesota Press.

Finter, Helga. 1985. 'Das *Kameraauge* des postmodernen Theaters'. In: Christian W. Thomsen (ed.), *Studien zur Ästhetik des Gegenwartstheaters*. Heidelberg: C. Winter, pp. 46–69.

Fischer-Lichte, Erika. 2008. *The Transformative Power of Performance: A New Aesthetics*. London: Routledge.

Greenblatt, Stephen. 1989. *Shakespearean Negotiations: The Circulation of Social Energy in Renaissance England*. Berkeley: University of California Press.

Jákfalvi Magdolna. 2004. 'A nézés öröme' [The Pleasure of the Gaze]. In: Imre Zoltán (ed.), *Átvilágítás. A magyar színház európai kontextusban* [Transillumination: Hungarian Theatre in European Context]. Budapest: Áron, pp. 96–126

Kristeva, Julia. 1984. *Revolution in Poetic Language*. New York: Columbia University Press.

Lehmann, Hans-Thies. 2006. *Postdramatic Theatre*. London: Routledge.

Mersch, Dieter. 2004. 'Medialität und Undarstellbarkeit. Einleitung in eine "negative" Medientheorie'. In: Sybille Krämer (ed.), *Performativität und Medialität*. München, Fink, pp. 75–96

Platon. n.d. *Timaeus*. APSU Electronic Classics Series Publication. http://www2. hn.psu.edu/faculty/jmanis/plato/timaeus.pdf (accessed 15 May 2012).

Ungvári Zrínyi Ildikó. 2011. *Bevezetés a színházi antropológiába* [An Introduction to Theatre Anthropology]. 2nd ed. Tg-Mures: Mentor.

Vanhaesebrouck, Karel. 2004. 'Towards a Theatrical Narratology?' *Image & Narrative*, 9. http://www.imageandnarrative.be/inarchive/performance/vanhaeseb-rouck.htm (accessed 28 March 2013).

Weber, Samuel. 2004. *Theatricality as Medium*. New York: Fordham University Press.

11 When Creation, Translation and Adaptation Meet

SignDance Collective's *New Gold*

Pedro de Senna

THIS IS NOT A CHAPTER

It is rather a series of articulations: ways of expressing (and by virtue of expression, formulating) ideas—but also hinges by which ideas are joined and made to move in different directions. I plan, therefore, to articulate some ideas from Performance Studies, Deaf Studies and Disability Studies, in the hope of making them move towards the field(s) of Translation and Adaptation Studies. These ideas have emerged as a by-product of the work I've been doing in a piece called *New Gold*, by SignDance Collective International, in which I perform, but also act as dramaturg. That simultaneity of expressing and formulating contained in the definition of 'articulation' is an important element of my dual role, but also of the work itself, as we will see.

As I am engaging in definitions, three key concepts must be defined here. I understand 'dramaturg' as a facilitator, somebody working alongside a director in a devising process, helping shape a performance or giving a production a sense of coherence.[1] Somebody who, in the words of Patrice Pavis, engages in "a new kind of stage writing" (2010: 404) and ultimately has the responsibility of putting on paper a semblance of script, emerging from a devising process.

I use the word 'Deaf' to refer to individuals who are culturally deaf, users of Sign Languages—as opposed to 'deaf', people who suffer hearing loss. Central to this vocabulary is the understanding that Deafness is not a physical condition, but a social construct. Corker and Shakespeare have succinctly explained this notion by analogy with gender studies: the same relation that exists between sex (biological) and gender (cultural) is in operation between impairment and disability (2002).[2]

Finally, by 'translation', I mean any process of transposition between linguistic systems, excluding here what Jakobson called intersemiotic translation (1963). I call the latter 'adaptation'. I am consciously establishing a fracture here, one which I intend to address as the articulations gain form.

There are no extensive studies in signdance theatre as an art form, so I develop my ideas with the support of analyses of sign poetry and Deaf theatre, as well as some writing on dance and devised theatre.

After definitions and caveats, a couple of introductions are necessary.

FIRST INTRODUCTION: SDC

SignDance Collective (SDC) International is a company that creates hybrid performances which include aspects of dance, theatre and Sign Language, as well as live music and, frequently, media and projections. They are also known simply as SDC, the name they have used since 2001 and which encompasses the work of all its collaborators for specific projects. Thus, as a participant in *New Gold*, I can consider myself a member of SDC. The invitation for me to work with them owes to a residency agreement established in January 2010 between SDC and Bucks New University, where I then worked.[3]

The company was founded in 1987 as Common Ground Sign Dance Theatre and re-established in 2001 by Isolte Ávila (dance director, disabled, non-Deaf) and David Bower (artistic director, Deaf). Their work pioneers a format called *signdance* (written together, as a compound name—though there are early references to sign dance), which they describe as "a way to extract choreography from signtheatre and at the same time keeping the integrity of the language" (Ávila 2011).

Kaite O'Reilly explains, "It fuses Sign Theatre . . . with dance, live music and spoken/sung language" (2001: 41).[4]

Live music is indeed fundamental for the work of the company. The performances are constructed in a way that facilitates dialogue between the various elements presented, and so music cannot be pre-recorded: it has to be in conversation with the choreography and the acting. The music is in fact composed after the basic choreography is sketched out and responds to the actors' and dancers' improvisation with improvisation, too. In Ávila's words, "The music within the company is unique, acting in partnership with the dance and theatre, rather than just accompaniment" (2011). This requires musicians of a very high calibre, and the company has had the pleasure of working with Mark Holub and Liran Donin, of contemporary jazz band *Led Bib*, Luke Barlow, and post-punk folk duo *Dead Days Beyond Help*, among others. Choreography is composed in silence, a practice adopted by many dance schools, with the intent to focus the choreographer's and the dancers' work on the body and its expressive capacity, independently of external factors. Silence which is, in fact, the daily experience of the d/Deaf individual; the rhythm exists in the body and the imagination.[5] David Bower describes the company's approach to choreography:

> Choreography begins with a simple idea like the movement of the sea and how the light plays on water. Or it could be creating a sign name for ourselves using sign language and taking that as a basis for a movement—and then creating interaction between that movement and other sign names.

> We don't believe interaction between the dancers has to be in time—
> beat wise. We find that interaction is enriched using a different but
> equally valid sense of timing. (2011)

Here we start to understand how the company's performances operate: words in spoken languages (English, sometimes Spanish, Italian, Portuguese) are translated into British Sign Language (BSL) and International Sign Language (ISL), and these are in turn adapted into choreographic form. In their devising processes, this continuum is at times reversed or disrupted, and the creative act originates in a choreographic idea, which may then be put into words. With their innovative aesthetics, the company regularly renegotiates the relationships between these systems of signification, constantly translating and adapting, operating what Bauman termed a "Poetics of Vision, Space and the Body" (1997).

In this fundamental text for Deaf Studies (and with important consequences for literary theory, Translation Studies and Performance Studies), Bauman discusses the relationship between Sign Languages and literary theory, and proposes avenues for an engagement of Sign Literatures with theoretical fields associated with written literature (1997). It is worth remembering that Sign Languages do not have well-established written forms (Davidson 2006; Mitchell 2006).[6] There is in fact debate among Deaf critics as to whether one should even use the term 'Sign Literature'—as it implies writing—with some preferring 'Sign Art'. In this respect, Bauman suggests that "[r]ather than offering a totalizing answer, it may be wise to tolerate the ambiguity that ASL [American Sign Language] 'art' both *is* and *is not* 'literature', that it is akin to hearing literary practices, but also cannot be contained by those practices" (1997: 322).

Two points are worthy of note here: first, the assertion (a common trope of Deaf Studies) that creative practices in Sign Languages go beyond the confines of hearing literatures. In other words, the former can offer something not accessible to the latter, disrupting notions about a supposed inferiority of Sign Languages. I will address some of the consequences of this for translators and adapters later in these articulations.

The second is the state of simultaneous being and nonbeing attributed to Sign Literature. This state is actually extended to Sign Language itself, as "[t]he eye, unlike the ear in the system of 'hearing-oneself-speak', can only partially 'see-oneself-sign'. There is always a trace of nonpresence in the system of signing" (Bauman 1997: 317). The phenomenological implications of signing, then, bear a striking resemblance with the widely acknowledged (Stanislavski, Grotowski, Schechner) experience of the actor's double consciousness: she simultaneously is and is not herself; she is and is not her character. When dealing therefore with actors making use of Sign during performance, we are in a very interesting liminal space, a state of 'betweenness' with which translators and adapters can easily identify. In this sense, an analysis of the use of Sign in performance might also offer insight for the study of translation and adaptation.

Bauman invites us to establish more connections and take her project forward. In relation to phenomenology, she proposes,

> Further phenomenological study of Sign poetry will, one hopes, explore other literary concepts in their visual-spatial quality, as opposed to their linguistic quantity. This approach will keep Sign criticism close to the original site of poetic creation: the meeting of body, time, space and language. In the end, we may arrive at a viewing practice in which Sign poems are not so much 'read' or 'seen' as they are *lived in* from the inside. (1997: 326–327)

There are Barthesian echoes here: "[Y]ou cannot talk 'about' a certain text, you can only talk 'in' it, *in its own manner*" (Barthes 1973: 37–38; my translation, always henceforth).

My proposition is precisely to look at translation and adaptation not from a linguistic point of view, but a phenomenological and aesthetic one. Moreover, my starting point is my dual experience in *New Gold*, as actor and dramaturg, and this shapes and colours my understanding. It is my contention however, that the aesthetic qualities and phenomenological experience of signance theatre as an art form may illuminate our understanding of those very semiotic processes.

SECOND INTRODUCTION: *NEW GOLD*

With the Olympic Games in London 2012, many artistic projects were supported or funded that dealt with themes relating to sport, Olympic values etc.[7] In the spirit of the 'Cultural Olympiad'—and with the support of Driving Inspiration, the Creative Campus Initiative and other 2012 associated funding streams—SDC conceived of a street performance that would question the very idea of competition, nationalism, being first; a piece that might enquire about the true value of gold, and perhaps look for a new gold. Our piece has five characters: four 'champions', the best in their field. We have the world's best secretary, World Champion Paper-pusher (Isolte Ávila); the world's best shopper, World Champion Consumerist (Francesca Osimani); the very poor World Champion Beggar (David Bower); and the world's best applause-taker and World Champion Ovationist (Laura Goulden).[8] These champions are joined by a Referee, MC, Fool, Jester, Commentator, Supporter—a Jack of all trades—me.

The performance begins with the Jester welcoming the audience, trying to attract them to the playing area and introducing the characters. After being introduced and demonstrating their abilities, the champions dance and interact, compete, forge alliances and mock the Referee. In the end, the Fool distributes medals and delivers a speech about gold, in the form of a letter dictated to the Paper-pusher, who 'takes notes' in Sign Language. Throughout the performance, there are moments of tension and release

200 Pedro de Senna

among the champions, but also between the champions and the MC, who tries in vain to order, police, organise the event (these attempts have Foucauldian echoes and implications for identity politics).

The tension and release are reflected also in the process of writing the piece. As well as acting in *New Gold* I was in charge of the dramaturgy. Just as my character tries to bring order to the chaos generated by the others, in my role as dramaturg I tried to order and give meaning to the improvisations that served as a basis for the performance. Throughout the devising process of collective creation, I attempted a process of 'creative collection'—namely my function, above all, was to gather, with aesthetic intention, the fragments generated in the rehearsal room.

Tim Etchells describes his own work as a dramaturg like this: "[For me] writing was so often about collecting, sifting and using from bits of other people's stuff—copied language like precious stones. Authentic has not really been in it" (1999: 101). Our approach (as a company) is in many respects similar to that; and this lack of interest in the 'authentic' needs addressing, because of its consequences for the translator and/or adapter. What can one say about a text—or do with a text that in its origin is not 'original' or 'authentic'?

Manuela Perteghella maintains, "Originality in particular poses problems in relation to the 'text' itself as made up of necessary, unavoidable, intertextuality, of textual (and cultural) borrowings, thus making rewriting/translation already inherent in the source text" (2008: 56). Thus, in contemporary theatre—and one might say in ancient theatre, too—intertextuality begins to destabilise precious notions about dramaturgical authorship and their inevitable associations with individual creativity, ascribed by western thinking. The notions of intertextuality and heteroglossia are inextricably connected in this way. In *New Gold* this is exacerbated by the fact that the performance is indeed a collage, where the intertext is perhaps less visible, but the heteroglossic character is clearly present.

As signdance theatre, *New Gold* is at the crossroads between performance categories. Whilst describing it as 'Deaf theatre' may be a useful point of departure for analysis—the show is, after all, very much informed by Deaf culture—we must not forget that *New Gold* is not exclusively Deaf, and much of its meaning and politics lie in the interactions between Deaf and hearing performers and audience. The experience it engenders in performers and audience alike is one of dis-location. Anater writes about the experience of cultural translation from a non-Deaf perspective, and describes the hearing individual within Deaf culture as "an agent of tension and contrast" (2008: 126). She goes on to state that "being both inside and out [of the language] makes possible a movement of identity, which enables us to change between various contexts (place, time, social dimension)" (143). And of course the ability to shift identities and contexts is intrinsic to the actor's work. Thus, by placing myself—a hearing actor—within a Deaf cultural context, I am in fact facilitating the construction of my own performance, through translation. In trying to write a text that might capture this performance, I am also being an agent of tension, through adaptation.

The processes of translation and adaptation that I write about here, then, occur on two different levels: at the very moment of rehearsal and performance, when what is spoken becomes a Sign, which becomes choreography (and vice versa); and at the moment in which I try to capture on paper something "generated in good part by performer improvisation . . . A kind of speaking that becomes writing" (Etchells 1999: 105). Translation and adaptation are therefore intrinsically linked to the creative act, a constituent part of that process, twice: in performance and in performance writing.

FIRST ARTICULATION: PERFORMANCE STUDIES AND DRAMATURGY > DEAF STUDIES

There is a debate in the world of performing arts that can be (crassly) summarised like this: on the one hand, there are those who believe that theatre comes from words. To use the biblical image: in the beginning there was the Word. According to this point of view, the theatrical act has its origin in text—not necessarily a script as such—but that actors and performers, even in ancient, ritualistic theatre, exist as a function of pre-existing narratives. Graham Ley calls the theatre "discursive embodiment", an act of adaptation (2009). Word made flesh. This position finds support from the field of Translation Studies in authors such as Ortrun Zuber-Skerritt, who had already referred to theatre as "translation" from page to stage (1984).

On the other hand, authors like Richard Schechner propose a pre-discursive theatre; that before any discourse there is an encounter, an event (1988). Eugenio Barba speaks of the pre-expressive body, the fundamental state of the performer (1991). In fact, the word 'performance' is preferred over 'theatre' and the field of Performance Studies (along with much of academia these days) suspects any logocentric tendency, typical of western thought, which began to be deconstructed in the latter half of the last century.

The question can be further reduced to a debate between a semiotic view of *theatre* (which tries to extract or construct meaning) and a phenomenological view of *performance* (dealing with the lived experience). One may well argue that this dichotomy is in fact false: that there is no lived experience to which one doesn't attribute meaning, nor meaning that is not experienced. Far from a simple exercise in naming, the debate, however, is real and fierce, and has ontological consequences for our understanding of *New Gold*, of what is fundamental about it.

Whatever the starting point, though, one understands that my dramaturg self needs words. Eugenio Barba defines dramaturgy as the relation between *concatenation* and *simultaneity* of actions in the plot (1991). Beyond—or rather, beneath—this, lies the more mundane question asked by Saulo Souza, "[H]ow do you put on paper something that is in motion?" (2009: 312). The solution he proposes in his poetic translation of Brazilian Sign Language (Libras) into Portuguese, 'retextualising' the Sign poem as concrete poetry is very interesting, and something to be explored in the future. However, when trying to translate into English (and other written languages) a performance created with Sign, the approach proposed by Souza, according to which "[translatability] is dictated not by the mode of the languages in contact, but the strategic approach and objective of the translator before the act of translation" (359) does not fully apply. Firstly, because what I did was not to write a *dramatic text* (made for the theatre), but describe a *theatre text* (made in the theatre), a distinction clearly pointed out by theatre semiotician Keir Elam (2002). The problem that presents itself to us now is one of description and interpretation, not merely translation.

Moreover, there is another force of resistance to describing a Deaf 'theatre text' in a 'dramatic text' form. There is a risk pointed out by Davidson, who warns, "The use of printed English text to 'interpret' the Deaf person's intentions would once again co-opt manual signs by linking them to English syntax and grammar" (2006: 226–227). From a hearing perspective, translating into and from Sign Languages poses difficulties which go beyond the well-rehearsed problems about lack of overlapping semantic fields and cultural differences between spoken/written languages: Sign offers structural challenges, too, with its possibility of simultaneity, fluidity and internal contradiction, none of which is achievable through the linearity of text and speech. The abundance of neologisms and morphisms[9] in Sign performance makes us think of translation to and from Sign Languages within the context of performance as adaptations.

Here lies a possible contribution Adaptation Studies may offer to Deaf Studies: if we agree that Sign Languages offer expressive possibilities not containable by the linearity of spoken and written text, it may be useful to look at linguistic exchanges between Sign and writing/speaking as adaptations, rather than translations. There is a potential danger in this proposition: Sign has historically struggled to be officially recognised as a 'proper language' in many countries. To think of adaptation instead of translation when dealing with Sign/spoken language relations risks dislodging this achievement. My proposition is that Adaptation Studies are used as an auxiliary tool for analysis which may illuminate some aspects of interlinguistic relations that are not containable by the more logocentric Translation Studies. The approximation between translation and adaptation proposed in this book finds in Sign (and signdance theatre) a particularly promising topos for further study. Perhaps we can reappropriate Graham Ley's expression, and refer to Sign as "embodied discourse".

In the dramaturgy of *New Gold*, as well as the intersemiotic translations from speaking to Sign (and back), we have to move from stage to page (reversing the established order)—a process of adaptation. Jakobson's rift (only just bridged by Sign) is in operation here in an unexpected way. In many respects, the situation is analogous to Barba's differentiation between *written* and *performance* texts (Elam's 'dramatic text' and 'theatre text'). The job of the dramaturg is to adapt the performance text into a written one.

Dramaturgy then operates as adaptation, and perhaps might cover some of the distance between the logocentric and the performance-centred views of theatre. Therefore, when Graham Ley asserts that "we have . . . the 'constitution' of theatre and drama by adaptation: what was not there before is derived by a process of adaptation from elsewhere" (2009: 203), his "elsewhere", the pre-existing narratives of script and myth, may be extended towards the characters themselves. What we have in *New Gold* is not strictly speaking narrative—only characters who are called into being. When Ley says "that there can be a drama with action but without character, but not with character and without action" (207), the statement needs the following qualification: if we understand the formation of identities (whether fictional or not) as essentially discursive projects—as gender, postcolonial and queer studies teach us (not to mention Deaf and Disability Studies)—characters are in themselves 'discursive embodiments' and so there can be a theatre "with character and without action". The characters in *New Gold* are born with their own discursive charge. As Rothfield put it, "Experience occurs in a body which is thoroughly marked by history" (2010: 309).

Thus, the World Champion Paper-Pusher has an extra pair of legs to help her multitask. The World Champion Beggar is Deaf. The applause-taker won't speak. In the continuum that goes from Ley to Schechner, texts created by dramaturgs in processes of 'creative collection', with characters made of scraps and written in "intersemiotic translation", resist classification.

In this capacity signdance theatre also starts to bridge the divide between the semiotic and phenomenological views of performance. With its challenge to linearity, it is by its very nature establishing a point of contact between the two elements of the plot (concatenation and simultaneity) identified by Barba as constituents of dramaturgy (1991). Watson refers to two codes: "There are essentially two types of actors' codes during performance: those generated by the role and those generated by the actor" (1995: 142). This dialectics gains particular emphasis in Deaf and disability theatre: if the lived, experienced (and experiencing) body of the actor possesses meaning, when the actor's body carries a marker of identity difference (race, gender, disability), the 'actor's code' becomes stronger, more present. Petra Küpers writes, in relation to disability theatre, "[S]emiotics and phenomenology start to leak into one another, start to overwrite one another, and begin to move" (2003: 4). This notion of ideas in motion, permeable frontiers, applies with great propriety to Deaf theatre in general and to the work of SDC specifically.

The improvisatory, devised nature of the company's work destabilises the notion that staging is translating/adapting a pre-existing narrative, but also that performance must precede discourse and text. As we have seen, in the creative process of *New Gold* these operations went both ways—at times text originated action, at times movement dictated text. But more importantly, translation and adaptation operate at textual and performance levels *simultaneously*.

What I am interested in at this point is what happens in the performance text, those questions that the performers (and audience) have to contend with—but also what happens to the text in performance. In *New Gold*, notions of source-text and target-text are undermined—actors in motion are also dramaturgs; on stage, the difference between 'translation as process' and 'translation as product' dissolve—everything happens in real time and, though strategies may be decided a priori as Souza suggests, translation and adaptation are articulated live. There is a "concern with language not as text then, but as event" (Etchells 1999: 105). Though Perteghella urges us to "distinguish between linguistic adaptation, on a verbal, textual level, and theatrical adaptation, on stage" (2008: 52), in the work of SDC the linguistic adaptation is theatrical.

One of the hallmarks of the performance is its multilingual character: as noted above, the company makes use of spoken English, Portuguese, Spanish; British and International Sign Languages; dance (or it may be more appropriate to say signdance). In performances of this nature, we can appropriate what Perteghella writes, "[T]here are target playtexts which are hybrid, syncretic and therefore seem to escape characterization" (2008: 61). We can think of the performance of *New Gold* as a hybrid text, too, one in which that syncretism extends itself so far as to engender the union between target and source-text.

Once again, Bauman, comes to the rescue: "[I]n the 'text-as-event', the borders between viewer and text, subject and object, inside and outside, become porous" (1997: 326). The position of the spectator here is important. If the text is multilingual, most of our audience certainly is not. When writing about the panorama of contemporary 'multicultural theatre', the versatile Marvin Carlson teaches that "with modern international touring, international festivals, international audiences and international companies, a significant heteroglossic theatrical tradition is emerging" (2006: 12). We may think of SDC's work as part of that tradition. However, it is my contention that this theatre tradition has at its base an elite culture, and a relatively homogenous public, composed in its majority by what we may call the 'global intellectual'.

This audience, though multicultural from an ethnic-linguistic point of view, is generally part of a theatrical mono-culture; it speaks and understands the 'language of theatre'.[10]

In his introduction, Carlson argues that "theatre has often . . . been seen and employed as an instrument of cultural and linguistic solidification" (2006: 3), with audiences in general being less diverse than the society to which they belong; and that multicultural theatre questions this solidification. As we have seen, this does not seem to be entirely true—it simply solidifies a different culture/language, one which is elite and globalised.

New Gold, however, is a street performance. We have performed in the central square of Graz (Austria), a shopping centre in Thessaloniki (Greece) in the street in High Wycombe, as well as schools for Deaf and non-Deaf children. The show has also been to the Ethos Theater Festival in Ankara (April 2012), where it was performed outdoors, and the Ana Desetnica Street Theatre Festival in Slovenia (July 2012). Though the piece also enjoyed a brief run at the Warehouse Theatre in Croydon (April 2012), exiting conventional theatre spaces is a common strategy in disability theatre. Küppers tells us that often the disabled actor uses "performance as a means to break out of allocated spaces [using] public spaces outside the theater in order to challenge ever more effectively the concept of allocation and categorization" (2003: 1–2). Much as this assertion is true, there is also an aspect of necessity here. Often, Deaf and disability theatre practitioners don't have access to conventional spaces, owing to prejudice on the part of programmers, who often see this type of theatre as having less artistic value or commercial appeal. In relation to dance, Benjamin notes that there is a "practice of placing companies associated with disability at the end of the programme" (2010: 111) following "the idea that disability and dance constituted a diversion from 'the real thing'" (113). The work of SDC and others, such as CandoCo, to which Benjamin refers, challenges these perceptions.

Küppers presents the interesting notion that this 'leaking' into the street subverts medical and cultural othering, not by containment (in ghettoes), but by "infection" (2003: 4). Whatever the reasons and consequences (political and economical) of this outing, the theatre of the street, square, shopping centre needs to communicate with its audiences at an aesthetic and poetic level—audiences who are often passers-by, who might stop for five minutes and then move on.

The performance and dramaturgy need to strongly operate at Barba's level of simultaneity, and not make use of lengthy narrative concatenation. Fragment becomes necessary. In relation to dance, Lansdale writes about the spectator's need "to observe the single moment intently, to register its completeness while also seeing its movement toward something else— another moment" (2010: 159). It is important to note that this immediacy does not in any way diminish the complexity of the show. In signdance theatre, we have a site where simultaneity and concatenation are at a crux. Complex concatenations are shaped at the speed of a gesture. Through its multilingual and hybrid nature, the text is amplified and gains force, the dramaturgical web is strengthened.

In the Jester's final speech, we have a clear example of this amplification, in a manner that illustrates quite straightforwardly the process of transforming words into movement—adapting. As he dictates a letter in English to his secretary, she 'takes notes' in International Sign Language; the rest of the cast then appropriate the Signs and expand them into choreography (signdance), creating a cascade of echoes. All three languages overlap to create a complex perceptual field, which viewers are asked to negotiate.

The "sequence of distorting mirrors: further textures" (de Senna 2007: 41), to which I referred when writing about translating plays which are explicitly intertextual is actualised within the performance itself, before the audience's eyes. These textures of the hybrid text, this grain, resistance "makes historical, cultural, psychological assumptions of the reader, and the consistency of his tastes, values and memories vacillate, it puts his relationship with language in crisis" (Barthes 1973: 25–26). They are, in Barthes' terms, a source of *juissance*. In the multilingual text, "the subject accedes to juissance through the cohabitation of languages, *which work side by side*: the text of pleasure, that's happy Babel" (10).

In multicultural and multilingual theatre, there is a sense in which not everything can or must be *understood* literally. Often, paralinguistic features such as tone of voice, speed and loudness of delivery allow hearing audience members to make up much of the meaning that may be lost in the linguistic code. This is still a phonocentric assertion, though. For Deaf spectators, just as in Deaf performance, the semiotic process of making meaning leaks into the phenomenal experience of watching. In hybrid formats such as signdance theatre, though, understanding often happens in the gaps, the interstices, "in the moment at the borders between hearing and deafness, between audience members and performers, through the listening bodies" (Kochar-Lindgen 2006: 187). This brings me to my second articulation point.

SECOND ARTICULATION: DEAF STUDIES AND THE THIRD EAR > DISABILITY STUDIES

It is crucial here that I tread carefully. Though at the time of writing I've been working with SDC International for almost three years, I am conscious of the risk of seeming to engage in cultural and intellectual tourism. There are many potential pitfalls in Deaf Studies for a non-Deaf person, who from a Deaf perspective is "often perceived as a foreigner" (Anater 2008: 128). Whilst trying to avoid falling into those traps, I would like to venture into this field, because I believe it has much to offer to the discipline of Translation and Adaptation Studies.

For many, the first point of contact between Deaf Studies and Translation Studies comes from the study of Sign Language interpretation. Furthermore, the association of Deafness and theatre in the eyes of most theatregoers does not extend far beyond the awareness of there being a few Sign interpreted performances of mainstream shows. In her study about Sign Language interpretation for the theatre, Siobhán Rocks highlights a series of difficulties resulting from current practices in Britain (and which, to a greater or lesser extent, are mirrored in other parts of the world, too) (2011). Quite apart from the practical problem of the time lapse between a character's speech and its 'translation', she points out the question of positioning for the interpreter, generally standing to one side of the stage, permanently lit, and forcing Deaf audience members to divide their attention between two foci. In *New Gold*, not only do we play with the notion of time-lag, disrupting it by having characters speak and sign simultaneously, or by having Sign precede speech, but also create multiple foci of attention, which at first glance might exacerbate these problems.

Rocks points towards solutions such as greater interpreter involvement in the rehearsal room: this would give him better knowledge of the theatrical text, and flexibility to adapt according to the scenic situation; another possible solution would be to give the interpreter more time with the dramatic text; and specific training for interpretation for the theatre. But she also suggests that theatre directors pay closer attention to the phenomenon of Sign interpretation, and have greater involvement in its staging, as it has a not insignificant bearing on the appreciation of the performances by the public. In order for this to happen it is necessary that the performance text is used as the source-text. She tells us, "[T]he acknowledgement of the performance as the source text forces a shift in focus from the functional notion of access, to the artistic notion of creating theatre for diverse audiences" (2011: 85). Particularly, as we have seen, if multicultural dramaturgy destabilises written texts, the only possible starting point for a process of translation of multicultural performance is the theatre text.

Though this may be a step in the right direction, the proposition still seems problematic to me. The quality of the interpreter's work notwithstanding, Rocks proposal still comes from an audist point of view, one that assumes theatre makers to be necessarily and by definition, non-Deaf. SDC's work of research and experimentation (they refer to their performances as a constant search towards high-quality inclusive theatre) revert this paradigm; they see Sign Interpretation as a potential instrument for further oppression. As David Bower once said to me, "What would you do, if nine out of ten plays you watch are not in your language?" (personal conversation, 2011). This is of course a conservative estimate.

SDC International define themselves as a Deaf- and disability-led company, one whose artistic decisions are primarily in the hands of a disabled (non-Deaf) dancer, and a Deaf actor.

> Inspired by a vision of integration between Deaf and Hearing cultures, the possibility of communication is offered on an equal, though not identical basis. The company do not use 'sign interpretation'—their work is the antithesis of this, in that there is not one dominant language. (O'Reilly 2001: 43–44)

This assertion might seem a little odd, given that in the example given above (where the Jester dictates and the Paper-pusher takes notes) there is a clear ordering in the process—though all three methods of communication overlap on stage, the text does originate in the speaker, then moves onto Sign, then onto signdance. At that point in the performance, there is a stretching out of processes that often have occurred simultaneously in the piece. Throughout the show, however, an ironic relationship between the Fool and the Paper-pusher has been established, one that runs through questions of identity, sexual and racial politics, with attempts on the part of the Referee to police and discipline his unruly four-legged (but only at times) secretary. There is a relation of complicity between performers, fundamental for the improvisational style of the company. Thus, SDC attempts to engender coalitions across difference, forming what Ostrove and Oliva have called "alliances", a term borrowed from feminist studies, and which they define as: "an effective, mutually respectful relationship across (at least one) difference of identity that acknowledges oppression, privilege, and the complicated nature of identity" (2010: 106). SDC forge alliances as a tactical move to challenge audism. And so we have to approach the relation between Adaptation, Translation, performance and Deaf Studies from a different angle.

There is a growing canon of criticism for American Sign poetry and theatre, due to there being a strong tradition of Deaf performance (with the establishment in 1967 of the National Theatre of the Deaf, as well as numerous poetry groups), and because of the existence in the United States of Gallaudet University, the world's first (and only) Deaf university. Thus, I make use of studies from that country's Sign theatre and poetry to trace some parallels to the poetics of signdance theatre. There are of course some studies in the UK, particularly at the University of Reading, who run a course in theatre arts, education and Deaf Studies, but the number of publications in the areas of British Sign poetry and Sign theatre is still small when compared to the output from the United States. Gallaudet University Press are rapidly creating a canon for Deaf Studies.

In his preface to Bauman's book on American Sign poetry, Mitchell writes about "the moment when language takes flight and creates new worlds out of words and images" (2006: xvi). He continues, "One could imagine a bilingual performance in which speech and gesture had a contrapuntal or even contradictory, ironic relationship" (xx). This exactly what we tried to achieve in *New Gold*—though we ask: why stay with two languages only?

Davidson warns us that "for Deaf nationalists such collaboration with the hearing world is problematic" (2006: 218), that these alliances and multilingual collaborations may pose a threat to Deaf identity. With regards to translation, Deaf nationalist sentiment is a process of identity formation and affirmation that follows the reverse path of the one Milton points out as occurring in nineteenth-century Europe, when inbound translation served as a formative element for an international canon in which national literatures might be inserted and to which they might respond (2003). Deaf American performers often resist performing translations and affirm American Deaf culture as independent and self-sufficient. This is consistent with that culture's status as a minority culture within the United States.[11] Thus, when the spoken word invades Deaf performance, this causes a degree of discomfort among Deaf audiences. Davidson states that "the eruption of speech in Deaf performance . . . challenges the conventional opposition of signing and speech and allows for more complex, hybrid combinations" (2006: 217). However, in *New Gold* we are, as stated, attempting to challenge nationalisms, and so hybridity becomes an important political aspect as well as an aesthetic quality of the work.

Words such as hybrid and complex are common in the vocabulary I am using to describe practices in signdance theatre. It is worth noting with Bauman that postcolonial studies already have a wealth of vocabulary of this kind to offer us, a lexicon which can be extremely useful for Deaf criticism (1997). The association between postcolonial studies and Translation Studies is, as we know, firmly established. Through this vocabulary, therefore, we may start to navigate between Deaf and Translation Studies in relation to performance. Enunciation and formulation are again coming together.

It is interesting to note that in her important book, *Hearing Difference: The Third Ear in Experimental, Deaf and Multicultural Theater*, Kanta Kochhar-Lindgren refers not only to Deaf theatre, but also to multicultural theatre and in particular those forms of dance-theatre that are typical of South Asia. In these types of performance, she claims, "[s]patial relations and visual codes become incredibly important. This shift in attention [towards a language of space rather than a language of hearing] leads to a different understanding of the body, inter-subjectivity, communication, and cross-cultural relations" (2006: 182). It is not a coincidence that Graham Ley also veers into writing about the work of British Asian theatre companies in his discussions of adaptation. He states that the aesthetic and production values present when such companies perform Western texts may in themselves constitute adaptations, cultural translation happening on stage (2009).

Both writers seem to be hinting at the importance of visual modes of communication in establishing a new 'text', which can be read across cultural divides. One might argue, in line with Carlson, that theatre possesses an "iconic identity" (2006: 13) and is therefore capable of direct representation. Deaf critic Joseph Grigely contests the very notion of iconic identity, though: "An interpretive model of iconicity does not require a factual similarity between a sign and its referent, but merely an impression that similitude of some kind or form exists—whether or not it actually does" (in Bauman 1997: 325). He is writing here about Sign Languages, but in retrieving iconicity from the image and placing responsibility over its meaning in the observer, Grigely begins to point towards a new way of perceiving which has implications for our understanding of translation and adaptation. Bauman, writing about American Sign poetry, states that there is "a profound preoccupation with pushing a linear, phonetic language beyond its conventional limitations to form an alternative linguistic perceptual field" (2006: 7). Again, it is not only language that is being stretched, but the phenomenological experience of language which is being altered at its source.

The interaction between Deaf and non-Deaf individuals that happens on stage (or the street) extends to the audience. The dynamism and heterogeneity required of the performers are also required as an attitude in hearing audiences who, in contact with Deaf Culture must become "capable of *auto* and *inter-constitution* through the relationships [they] establish" (Anater 2008: 128). The audience (Deaf and hearing) are in fact engaging in processes of constitution which are not dissimilar to those of the performers and their characters, who exist as a function of each other.

We have noted that communication in *New Gold* takes place in the physical space, but also in a metaphorical one, that which exists between the performers among themselves, and that which exists between them and the public. Kanta Kochhar-Lindgren states that this intersubjectivity leads us towards "a method of *hearing* across perceptual domains" (2006: 180; my emphasis). She calls this method the 'third ear'. What interests me in her approach, and which seems important for a new way of thinking about theatre translation and adaptation is the emphasis given to the spectator in this process. Translation, this hybrid 'in-between' place, comes into being through an act of improvisation, not by the performer, but by the public. A way of guessing, filling the gaps, reorganising information: adapting and translating. "We are, at these [liminal] moments, in between senses, in between meaning, in between hearing and deafness" (5). Spectators of Deaf theatre are, just as the audiences of British Asian company Tara Arts might be, constantly shifting their perceptual positioning, using the third ear to create cross-sensory and synaesthetic adaptations. Deaf spectators, she argues, are particularly well equipped and versed in these processes.

This improvisational mode of understanding is strongly activated in *New Gold*. The carnivalesque (in the Bakhtinian sense) nature of the performance, its destabilizing of roles—a Commentator who is also a Supporter who is also a Referee—is typical not only of Deaf theatre but of street theatre also. Carnival is, after all, a street event, with a strong participatory element and where the borders between performers and spectators are blurred—all are participants. In his analysis of Deaf American theatre, Peters makes these associations: "[T]he dynamic, polyvocal, hybrid, and heterogenous forms . . . provide lively entertainment in the commedia dell'arte style—political, comic and parodic" (2006: 89). Furthermore, he asserts that "the creation of and delight in a feeling of collectivity take precedence over the more narrow assessment of literary and artistic values" (78). This latter statement needs to be treated carefully, because it risks corroborating the audist attitude which permeates theatre programming around the world. In relation to the work of SDC at least, it requires attention and explanation: this precedence does not take place at a hermeneutic level, but ontological. The delight in collectivity is precisely what enables the artistic quality, it is a fundamental constituent part of that quality, which one never renounces or relegates to a secondary level. With the collective as creator, we are back in territory explored earlier—where individual authorship was contested. And if that is the case, the adapters and translators, both on and off-stage, must also be collective.

New Gold incorporates elements of Deaf theatre, multicultural theatre and dance theatre. Kochhar-Lindgren's vocabulary and approach offer interesting subsidies for us to talk about translation and adaptation in performances of this nature, and are an excellent contribution of Deaf Studies towards theatre Translation Studies. The spectator as adapter.

I'd like to pay closer attention to this different way of perceiving. If Sign, being a site of embodied discourse alters the experience of language at its source, it also promotes a new phenomenology of seeing, a new aesthetic appreciation, as we have just noted. The same applies to disability. Petra Küppers explains,

> Disability as a concept asks for a thorough and careful analysis of reading practices, the investigation of different blind spots, different ways of making meaning and an analysis and awareness of the power structures inherent in any act of performativity, performance and mediation. (2003: 17)

As we know, the relationship between Deaf Studies and Disability Studies is a complex one, involving questions of identity which have real and serious political consequences. Still, Deaf Studies, with its linguistic slant, associated to a phenomenology of perception and the body, can serve as a hinge that may help angle Disability Studies in the direction of Translation and Adaptation Studies. I would like to make use of this hinge for my final (brief) articulation.

THIRD ARTICULATION: DISABILITY STUDIES AND AESTHETICS > TRANSLATION AND ADAPTATION[12]

As with most academic criticism concerned with the politics of identity, Disability Studies approaches the artistic canon with a double mission: first, to 'rescue' disabled artists from the ghettoising tendencies of mainstream, also known as the 'conspiracy of normalcy'; then to challenge and reassess representations of disability and the implications of these representations in a socio-political context. As part of a political project, Benjamin argues that "work that includes disabled performers holds with it an imperative: it must offer a new reading of everyday stereotypes if it wishes to disturb preconceptions and overturn prejudice" (2010: 115).

Küppers describes this mission as operating a "move from non-disabled certainties about disability to disabled perspectives on these certainties"

(2003: 12). She and Benjamin write about disability and performance, but if we accept that translation and adaptation are phenomena that occur during performance, in the intersubjectivity of actors, dancers and audience, then those disabled perspectives might also apply to these phenomena. Furthermore, given that in *New Gold* translation, adaptation and creation collapse into each other, one might reasonably talk about disabled perspectives on the poetics of the show. To put it another way: quite apart from the fact that SDC is a Deaf- and disability-led company, whose thematic preoccupations are inevitably associated with these perspectives, the fact that *New Gold* makes extensive use of translation and adaptation also qualifies the performance for Disability Studies analysis.

More than an analysis of power structures and making meaning, though, Tobin Siebers proposes in his recent *Disability Aesthetics* to elaborate a discourse that sees disability as an "aesthetic value in itself worthy of future development" (2010: 3). He argues, "If modern art has been so successful . . . it is because of its embrace of disability as a distinct version of the beautiful" (9). It might be easier to understand the argument by its reverse: as the twentieth century progressed, every art that aspired to an 'idealised perfection' of the body, such as Nazi art or Soviet social realism (perhaps more appropriately termed an 'ideologised perfection' of the body), is considered bad art. The art that we appreciate today is the kind of art that Hitler called degenerate: distorted images, incomplete, disabled.

A disabled perspective on the poetics of *New Gold*, then, looks for moments of incompleteness and distortion in its creation. These moments are precisely those constructed in the interstices of language, those gaps that require the third ear as an instrument of adaptation. From this point of view, one perceives imperfection as a virtue. The non-materialist aesthetics established in the eighteenth century that Siebers challenges looks for an immaterial, idealised notion of beauty, which is by definition unobtainable in translation and adaptation. In particular, it is unobtainable in translation and adaptation that are created by bodies in the full materiality of their movement, in signdance. These feelings of fragmentation, break, imperfection, this moment of pleasure in which, as Barthes puts it, "my body will follow its own ideas—for my body doesn't have the same ideas as me" (1973: 30), are sentiments that are also present when one talks about translations and adaptations, which are said to be imperfect or incomplete by comparison to an idealised original.

I have argued elsewhere that "[i]f translation is only able to reveal certain aspects of the original, this is not necessarily an evil" (de Senna 2007: 40). Translation wants the grain, the texture, the voice within the language, the body within the movement. It wants the gap. "Treason", as I had called it, is a virtue of the translator, a necessity at times. Now, with Siebers, it is also an aesthetic value, a disability.

In relation to SDC's work, we can appropriate what Tim Etchells said, "I think that the meaning of what you do *is* the aesthetic and *is* the form—in a way it's dangerous to think otherwise" (Billingham 2007: 173)

In *New Gold*, the imperfect translation, the incomprehensible Sign, the speech that isn't heard, the impossible adaptation are aesthetically disabled, and because of that they are beautiful.

NOTES

1. Often in contemporary practice director and dramaturg are the same person. This was not the case in *New Gold*, which was directed by Slovenian director Goro Osojnik.
2. I am extending a definition of 'disability' to include Deafness here, a problematic proposition. I will address some of these problems later in these articulations.
3. As Company in Residence, SDC have access to administrative, storage and rehearsal space, and they offer workshops, classes and work placement opportunities for students, as well as developing shows in partnership with the university and its staff.
4. Kaite O'Reilly worked with Isolte Ávila in Common Ground Sign Dance Theatre. It is about that stage of the company's work that she writes. It was in Common Ground Sign Dance Theatre that Isolte Ávila initiated her search for a new scenic language. O'Reilly has written the only (to my knowledge) academic article describing the art form.
5. A lengthier discussion about the relation between music and choreography in SDC's work is outside the scope of this article, but would certainly be of interest to choreographers, musicians and adaptation and performance theorists.
6. This, in spite of interesting proposals and fairly widespread use of Valerie Sutton's *SignWriting* (1974) and, more recently, the Brazilian 'ELiS—Escrita das Línguas de Sinais' (Barros 2008)
7. This prioritised allocation of funds is by no means unproblematic. As David Bower once told me, "To determine that a work of art should be about sport is the same as asking for an athlete to wear ballet shoes for a race".
8. Each of these champions represents a country, and there is a degree of ethnic stereotyping that goes into the performances. This is done, however, in a rather ironic tone, as the very idea of nationalism is being questioned by the show.
9. For a study of neologisms and morphisms in Sign poetry, see Sutton-Spence and Quadros (2006).
10. I refer here to the audiences who flock to watch the latest Peter Brook, Arianne Mnouchkine, Robert Lépage, Complicité and so on. I am not at all disavowing the quality of their work, there is no value judgement in my assertion; I believe, however, that SDC's work is of a different nature.
11. Although one writes of Deaf nationalism, one may also refer to Deaf culture as a transnational minority culture.
12. Further study of the relation between disability and Translation/Adaptation Studies is needed. I intend to pursue this line of inquiry, again with the work of (and with) SDC as a starting point.

WORKS CITED

Anater, Gisele Iandra Pessini. 2008. 'Pensando em Tradução Cultural a partir do sujeito não-surdo'. In: Ronice Quadros (ed.), *Estudos Surdos III*. Petrópolis: Arara Azul, pp. 124–147.

Ávila, Isolte. 2011. *Signdance Theatre Company CVs*. http://sites.google.com/site/signdancecollective/signdance-productions/signdance-tech-spec/signdance-diary/signdance-the-collective-artists-collaborators/signdance-company-cv-s (accessed 5 August 2011).

Barba, Eugenio. 1991. *A Dictionary of Theatre Anthropology: The Secret Art of the Performer*. London: Routledge.

Barros, Mariângela Estelita. 2008. *ELiS—Escrita das Línguas de Sinais: proposta teórica e verificação prática*. PhD Thesis. Florianópolis: Universidade Federal de Santa Catarina. http://www.ronice.cce.prof.ufsc.br/index_arquivos/Documentos/Mariangela%20Estelita%20.pdf (accessed 10 August 2011).

Barthes, Roland. 1973. *Le Plaisir du texte*. Paris: Éditions du Seuil.

Bauman, H-Dirksen L. 1997. 'Towards a Poetics of Vision, Space, and the Body: Sign Language and Literary Theory'. In: Lennard J. Davis (ed.), *The Disability Studies Reader*. London: Routledge, pp. 315–331.

Bauman, H-Dirksen L., Jennifer. L. Nelson and Heidi. M. Rose (eds.). 2006. *Signing the Body Poetic: Essays on American Sign Language Literature*. Berkeley: University of California Press.

Benjamin, Adam. 2010. 'Cabbages and Kings: Disability, Dance and Some Timely Considerations'. In: Alexandra Carter and Janet O'Shea (eds.), *Routledge Dance Studies Reader*. London: Routledge, pp. 111–121.

Billingham, Peter. 2007. *At the Sharp End: Uncovering the Work of Five Leading Dramatists*. London: Methuen.

Bower, David. 2011. *David Bower Blogs About the Signdance Collective's Approach to Choreography*. http://www.disabilityartsonline.org.uk/signdance_theatre-international?item=829&itemoffset=5 (accessed 5 August 2011).

Carlson, Marvin. 2006. *Speaking in Tongues: Languages at Play in the Theatre*. Ann Arbor: University of Michigan Press.

Corker, Marian and Tom Shakespeare. 2002. *Disability/Postmodernity*. London: Continuum.

Davidson, Michael. 2006. 'Hearing Things: The Scandal of Speech in Deaf Performance'. In: H-Dirksen L. Bauman, Jennifer L. Nelson and Heidi M. Rose (eds.), *Signing the Body Poetic: Essays on American Sign Language Literature*. Berkeley: University of California Press, pp. 216–234.

De Senna, Pedro. 2007. 'In Praise of Treason: Translating Calabar'. *Journal of Adaptation in Film & Performance*, 1:1, pp. 33–44.

Elam, Keir. 2002. *The Semiotics of Theatre and Drama*. 2nd ed. London: Routledge.

Etchells, Tim. 1999. *Certain Fragments: Contemporary Performance and Forced Entertainment*. London: Routledge.

Kochhar-Lindgren, Kanta. 2006. *Hearing Difference: The Third Ear in Experimental, Deaf and Multicultural Theater*. Washington, DC: Gallaudet University Press.

Küppers, Petra. 2003. *Disability and Contemporary Performance: Bodies on Edge*. London: Routledge.

Lansdale, Janet. 2010. 'A Tapestry of Intertexts: Dance Analysis for the Twenty-First Century'. In: Alexandra Carter and Janet O'Shea (eds.), *Routledge Dance Studies Reader*. London: Routledge, pp. 158–167.

Ley, Graham. 2009. '"Discursive Embodiment": The Theatre as Adaptation'. *Journal of Adaptation in Film and Performance*, 2:3, pp. 201–209.

Milton, John. 2003. *Nationalism and Literary Translation*. http://dlm.fflch.usp.br/sites/dlm.fflch.usp.br/files/2003-nationalism_and_literary_translation.pdf (accessed 30 July 2011).

Mitchell, William J. Thomas. 2006. 'Preface: Utopian Gestures'. In: H-Dirksen L. Bauman, , Jennifer. L. Nelson and Heidi. M. Rose (eds.), *Signing the Body*

Poetic: Essays on American Sign Language Literature. Berkeley: University of California Press, pp. xv–xxiii.

Nicoloso, Silvana. 2010. 'Traduzindo Poesia em Língua de Sinais: uma experiência fascinante de verter gestos em palavras'. *Cadernos de Tradução*, 2:26, pp. 307–332.

O'Reilly, Kaite. 2001. 'What Words Look Like in the Air: The Multivocal Performance of Common Ground Sign Dance Theatre'. *Contemporary Theatre Review*, 11:3–4, pp. 41–47.

Ostrove, Joan and Gina Oliva. 2010. 'Identifying Allies: Explorations of Deaf-Hearing Relationships'. In: Susan Burch and Alison Kafer (eds.), *Deaf and Disability Studies: Interdisciplinary Perspectives*. Washington, DC: Gallaudet University Press. pp. 105–119.

Pavis, Patrice. 2010. 'The Director's New Tasks'. In: Maria Delgado and Dan Rebellato (eds.), *Contemporary European Theatre Directors*. London: Routldge.

Perteghella, Manuela. 2008. 'Adaptation: "Bastard Child" or Critique? Putting Terminology Centre Stage'. *Journal of Romance Studies*, 8:3, pp. 51–65.

Peters, Cynthia. 2006. 'Deaf American Theater'. In: H-Dirksen L. Bauman, Jennifer L. Nelson and Heidi M. Rose, (eds.), *Signing the Body Poetic: Essays on American Sign Language Literature*. Berkeley: University of California Press, pp. 71–92.

Rocks, Siobhán. 2011. 'The Theatre Sign Language Interpreter and the Competing Visual Narrative: The Translation and Interpretation of Theatrical Texts to British Sign Language'. In: Roger Baines, Cristina Marinetti and Manuela Perteghella (eds.), *Staging and Performing Translation: Text and Theatre Practice*. London: Palgrave Macmillan, pp. 72–86.

Rothfield, Philipa. 2010. 'Differentiating Phenomenology and Dance'. In: Alexandra Carter and Janet O'Shea (eds.), *Routledge Dance Studies Reader*. London: Routledge, pp. 303–318.

Siebers, Tobin. 2010. *Disability Aesthtics*. Ann Arbour: University of Michigan Press.

Souza, Saulo Xavier. 2009. 'Traduzibilidade poética na interface Libras-Português: aspectos linguísticos e tradutórios com base em *Bandeira Brasileira* de Pimenta (1999)'. In: Ronice Quadros and Marianne Rossi Stumpf (eds.), *Estudos Surdos IV*. Petrópolis: Arara Azul, pp. 310–362.

Sutton-Spence, Rachel and Ronice Quadros. 2006. 'Poesia em língua de Sinais: traços da identidade surda'. In: Ronice Quadros (ed.), *Estudos Surdos I*. Petrópolis: Arara Azul, pp. 110–165.

Watson, Ian. 1995. '"Reading" the Actor: Performance, Presence and the Synesthetic'. *New Theatre Quarterly*, 11:42, pp. 135–145.

Zuber-Skerritt, Ortrun. (ed.). 1984. *Page to Stage: Theatre as Translation*. Amsterdam: Rodopi.

Contributors

Dennis Cutchins is an associate professor of English at Brigham Young University, where he regularly teaches courses in adaptation, American literature, and Western American literature. He has published on a wide range of topics, and recently co-edited three collections on adaptation. In 2000, he won the Carl Bode Award for the best article published in the *Journal of American Culture* for an essay on Leslie Silko's *Ceremony*, and in 2004 received the Charles Redd Center's Mollie and Karl Butler Young Scholar Award in Western Studies. In 2007, he founded the 'Adaptation' section of the American Culture Association, and has served as the chair/co-chair for that section since. In 2010, he became the chair of the Rollins Documentary Film Award, and serves on the editorial board of the *Journal of Popular Culture*. His current book project explores Westerns as adaptations.

Tony Gurr is a seasoned teacher, trainer, writer, keynote speaker—and learner. He has worked with a wide range of disciplines and academics on improving classroom learning and teaching in the UK, Middle East, the US, Australia and Turkey. He is currently based in Ankara and heads up Momentum Learning Solutions as its lead consultant and chief learning officer. He is an avid blogger, and his blog—allthingslearning. wordpress.com—is popular with educators, trainers, curriculum and assessment specialists and educational managers. In collaboration with Laurence Raw, he is the author of *Adaptation Studies and Learning: New Frontiers* (Scarecrow, 2012).

Richard J. Hand is professor of theatre and media drama at the Cardiff School of Creative and Cultural Industries in Wales. He is the founding co-editor of the *Journal of Adaptation in Film and Performance*, an international peer-reviewed journal which features 'traditional' academic articles as well as explorations of creative practice and pedagogy. In addition to Adaptation and Translation Studies, his interests include interdisciplinarity and cross-disciplinarity in performance media, using critical and practical research methodologies.

Katja Krebs is senior lecturer in Theatre and Performance Studies at the University of Bristol. She is the founding co-editor of the *Journal of Adaptation in Film and Performance*, an international peer-reviewed journal which endeavours to establish a relationship between translation and adaptation as well as theory and practice. In addition to her editorial roles, she has published widely on translation and adaptation and is particularly interested in the relationship between translation and constructions of theatre histories.

Adrienne Mason is the language director for translation at the University of Bristol and a practising translator. Her research interests are primarily in the area of translation history.

John Milton is titular professor in the area of Translation Studies at the Universidade de São Paulo (USP). He is the author of *O Poder da Tradução* [*The Power of Translation*] (1993), republished as *Tradução: Teoria e Prática* [*Translation: Theory and Practice*] (1998 and 2010); *O Clube do Livro e a Tradução* [*The* Clube do Livro *and Translation*] (2002); *Imagens de um Mundo Trêmulo* (2006), a travel book on Japan; and *Journey to Turkey, the Balkans and Egypt* (2011). He also edited *Agents of Translation* (John Benjamins 2009) with Paul Bandia. He has also translated the poetry of Keats, Wordsworth and Shelley to Portuguese, together with Alberto Marsicano.

Márta Minier is lecturer in drama at the University of Glamorgan. She holds a PhD from the Centre for Performance Translation and Dramaturgy at the University of Hull. Her PhD thesis discussed the translation of *Hamlet* into Hungarian culture. Márta's established and emerging research interests include Translation Studies, Adaptation Studies, Shakespeare Studies, biography on page, stage and screen, as well as European drama with a special emphasis on the small nations of Central and Eastern Europe. She is assistant editor of the *Journal of Adaptation in Film and Performance* and one of the associate editors of the theatre studies journal *Symbolon*.

Laurence Raw teaches in the Department of English, Baskent University, Ankara, Turkey. His recent publications include *Nights at the Turkish Theatre* (2009), a book on Nathaniel Hawthorn adaptations, as well as a number of edited collections such as *The Theme of Cultural Adaptation in American History, Literature and Film: Cases when the Discourse Changed* (Edwin Mellen, 2009); *The Pedagogy of Adaptation* with Dennis Cutchins and Jim Welsh (Scarecrow, 2010).

Pedro de Senna is a theatre practitioner and academic. He was born in Rio de Janeiro, where he started performing in 1993, and he has been a member of SignDance Collective since 2010. He is a lecturer in contemporary theatre at Middlesex University.

Ildikó Ungvári Zrínyi graduated from the Babes-Bolyai University Cluj, Romania. She is an assistant professor at the University of Arts, Faculty of Arts in Hungarian, Theatre Department. She has been teaching theatre studies, theatre anthropology and performance analysis at this institution from 1992. Her books are *A látott lét dramaturgiája* [*The Existence of Life to be Seen*] (2001), *Látványolvasás* [*Reading Theatre Scenery*] (2004), *Bevezetés a színházantropológiába* [*The Anthropology of Theatre*] (2006) and *Képből van-e a színház teste?* [*Is the Body of Theatre Made of Images?*] (2011). She is responsible editor of the theatre studies review *Symbolon* and the Transylvanian theatre periodical *Játéktér* [*Playing Area*]. Alongside her academic activity, she is an active dramaturg and translator.

Eckart Voigts-Virchow is professor of English Literature at TU Braunschweig, Germany. He also taught at Siegen University, the Universities of Madison and Milwaukee (Wisconsin) and at Leeds University. His *Introduction to Media Studies* (Klett) was published in 2005. He is also editor of *Dramatized Media / Mediated Drama* (2000), *Janespotting and Beyond. British Heritage Retrovisions since the Mid-1990s* (2004) and co-editor of *The New Documentarism ZAA* (56.2, 2008) and *Adaptations: Performing across Media and Genres* (2009).

Jessica Wiest received her MA in American literature with an emphasis in Film Adaptation Studies from Brigham Young University. Other academic interests include American Western literature and Folklore Studies. Jessica enjoys writing and teaching, and is currently working as a freelance writer out of Iowa, where she lives with her husband and two boys.

Index